Contemporary Issues Series

YO-DBX-931

The Agriculture Crisis

A Critical Analysis of the Agricultural Policy of the United States

Thomas J. Hynes
William F. Campbell

NATIONAL TEXTBOOK COMPANY • *Lincolnwood, Illinois U.S.A.*

6 7 8 9 0 VP 9 8 7 6 5 4 3 2 1

Table of Contents

Introduction

Any discussion of American agriculture is by necessity incredibly complex. More than just finding out what's for dinner, discussions of American agriculture necessarily cover a wide range of technological, environmental, economic, and political issues. This occurs at the same time Americans attempt to discover who is the American farmer and how may we help him/her to survive. This work will provide an introduction to some of the issues involved in the development of an American agricultural policy for the future. The introduction is divided into three parts. The first section will include an overview of current governmental policies affecting American agriculture. The overview will consider the history of legislative action, including a summary of the more recent implications of the 1985 Food Security Act.

It is nearly impossible to consider the development of new strategies for American agriculture without examining the implications of the those changes on foreign agricultural markets. These changes, in turn, have implications on the development of food supplies for a growing world population. The essays contained in the second section will focus on the foreign effects of American agricultural policy.

Our drive to provide food for ourselves and the world is often discussed without adequate concern for the farmer—the individual who ultimately provides the bounty upon which literally billions of human beings depend. The third section of essays includes several essays concerned with the farmer—who is the American farmer, what are the chances of his/her survival in the coming years, and in what form will this survival take.

As with virtually every other area of governmental policy, actions related to one area of agricultural policy have implications for others. Changes in the size or demographics of farms, for example, affects the types of technologies which are used, or even the crops which are grown. When we alter our export policies we alter the nature of domestic markets, and ultimately the farmers who send goods to these markets. We hope that these introductory essays will provide a general background for understanding some of the many dimensions of American agricultural policy.

I. CURRENT GOVERNMENT POLICIES AND THEIR EFFECT ON AMERICAN AGRICULTURE

American agriculture has had a long association with government regulation. Since the time of the New Deal, American farmers have been the subject of broad ranging legislative actions. These actions, notes Julian Juergensmeyer, should be studied as a backdrop for anticipating any further policies which the U.S. Government should initiate in the next decade.

Focusing on the new developments in Federal law relating to American agriculture, the next essay provides a broad overview of the history of farm policy. The staff writers for *Agricultural Outlook* summarize provisions of the Food Security Act of 1985, which they argue will have sizeable effects on soil conservation, international trade competitiveness, as well as commodity price stability.

Some argue that solutions to the problems of American agriculture will take more than Federal legislation. John Lee, also commenting on the implication of the Food Security Act, argues that little can be done to change the farm economy without some dramatic effects on the general economic picture.

A final essay for this section provides information on an area of potential government policy not often the first concern of decision makers. The relationship between animal rights and new developments in the agricultural economy are not frequently discussed. Jonny Frank, however, draws attention to the potential increases in animal cruelty and the growth of agribusiness. Frank argues for model reform legislation to deal with what he argues is the inevitable clash between animal rights proponents and agribusiness.

II. FOREIGN EFFECTS OF AMERICAN AGRICULTURAL POLICY

Both political and economic reasons justify a concern for an expanding American role in exporting agricultural production. This section will consider a number of the reasons, as well as some of the competing means of considering American exportation of its agricultural production.

The interdependence of the world community, as well as the traditional American view of its responsibility to assist those in times of need, has made decisions about American agricultural policies interconnected with policies for agricultural assistance. The next several essays begin our discussion of various elements of assistance policies.

Lester Brown of the Worldwatch Institute, describes the complex relationships between future population growth, agricultural demand, and the prospects of successful survival of continued world population growth. The critical concept to be found in Brown's testimony is the extent of interactions among changes in one variable of development with all others in the Third World.

From the same perspective, Robert Taft indicates that food assistance without some associated developments in population control measures suggests potential disaster for the Third World. According to Taft, without changes in population planning, ". . . our well meaning assistance will merely complicate the long-term problems of the developing countries."

When discussions about changes in American export policy arise, they frequently are made with the assumption that American farmers will respond as they have historically done—increase production to meet almost any potential demand. Clark Edwards and David Harrington explore the implications of these assumptions. They note that such future responses will require varied responses in technology, resource availability, regional location, and institutional arrangements.

The development of international markets for American agriculture is often related to the ability to align market demand with agricultural production. The 1985 Food Security Act, along with its other provisions, represents an effort to align supply and demand. It also represents an effort to anticipate the coming changes in the world agricultural market—from one of constantly increasing demands to one where growth rates, while declining, will still be subject to occasional supply disruptions.

C.W. McMillan observes that major changes are needed in the direction of American agricultural policy. According to McMillan, America must recognize that agriculture is an international industry, with cooperative programs needed to solve problems created by fluctuations of international supply, price and production.

Selections from the Staff Report of the House Select Committee on Hunger completes this section. This essay provides a summary of the Staff's findings on world hunger, the extent and nature of U.S. actions to anticipate future demands, as well as other developmental efforts which necessarily intersect with American agricultural programs.

III. THE AMERICAN FARMER—PROSPECTS FOR THE FUTURE

Recognizing the international nature of agriculture does not absolve us of our obligation to examine the domestic implications of American agricultural policies. This examination will be the subject of the third section of this collection.

The media is alive with claims of the financial plight of the American farmer. Reported in *Farmline* economists of the US Department of Agriculture's

Research Service note the extent of the farmers concerns. Among other things, the survey reports that nearly 20% of all farms with annual sales of more than $40,000 were under severe financial stress.

Based on the work of Paul Velde of the US Department of Agriculture, *Farmline* reports the increasing importance of the large farm in American agriculture. This changing composition of the American agricultural sector has clear implications for American agriculture's future—what cost to the consumer? what effect on the family farm? what efficiencies of production?

In its drive to feed America and the rest of the world, American farmers have utilized a variety of chemical techniques to expand production. One of the by-products of such chemical use has been substantial environmental degradation. John Keene outlines the nature of the environmental threat from agricultural production, as well as the variety of techniques available to fight such assaults.

Vernon Ruttan argues that the growth of American agriculture has been based upon the growth and application of technological developments to the farm sector. In order to be able to maintain further gains in production, each actor in the business of agricultural research and development efforts—federal, state and private—must recognize their responsibility for supporting policies that will maintain the strength of the others.

In a discussion of a variety of views on the financial crisis in American agriculture, Mark Drabenstott and John Blake provide a number of important insights. They explore, for example, the implications for providing a safety net for American producers during times of farm sector downturns. They further discuss the competing claims about the long-run structure of the farm sector, the risks and associated benefits facing lenders to American farmers. Any changes in the financial arrangements available to American farmers will have obvious effects on financial institutions charged with dealing with this sector of the American economy.

The testimony of former secretary of agriculture Orville Freeman will serve as the final essay. Freeman provides the business perspective of agriculture's future. He argues that the farmers' financial difficulties must be combatted by national and international initiatives which makes demand for agricultural production more predictable. National commitments must also account for the different needs of the small, medium and large agricultural producer.

IV. SELECTED BIBLIOGRAPHY

This work ends with a selected bibliography of works related to agricultural issues. As should be clear from the previous essays, U.S. agricultural policies must consider a wide variety of related issues—population, climate, environment among others. The selected bibliography reflects such interactions.

As is the case in many dimensions of American agricultural policy, there are no easy answers. This series of readings is an effort to direct readers to new questions about such policies, as well as the important connections which relate changes in one area of agricultural policies with all others.

I
Current Government Policies and Their Effects on American Agriculture

The Future of Government Regulation of Agriculture: An Introduction*

Julian Conrad Juergensmeyer**

American agriculture is in a sorry state. Production costs have risen while market prices have fallen (at least when measured in constant dollars). The volume of exports has declined. As a result, farm income in nearly all states has plummeted drastically. Farm to urban area migration which plagued our country several decades ago, but stabilized somewhat in the 1970's, is again on the increase.[1] A symposium devoted to agricultural law issues could focus on the current plight of American agriculture from numerous perspectives. One such important perspective is to view the current agricultural malaise and its future from the point of view of government regulation. The theory for doing so is that government regulation of agriculture is a common thread which runs through most, if not all, agricultural issues in the 1980's. "Government regulation" is used in this symposium as the equivalent to "government activity," whether the activity restricts, protects, subsidizes, confiscates, promotes or simply confuses agricultural activities.

The importance of government regulation to American agriculture should need little if any comment. From the very beginning of our republic, government

* Professor Juergensmeyer's article and the subsequent articles by Dean Looney and Professors Wadley and Harl were originally presented as speeches at an Agricultural Law Seminar for the dedication of Northern Illinois University's College of Law Building, March 18, 1983.
** Professor of Law and Co-Director of the Center for Agricultural Law, University of Florida, Spessard L. Holland Law Center; J.D., A.B., Duke University; Certificate d'Etudes Polit., Bordeaux, France; Diplomas I & II, Comparative Law, Strasbourg, France.
*** From *Northern Illinois University Law Review,* 3, 1983, pp. 253-261. Reprinted by permission.

policy toward agriculture has been of extreme importance to those who govern as well as those governed.[2] Since the Supreme Court of the United States sustained government regulation of agriculture by upholding New Deal legislation in *Wickard v. Filburn*,[3] the American farmer has been subjected to more laws and regulations than the farmers of most other countries of the world, including those of many so-called totalitarian systems.

Whether this extreme amount of regulation is good, bad, inevitable, avoidable, or reversible involves value judgments that will no doubt vary the answer from person to person. One should note, however, that in recent months various proposals for so-called "deregulation" of American agriculture have raised the issues more than perhaps ever before. The complexities presented by deregulation and the difficulty of evaluating the effects of various deregulation proposals on farmers and on consumers are illustrated by a 1974 analysis of the potential effects of deregulating the production of tobacco, peanuts, and fresh fruit and vegetables.[4]

In regard to tobacco, the study concluded that deregulation by the government would release the tobacco farmers from any acreage or poundage restrictions and almost certainly would result in larger, mechanized tobacco farms which would have a drastic effect on the tobacco farmers but little effect on the consumer. A shift to larger, mechanized farms eventually would result in a complete relocation of tobacco farms; they would shift from their hilly, small tracts to large, flat coastal plains better suited to tobacco cultivation. This complete uprooting of tobacco farming would be offset by little or no benefit to the consumer. Aside from the fact that tobacco is not an important good for consumption, the cost of the tobacco leaf itself is a very small part of the cost of cigars and cigarettes, since most of the cost of tobacco products is the labor required to produce them.[5]

Peanuts are another crop that was examined for the varying effects of government deregulation. Peanuts have high acreage allotments and high price supports that along with increasing yields have combined to create a surplus of edible peanuts and have encouraged the production of an inferior, inedible product. This led those conducting the study to conclude that the price of peanuts to consumers would be largely the same with or without regulation.[6]

Finally, an analysis of the fresh fruit and vegetable sector of agriculture was made to illustrate potential effects of deregulation. Import restrictions have proved to be the most significant regulation affecting fresh fruit and vegetable production. Mexico and other temperate areas close to the United States could be competition for America's fresh fruit and vegetable industry because of their plentiful supply of cheap labor. If import restrictions were removed, the fresh fruit and vegetable sector could become unstable. The increased supply of goods, especially during harvest, would drive the price down. This might seem to benefit consumers, but the fluctuation and range of prices, normally limited because of supply controls, would be wide. The variety of products available also would fluctuate widely, and this, too, would be of questionable benefit to the consumer.[7]

The dubious benefits to the consumer discussed above should be compared to the farmers' dislocation, another result of the relaxing of regulations. To remain competitive with the cheap labor areas abroad, American farmers in this sector most surely would move toward increased mechanization of large land areas, a move that would affect property values and employment.

In general, the three examples cited indicate that consumers would benefit from deregulation indirectly rather than directly, that is, through reduced federal program costs rather than lower prices at the grocery store. Even in the one instance where the price surely would go down (halting import restrictions for fresh fruit and vegetables), the advantages of deregulation would be offset by prices that would fluctuate throughout the year and by a decrease in the variety of products available at any one time. The indirect benefit to consumers also must be measured against the dislocation of farmers and the arguable misallocation of time and capital that would arise from effecting the various change-overs. It seems that any deregulation should be carefully considered and examined before wholesale changes are effected.

A further factor to consider in the deregulation calculus is the indirect harm to consumers that results from the sale of more and more of America's farmlands. One of the main reasons farmers are selling their lands is that they can acquire more lucrative positions elsewhere. One aid to keep farmers farming would be for government programs to continue. Alternatively, if deregulation occurred, the amount of farmland would continue to shrink and the supply of agricultural products, as well as their variety, could be reduced; the end result could be unfortunate for the consumers, with prices rising and diet choices diminishing.[8]

The complexity of the issues inherent in government regulation makes any attempt at comprehensive coverage impossible. Consequently, this symposium, in addition to this segment, will concentrate on three specific topics: the recent federal taxation developments, an analysis of farm credit and bankruptcy problems, and an examination of United States Department of Agriculture programs as they impact on small farms and small farm communities. This part of the symposium involves a brief examination of the present and predicted future of U.S. government activity relating to the export of American agricultural commodities.

If this symposium were to be held in many states, it would be necessary to justify choosing international trade of agricultural commodities as a topic of primary concern to American agriculture. No such necessity should exist in Illinois, since this state ranks first in the dollar value of agricultural exports. In 1980, the total value of agricultural exports from Illinois was $3.64 billion. This figure represented nine percent of the total U.S. agricultural exports for that fiscal year.[9] Nationally, the importance of agricultural exports is clear, as they are responsible for more than one million jobs within the United States—about one-half million on the farm and over 630,000 off-farm jobs relating to assembling, processing, and distribution of agricultural products for exports. United States agricultural exports for fiscal 1980 represented the output of approximately 138 million of the slightly more than 400 million United States cropland acres.[10]

Since our focus is on governmental activity, it should be noted at the outset that international trade of agricultural commodities is an area in which government activity is essential and unavoidable. From the very basic fact that international activities are involved, the individual American farmer, cooperative, or agribusiness concern must have the United States as a partner. In fact, it is submitted that in the years to come, more and more government activity and concern will and should occur in regard to the import and export of agricultural commodities.

In short, "deregulation," if that term means no activity, is not possible as far as international trade is concerned. What is needed is not less activity by the U.S. government but more enlightened government activity. For example, the use of American food exports as a weapon of international diplomacy has accomplished little, if anything, by way of attaining foreign policy goals but has been extremely harmful to American farmers. Recent anti-embargo and sanctity of export contract legislation is a step in the right direction.[11] Further steps need to be taken to guarantee the reliability of the United States as an exporter. The current inadequacy of U.S. government policy toward agricultural exports was recently summarized and highlighted by a leading American agribusiness executive in a speech delivered to the American Agricultural Law Association. The speaker, Thomas N. Urban, noted:

> We lack a clear policy that recognizes the new realities of food production, allowing it to make its maximum contribution to the economy of this country and to the world economy that is a tragedy. We are in danger of squandering our food production advantages because our political system seems unable to recognize change.
>
> An example of what happens when such a policy void exists is the attitude of certain government officials regarding agricultural embargoes. Although admitting that embargoes have failed as an instrument of foreign policy, a State Department official recently declared that he believes we must apply an embargo occasionally to show the world that we are willing to use such means. That kind of a statement doesn't make sense and destroys whatever food policy there might be in this country. I doubt if the official had any idea at all of the impact of his statement on food and agricultural economic health.[12]

An example of positive action that the United States government has taken recently to encourage foreign purchases of American farm products is to arrange so-called blended credits for foreign purchasers. Such arrangements have already provided significant results.[13] The interrelationship and complexity of United States government programs is demonstrated by the parallel controversy which has arisen in connection with the exports made possible by the blended credits—namely the problem of cargo preference. In short, the Cargo Preference Act of 1954[14] mandates that one-half of all farm commodity exports from stocks owned by the government or sales subsidized by the U.S. government must be transported by ships flying the United States flag.[15] Due to the various economic factors, shipping agricultural commodities on American vessels costs as much as 150% more than shipping them on foreign vessels. For example, in the recent blended credit financed sale of wheat flour to Egypt, the cost for freight per metric ton for bagged wheat flour from Beaumont, Texas, to Alexandria, Egypt, was $108 on American registered ships and only $42.50 on foreign registered ships.[16] This cost differential means that the price advantage created by blended credit arrangements can be completely or largely eliminated by the extra shipping cost necessitated by requiring the use of American flag ships.

The cost differential is not the only problem posed by the Cargo Preference Act. Very few U.S. flag-flying ships are equipped to carry agricultural commodity cargoes. Thus, even if the government paid the extra freight costs—which is of course *not* the current policy—the requirements of the Act would still hamper U.S. exporters.

The applicability of the cargo preference principle to sales financed by the United States government is harmful enough to American farmers; in addition, there are proposals in Congress to expand the concept even to private export arrangements. The Competitive Shipping and Shipbuilding Act of 1983[17] would mandate that five percent of United States dry and liquid bulk exports be carried by U.S. ships. The mandated percentage would climb one percent per year to a total of twenty percent.[18] The U.S. shipping and shipbuilding industry may need and deserve assistance, but to so subsidize at the expense of farm commodity exports could be economically disastrous to American agriculture. Cargo preference, like the grain embargoes, is an example of government regulation that can only be labeled harmful interference.

In short, the U.S. government must and should participate in and regulate the importation and exportation of agricultural commodities. Government activity should promote, not discourage, exports and should seek to guarantee that American agribusiness is treated fairly in international markets. At times it seems that the key trade war is the conflict between American farmers and their own government. If the agricultural segment of our economy is to win any of the international trade wars and the fight against domestic surpluses, the U.S. government must make peace with American agriculture.

NOTES

1. For a discussion of the major issues currently facing American agriculture, see J. JUERGENSMEYER & J. WADLEY, AGRICULTURAL LAW §1.4 (1982).
2. Some of the current policy concerns are discussed in Batie & Healy, *The Future of American Agriculture*, SCI. AM., Feb. 1983, at 45. The authors suggest that there is much disagreement over whether our major problem is over-production or long-term shortages:

> The debate over American agricultural policy should not await research findings, if for no other reason than that policy debates can help to identify areas of ignorance. With the present farm

economy beset by production surpluses and cost and credit squeezes on the farmer, it may seem strange to suggest debating how the U.S. might confront possible long-term shortages. The urgency of short-term problems, however, must not obscure the importance of considering how to organize an agricultural sector that can survive and flourish for as long as we expect our society to endure.

Id. at 53.

3. 317 U.S. 111 (1942). In *Wickard,* the Supreme Court of the United States upheld regulation by the U.S. government of the size of the farmer's crop even though it was intended solely for on-farm consumption. The wheat acreage allotted the farmer (Filburn) was 11.1 acres. Agricultural Adjustment Act of 1938, 7 U.S.C. §§1281-1385 (Supp. IV 1981). However, he sowed 23 acres. From the excess planting, he harvested 239 bushels of wheat which under the terms of the Act constituted a farm marketing excess subject to a $.49 per bushel penalty.

In upholding the regulation and the penalty imposed on the farmer, the Supreme Court reiterated its view that the commerce power of the federal government "extends to those activities intrastate which so affect interstate commerce, or the exertion of the power of Congress over it, as to make regulation of them appropriate means to the attainment of a legitimate end, the effective execution of the granted power to regulate interstate commerce." 317 U.S. at 124 (quoting United States v. Wrightwood Dairy Co., 315 U.S. 110, 119 (1942)).

For a full discussion of the *Wickard* decision and its precedent-setting effect on federal regulation of agriculture, see J. JUERGENSMEYER & J. WADLEY, *supra* note 1, §2.2.

4. Sundquist, *Removing Legal Constraints on Agriculture,* 19 S.D.L. REV. 512 (1974).

5. *Id.* at 531.

6. *Id.* at 533.

7. *Id.* at 536.

8. J. JUERGENSMEYER & J. WADLEY, *supra* note, 1, §2.6.

9. USDA (FAS), THE U.S. AGRICULTURAL TRADE BOOK (1981). The total dollar value of all agricultural exports in fiscal 1980 was $40.48 billion.

10. NATIONAL AGRICULTURAL LANDS STUDY, FINAL REPORT 7 (1981).

11. In the last few years the controversial embargoes have been directed toward the Soviet Union and Eastern Europe. The first controversy was over the embargo of soybeans to Japan. The Japanese embargo and its unfortunate consequences is analyzed in considerable detail in E. CASTLE & K. HEMMI, U.S.-JAPANESE AGRICULTURAL TRADE RELATIONS (1982).

A few statistics serve to highlight the effect of the recent Russian and Polish embargoes. In 1980, the dollar value of U.S. agricultural exports to the Soviet Union was approximately $1.5 billion. This figure rose to $1.7 billion in 1981, and to nearly $3.3 billion in 1982, but will probably tumble back to $1.7 billion for fiscal 1983. The value of exports of agricultural commodities to Eastern Europe in 1980 was nearly $2.5 billion but dropped to $2 billion in 1981 and plummeted to $900 million in 1982 where it will probably remain in 1983. USDA (FAS), THE U.S. AGRICULTURAL TRADE BOOK (1981).

The drastic drop in exports to Eastern Europe is easy to understand when it is realized that Poland was the biggest importer of U.S. agricultural products in Eastern Europe. The entire Polish poultry industry, for example, was based on feed imported from this country. Embargoes and punitive measures, such as the lifting of Poland's Most Favored Nation trade status, plus the increased value of the U.S. dollar in international monetary markets, created a drop in demand which will be difficult, if not impossible, to restore in the foreseeable future.

A degree of embargo protection was extended to American farmers by the Farm Bill of 1981. Agriculture and Food Act of 1981, 7 U.S.C. §1281 (Supp. V 1981), Section 1736(j) provides:

Notwithstanding any other provision of law—

(a) If the President or other member of the executive branch of the Federal Government causes the export of any agricultural commodity to any country or area of the world to be suspended or restricted for reasons of national security or foreign policy under the Export Administration Act of 1979 or any other provision of law, and if such suspension or restriction of the export of such agricultural commodity is imposed other than in connection with a suspension or restriction of all exports from the United States to such country or area of the world, and if sales of such agricultural commodity for export from the United States to such country or area of the world during the year preceding the year in which the suspension or restriction is imposed exceed 3 per centum of the total sales of such commodity for export from the United States to all foreign countries during the year preceding the year in which the suspension or restriction is in effect, the Secretary of Agriculture shall compensate producers of the commodity involved by—

(1) making payments available to such producers, as provided in subsection (b) of this section;

(2) on the date on which the suspension or restriction is imposed, establishing the loan level for such commodity under the Agricultural Act of 1949, if a loan program is in effect for the commodity, at 100 per centum of the parity price for the commodity, as determined by the Secretary on the date of the imposition of the suspension or restriction; or

(3) undertaking any combination of the measures described in clauses (1) and (2) of this subsection.

7 U.S.C. §1736(j) (Supp. V 1981).

A sanctity of agricultural export contracts provision was added to the Futures Trading Act of 1982, Pub. L. No. 97-444, 96 Stat. 2294 (1983). Section 238 of the Act prohibits the President from prohibiting the export of agricultural commodities covered by an export sales contract: (1) if the contract was made prior to the announcement of the embargo, (2) if the contract calls for delivery within 270 days after the embargo is announced. 96 Stat. 2326. *See* Juergensmeyer, *International Trade Developments*, 5 J. AGRIC. TAX'N & L. 70 (1983).

12. Urban, *Wanted: A New Coalition to Develop Food and Agriculture Policies*, 2 AGRIC. L. NEWSLETTER 1, 2 (1983).

13. *Cargo Preference Could Sink Bigger Export Sales*, 98 PROGRESSIVE FARMER: MIDMONTH SOYBEAN EDITION 1, 4 (No. 4) (Apr. 1983).

14. 46 U.S.C. §§1241 to 1244 (1976).

15. *Id.* §1241(b)(1).

16. *See* PROGRESSIVE FARMER, *supra* note 13, at 4.

17. H.R. 1242, 98th Cong., 1st Sess. (1983).

18. Section 4(a) of H.R. 1242 provides:

In the calendar year following the year of enactment of this Act, each importer or exporter of bulk cargoes shall transport at least 5 per centum of these bulk cargoes in United States-flag ships. In each calendar year thereafter the percentage of bulk cargoes required to be transported in United States-flag ships shall increase by 1 per centum until the percentage of the bulk cargoes required to be transported in United States-flag ships during each calendar year is at least 20 per centum.

Implications of the 1985 Farm Bill

The Food Security Act of 1985 (P.L. 99-198) begins a 5-year program by the Federal Government to allow U.S. prices for wheat, feed grains, cotton, and rice to follow the world market. The act contains several innovations. Loan rates are tied to market prices, and the Secretary of Agriculture can allow loans to be repaid at existing market prices when these prices fall below loan rates. New formulas for computing acreage bases and program yields effectively break the link between production and receipt of Government payments.

Tying loan rates to a formula based on historical prices allows support prices to increase or decrease in response to changing world supply and demand. The previous farm bill used the formula concept only for determining soybean and cotton loan rates.

The 1985 act is also innovative in that it authorizes a conservation reserve of up to 45 million acres. Farmers will receive an annual rental payment for land placed in this reserve.

THE ADMINISTRATION SETS GOALS

The Administration began the farm bill debate wanting to achieve three major goals:

1) flexible commodity price supports to allow greater export potential,
2) consistency among commodity programs and trade, conservation, research, credit, and grain reserve policies, and
3) reduced Government spending on agriculture.

From *Agricultural Outlook,* March 1986, pp. 23-33. Reprinted by permission.

The goal of increasing or maintaining farm income was not specifically enumerated in the Administraiton's initial proposal. For many farmers, the deficiency payment, a direct income transfer from the Government to a qualified producer, has become an important component of total income. Many farmers and farm organizations were unwilling to accept sharp reductions in deficiency payments. However, most participants in the farm bill debate did agree that lower price supports were needed to boost U.S. exports. Maintaining target prices at current levels while allowing market prices to drop will nearly double deficiency payments.

PRICE AND SUPPORT PROGRAMS ROSE SHARPLY IN THE 1980'S

Annual price and income support programs for agriculture, on average, cost less than $4 billion a year before 1981. However, they reached between $10 and $20 billion a year during 1982-85. Total USDA spending moved from a midlevel position in the Federal budget to just behind the Departments of Health and Human Services and Defense. Since most participants in the farm bill debate agreed that price supports needed to drop, negotiations focused on target prices.

In April and May 1985, the House and Senate Agriculture Committees began separate meetings to draft the new farm bill. Early in the session, the House and Senate agreed to limit spending for years 1986-88 to $34.4 billion. This total applied to 1986, even though that year was covered by previous legislation.

During April-June, the House Agriculture subcommittee on wheat, feed grains, and soybeans agreed to include two items—the Findley Amendment and the marketing loan provision—in their draft. Under the Findley Amendment, the Secretary can lower wheat and feed grain loan rates up to 20 percent to specifically achieve price competitiveness in export markets. But, this adjustment cannot be used in calculating the following year's loan rate with respect to the 5-percent-a-year reduction. Under the marketing loan provision, the Secretary can accept repayment of the price support loan at a reduced rate.

MARKETING LOANS AIM FOR COMPETITIVENESS

Traditionally, nonrecourse commodity loans were made by the Government to producers using the crop as collateral. If, at the end of the loan period, the market price was not sufficient to cover the cost of the loan plus interest, the producer simply kept the loan proceeds and turned the crop collateral over to the Government. This kept the market price from falling much below the loan level. By contrast, the marketing loan is intended to encourage farmers to redeem their loans and market the commodity, thus lowering market prices and increasing

U.S. commodities' export competitiveness. However, lower repayment offers the potential for higher budget outlays.

In a key vote on July 24, Senate Agriculture Committee members voted to freeze target prices at their 1985 levels for 4 years. The vote was along party lines, with only one Republican crossing over to vote with the Democrats in favor of the price freeze. In the 17-member committee (9 Repubicans, 8 Democrats) the crossover was sufficient to pass the 4-year target price freeze.

By the end of July, the Senate Agriculture committee, essentially abandoning its own budget restraint, had developed a farm bill estimated to cost $40.5 billion over the next 3 years—only $1 billion less than estimates for continuing provisions of the 1981 farm bill. It was not until late in the debate, on November 23, that the Senate moved away from a 4-year freeze on target prices and instead instituted a 1-year freeze for 1986, with cuts in subsequent years.

TARGET PRICES KEPT HIGH

Debates on maintaining farm income was contentious at times. Several alternative plans were extensively debated, such as the Targeted Option Plan, which would have allowed producers to choose higher target prices in return for greater acreage cutbacks. The final compromise froze target prices for 1986 and 1987, with in-kind payments compensating for small reductions in the following years.

By the end of the farm bill process, USDA estimates of potential outlays for fiscal 1986-90 had risen to $101 billion for price and income support and related programs, and $68.6 billion for food assistance. Price and income support alone was estimated to cost about $69 billion, and the credit component, $10.2 billion over the 5-year life of the bill. The export, research, and conservation provisions are expected to cost $21 billion.

CONSERVATION PROGRAM IS LARGEST EVER ESTABLISHED

For the first time since 1956, major soil conservation provisions are included in a farm bill. This legislation has the potential to create the largest soil conservation program ever, as well as to support farm income. An underlying objective is to make conservation and other farm programs mutually supportive.

The conservation title can be considered in four parts:

1. The main measure for fulfilling the dual objectives of erosion abatement and income support is the conservation reserve. The goal is to enroll 40 to 45 million acres by 1990/91. This is nearly twice the acreage stipulated in earlier proposed Senate and House farm bills. About 70 million highly erodible acres are eligible for the reserve in 1986.
2. Other measures discourage farmers from: (a) plowing up additional highly erodible grasslands, pasture, and forest lands, and (b) draining and cultivating

wetlands for crop production. These sodbuster and swampbuster provisions will eliminate access to virtually all Government programs and benefits if agricultural producers bring highly erodible lands into crop use without a conservation plan, or convert wetlands to crop use.

3. The conservation compliance provision denies future program benefits to producers if specific conservation plans are not being implemented by 1990 on highly erodible land now in production.
4. Several existing conservation programs are continued or augmented, and Federal and State cooperation in more traditional conservation programs is strengthened.

Together, these new conservation provisions have the potential to greatly reduce crop production on highly erodible land, thereby decreasing soil erosion, crop surpluses, and environmental damage. Roughly 25 percent of all cropland could be affected.

CONSERVATION RESERVES WILL PAY LAND RENT & HALF OF COVER COSTS

For farmers producing agricultural commodities on highly erodible land, the conservation reserve will provide rental payments and half of the cost of establishing a cover when converting the land to grass or trees for 10 to 15 years.

Farmers who choose not to enroll their highly erodible acres in the reserve will lose program benefits on their whole farm after 1990, unless they begin implementing individual conservation plans to adequately protect that land. To keep the conservation reserve from hurting local economies, no more than 25 percent of the total cropland in any county may be placed in the reserve.

No grazing or harvesting of forage or any other commercial activity on reserve lands is permitted for the duration of the contract, unless specifically allowed by the Secretary of Agriculture. Also, a farmer's cropland base and allotment history will be reduced by the ratio of the land retired to total cropland acreage.

The legislation requires the selection of the most highly erodible acres for the reserve, but it also gives weight to choosing those bids that will remove the largest amount of area from production. Bidding may be used to select which acres enter the conservation reserve, but specific criteria for selecting acres can vary from year to year. Annual erosion on U.S. cropland in excess of quantities replenished totals about 900 million tons. Targeting the most erodible land could reduce excessive soil loss by 60 to 90 percent.[1]

Those farmers who do not place their highly erodible croplands into the reserve have until 1995 to complete a plan approved by their conservation district, or they forego all program benefits. By adding new program requirements as well as benefits for the farmers who account for much of U.S. soil erosion, the conservation compliance provision reduces the cost of both the conservation reserve and commodity programs.

LAND CONVERSION DISCOURAGED

The sodbuster provision makes sodbusters ineligible for: price support loans, purchases, and payments for program crops; Federal crop insurance; disaster payments; and loans made, insured, or guaranteed by the Farmers Home Administration (FmHA). In the swampbuster provision, if a converted wetland cannot maintain its integrity as a natural wetland while cultivated, such as during a drought, producers will be ineligible for Government program benefits.

SOME LAND TO BE USED FOR TIMBER PRODUCTION

The conservation provisions encourage tree cultivation in several ways, and a portion of the reserve will be planted in trees. In fact, the title stipulates that, if possible, at least one-eighth of the total reserve acreage should be devoted to trees. A specific softwood timber provision will also allow farms with distressed FmHA loans to reamortize these loans and reschedule them using future timber revenues as collateral. The program can total no more than 50,000 acres.

In areas such as the Southeast, where softwood pines compete for crop acres, the trees will provide farmers some income from program acres that would otherwise stand idle. Strips of trees are also proposed to prevent wind erosion. In the long run, tree cultivation reduces timber-harvesting pressure on existing forested land, which must be used for both wood production and other purposes (recreation, wildlife habitat, etc.). Thus, forestry is a further environmental benefit of the new farm bill.

The conservation reserve will also give wildlife and small game that nest on farms the advantage of long-term cover on idled acres. Annual acreage reduction programs provide little wildlife shelter because of the limited period for which groundcover is provided.

The conservation reserve can include land other than highly erodible acres if such inclusion would reduce environmental damage. Buffer strips or extra protection for fragile water resources are potential uses of the reserve. However, because the reserve will be directed at areas accounting for the most soil erosion, the major contribution to natural resources will be reducing erosion sedimentation and nutrient pollution in streams, lakes, and estuaries. This benefit will support State and local water quality programs.

CONSISTENCY SOUGHT WITH OTHER PROGRAMS

The conservation title in the farm bill is also designed to cut price support outlays. The sodbuster and swampbuster provisions reduce the price-depressing effect of having more land brought under the plow during crop surplus years. The

HOW THE NEW FARM BILL DIFFERS FROM THE OLD . . .

Provision	Old law	New law
General Commodity Provisions		
Advance deficiency & diversion payments	Sec. given authority to make up to ½ of estimated payments in advance.	Sec. must make advance deficiency payments in 1986; diversion payments discretionary in 1986; both discretionary for 1987-90. Payments may be in cash or in kind. No more than 50% of advance payment may be made in kind. Advance may not exceed 50% of estimated total payment.
Interest payment certificates	No provision.	Sec. may issue certificates to producers who repay interest on CCC loans for wheat, feed grains, cotton, & rice. Certificates redeemable for CCC commodities.
Haying & grazing	Sec. given discretion to implement haying & grazing restrictions.	Except for 5-month period designated by each county ASCS committee, Sec. must permit haying & grazing on diverted acres in 1986, & grazing in 1987-90.
Farmer-owned reserve (FOR)	Minimum FOR of 700 million bu. wheat, 1 billion bu. corn; release price discretionary.	FOR is continued. If FOR wheat is less than 17% of total use or FOR feed grains are less than 7% of total use, & farm prices are less than 140% of the loan rate for the commodity, Sec. must offer incentives to encourage FOR placements; FOR wheat may not exceed 33% of total wheat use; FOR feed grains may not exceed 16.5% of total use.
Payment limitations	$50,000/person for payments from wheat, feed grains, cotton, & rice; disaster payments $100,000/person for the above commodities.	$50,000/person/yr. for deficiency & diversion payments from wheat, feed grains, cotton, & rice; disaster payments $100,000/person for above commodities. Exempt from limit are: loans or purchases, loan payments (payments received as a result of prices falling below basic loan rates), & inventory reduction payments.
Base acreage & yields	Separate provisions in each commodity title.	Farm acreage base = sum of crop acreage bases. Beginning in 1987, soybean & conservation use acres included. Crop acreage base = av. of acres planted & considered planted during preceding 5 yrs., but not to exceed av. planted & considered planted

Provision	Old law	New law
General Commodity Provisions (cont.)		during preceding 2 yrs. For cotton & rice, any yrs. of zero plantings during 1981-83 will not be counted. Sec. can allow 10% offsetting adjustments in individual crop bases on a farm. Farm program payment yield for 1986 & 1987 = av. of farm program yields during 1981-85, excluding high & low. Sec. has discretion to continue to freeze payment yields in 1988-90 or to base yields on 5-yr. moving av.
Cross compliance	Sec. discretion.	If acreage reduction program (ARP) in effect for wheat or feed grains, planting of other program crops may not exceed base acreage of those crops on farms participating in wheat or feed grain programs. Sec. discretion whether to apply provision to rice & cotton. If set-aside in effect for wheat or feed grains, Sec. has discretion whether to require cross compliance.
Offsetting compliance	Sec. discretion.	Sec. cannot require all cotton & rice farms operated by an individual to be enrolled in those programs in order to receive benefits on any 1 farm.
Dairy		
Price support	Reduced to $11.60/cwt on 7/1/85.	$11.60/cwt for 1986. $11.35 from 1/1/87 to 9/30/87. $11.10 beginning 10/1/87. Beginning 1/1/88, may fall $0.50/cwt/yr., if CCC removals are projected to exceed 5 bil. lbs. per yr. If annual removals are projected at 2.5 bil. lbs. or less, must increase $0.50/cwt/yr.
Diversion	1/84-3/85, producers who voluntarily reduced production 5-30% received $10/cwt.	Sec. discretion for 1988-90.
Milk production termination program	No provision.	Sec. required to implement a whole-herd buyout program beginning 4/1/86, under which producers (on a bid basis) may take their entire herds out of production for 5 yrs. Program is discretionary for 1988, '89, & '90. Program is funded by a producer assessment of $.40/cwt beginning 4/1/86; assessment drops to $.25/cwt on

Provision	Old law	New law
Dairy (cont.)		1/1/87, terminates 10/1/87. Sec. required to purchase 400 mil. lbs. of red meat to be distributed equally between export use (principally military) & domestic feeding programs during buyout program.
Wheat		
Loans	Sec. has discretion to lower rate up to 10% per yr., but not below $3.00/bu. 1985 rate = $3.30.	Basic loan rate = $3.00/bu. in 1986; for 1987-90, equals 75-85% of recent 5-yr. moving average, excluding high & low, but cannot fall more than 5% from previous yr. Actual loan rate can be reduced 20% from basic loan. Actual loan in 1986 = $2.40. Loan repayment, at Sec. discretion, can be allowed at rates as much as 30% below basic rate.
Target prices	Minimum $4.38/bu. for 1985.	Minimum = $4.38/bu. in 1986 & 1987, $4.29 in 1988, $4.16 in 1989, & $4.00 in 1990. Sec. may offer target option program which sets target prices for different gross agricultural sales & for different ARP levels.
Deficiency payments	Rate = target price minus higher of loan rate or average price received by farmers during first 5 months of each marketing yr.	Deficiency payment rate = target price minus higher of basic loan rate or average farm price during first 5 months of each marketing yr. Sec. has discretion to set minimum def. payment rates of $1.83/bu. in 1986, $1.73 in 1987, & $1.47 in 1988. Loan payment rate = basic loan rate minus lower of actual loan or loan repayment rate. Total deficiency payments & loan payments = farm program acreage times program yield times payment rates. If farmer plants between 50 & 92% of permitted acreage, program acreage equals 92% of permitted. Otherwise, program acreage equals actual planted.
ARP, set-aside, & paid land diversion (PLD)	1985 = 20% ARP plus 10% PLD with payment rate of $2.70/bu.	Sec. authorized to establish ARP, set-aside, & PLD. If ending stocks are forecast to exceed 1 billion bu., acreage limitations required to total 15-22.5% plus 2.5% of PIK diversion in 1986; 20-27.5% in 1987; 20-30% in 1988-90. Actual 1986 announced as

Provision	Old law	New law
Wheat (cont.)		25% acreage reduction including 2.5% PLD, plus 10% PLD at $2.00/bu. for producers who planted prior to 1/13/86.
Inventory reduction payments	No provision.	At Sec. discretion, producers who reduce plantings by ½ announced acreage reduction percentage & forego loans & deficiency payments may receive loan payment in kind.
Quota & referendum	No provision.	Sec. required to conduct poll by 7/1/86 to determine if producers support mandatory production limits in exchange for higher price support. Sec. has discretion to proclaim national marketing quotas for 1987-90 crops.
Feed Grains*		
Loans	Sec. had discretion to lower rate up to 10% yr., but not below $2/bu. for corn. 1985 rate = $2.55/bu.	Basic loan rate = $2.40/bu. for corn in 1986. 1987-90 calculated same as wheat. Actual loan rate = $1.92 for corn in 1986. 1987-90 same method as for wheat. Loan repayment rate calculated same as for wheat.
Target prices	Minimum $3.03/bu. for corn in 1985.	Minimum = $3.03/bu. in 1986 & 1987, $2.97 in 1988, $2.88 in 1989, & $2.75 in 1990.
Deficiency payments	Same calculation as for wheat.	Deficiency payment rate calculated same as for wheat. Sec. has discretion to set minimum rates of $0.99/bu. for corn in 1986, $0.84 in 1987, & $0.73 in 1988. Loan deficiency payment rate calculated same as for wheat. Total deficiency payment, loan payment, & 50-92% rule, same as for wheat.
ARP, set-aside, & PLD	1985 = 10% ARP.	ARP, set-aside, & PLD authorized. If corn stocks forecast to exceed 2 billion bu., acreage limitations required to total 12.5-17.5.% plus 2.5% PIK diversion in 1986; 12.5-20% limitations in 1987-90. Actual 1986 = 20%, including 2.5% of PLD.
Inventory reduction payments	No provision.	Same calculation as for wheat.

*Provisions described for corn; loan rates & target prices for sorghum, oats, barley & rye set proportional to corn.

Provision	Old law	New law
Upland Cotton		
Loans	Lower of 85% of 3-yr. av. spot mkt. price or 90% of av. world price. Minimum = $0.55/lb. 1985 = $0.573.	Basic loan rate = $0.55/lb. in 1986. 1987-90 = formula unchanged from old law; minimum = $0.50. Each crop yr., Sec. chooses Plan A or B. Plan A: loans can be repaid at rate as much as 20% below basic loan rate. If world prices are below repayment rate, Sec. must issue certificates to first handlers of cotton to make U.S. cotton competitive. Plan B: loans can be repaid at rates equal to world market prices.
Target prices	Minimum $0.81/lb. for 1985.	Minimum = $0.81/lb. in 1986, $0.794 in 1987, $0.77 in 1988, $0.745 in 1989, & $0.729 in 1990.
Deficiency payments	Target price minus higher of loan rate or av. farm price during yr. in which crop was planted.	Deficiency payment rate = target price minus higher of basic loan rate or av. farm price during yr. in which crop was planted. Loan payment rate = basic loan rate minus repayment rate. Total deficiency payment, loan payment, & 50-92% rule, same as for wheat.
ARP & PLD	1985 = 20% ARP plus 10% PLD with payment rate of $0.30/lb.	Maximum ARP of 25% authorized. Voluntary PLD can be offered. Sec. encouraged to operate programs so as to reduce ending stocks to 4 mil. bales.
Inventory reduction payments	No provision.	Same provision as for wheat.
Rice		
Loans	Sec. discretion with $8.00/cwt minimum. 1985 = $8.00.	Beginning 4/15/86, 1985-crop loans can be repaid at world market prices. Producers may be required to purchase marketing certificates equal in value to 1985 loan rate minus repayment rates. Certificates would be redeemable for CCC inventory. Basic loan rate in 1986 = $7.20/cwt minimum. For 1987-90, minimum = higher of 85% of 5-yr. moving av. of market prices excluding high & low, or $6.50/cwt. Maximum 5% reduction each yr. Loan repayment rate = higher of world

Provision	Old law	New law
Rice (cont.)		price or 50% of basic loan rate in 1986 & 1987, 60% in 1988, & 70% in 1989 & '90. Purchase of <u>marketing certifi-cates</u> equal in value to ½ difference between basic loan rate & loan repayment rate may be required in 1986-90.
Target prices	Minimum $11.90/cwt for 1985.	Minimums: 1986, $11.90/cwt; 1987, $11.66; 1988, $11.30; 1989, $10.95; & 1990, $10.71.
Deficiency payments	Same calculation as for wheat.	<u>Deficiency payment rate</u> calculated same as for wheat. <u>Loan payment rate</u> calculated same as for cotton. Total deficiency payments, loan payment, & 50-92% rule, calculated same as for wheat.
ARP & PLD	1985 ARP = 20%. PLD = 15%.	Maximum ARP of 35% authorized. Voluntary PLD can be offered. Sec. encouraged to operate programs so as to reduce ending stocks to 30 million cwt.
Inventory reduction payments	No provision.	Same provision as for wheat.
Soybeans		
Loans	1985 = $5.02/bu.	<u>Basic loan rate</u> = $5.02/bu. in 1986 & 1987. For 1988-90 = 75% of 5-yr. moving av. of farm prices excluding high & low. 5% maximum drop from previous yr. $4.50 minimum. <u>Actual loan rate</u> may be reduced 5% below basic loan in 1986 & may drop 5%/yr. to minimum of $4.50 during 1987-90. <u>Loan repayment</u> can be allowed at world prices.
Peanuts		
Price support	Quota peanuts supported at $559/ton in 1985. Additional peanuts supported at $148/ton.	1986-crop quota peanuts supported at 1985 rate adjusted for production cost increases between 1981 & 1985. 1987-90 quota peanuts based on previous yr's rate adjusted for production costs, with maximum annual increase of 6%. Additional peanuts supported at rate set by Sec.

Provision	Old law	New law
Peanuts (cont.)		
Quota	National poundage quota in 1985 = 1.1 mil. tons with acreage quotas suspended.	Minimum = 1.1 mil. tons. 1986 national poundage quota increased to 1.4 mil. Each yr's quota to equal estimated domestic disappearance. National quota will be apportioned among States in same percentage shares as 1985 quota. Increases in quota will be shared by old & new growers.

Sugar

Loans	Sugar cane $.18/lb. in 1985; sugarbeet set relative to cane.	Minimum loan rate = $.18/lb. for sugar cane. Sugarbeets set relative to cane. Sec. authorized to make annual adjustments reflecting cost of production, cost of sugar products, & inflation. Import quotas must be set so that loan forfeitures & cost of sugar program will be minimized.

Wool & mohair

	Producer incentive payment was difference between incentive price (based on parity) & price received by producers.	Extends current law.

Honey Loan Rate

	Set at 60-90% of parity; in 1985 rate was $.683/lb. (60% parity).	$.64 in 1986, $.63 in 1986; may drop 5% per yr. during 1988-90, but cannot be less than 75% of 5-yr. moving av. dropping high & low. Sec. may implement a marketing loan.

Trade

Export program	Authorized Sec. to extend intermediate credit (3-10 yr. terms) for sale of CCC & private stocks to develop, expand, & maintain foreign markets for long-term commercial sale of agricultural products. Provided for direct short-term export credit guarantees to expand commercial exports with deferred payment for up to 36 months; annual	Funding for an intermediate credit guarantee program (3-10 yrs.) set at not less than $500 mil./yr. for FY 86-88 & not more than $1 bil./yr. for FY 89-90, with repayment in dollars & with interest rate set by Sec. $5 bil. for short-term credit guarantees authorized through FY 90. Targeted assistance program funded at $325 mil./yr. Export credit revolving fund reauthorized. Export sales of 150,000 tons of dairy surplus mandated annually through FY 88.

Provision	Old law	New law
Trade (cont.)	funding authority for guarantees was $5 bil. Mandated FY 83-85 expenditure for export assistance of $175-$190 mil. through CCC charter. Provided for barter of CCC dairy stocks for 40,000 metric tons of ultra-high-temperature milk for donation overseas.	Sec. required to establish an export promotion program providing total of $2 bil. of CCC commodities through FY 88 at no cost to exporters & others to encourage development, maintenance, & expansion of export markets. Commodities to be used to counter or offset unfair trading practices, high U.S. price support levels, & unfavorable changes in exchange rate; under program, Green Dollar Export Certificates may be issued by Sec.; of those programs involving bonuses to promote exports, 15% of program funds may be used to enhance commercial exports of poultry, beef, pork, or meat products. Food Security Wheat Reserve extended; contract sanctity affirmed & producer embargo protection adjusted.
P.L. 480	Title I allowed for credit sales repayable in 20 yrs. with dollars, or in 40 yrs. in local currencies convertible to dollars at concessional interest rates. Minimum Title II tonnage 1.7 mil. tons, of which 1.2 mil. for nonemergency programs distributed through private voluntary organizations (PVO's) & World Food Program (WFP). Funding limit for Title II programs was $1.0 bil.; no minimum annual level for processed, fortified, or bagged commodities. Title III (Food for Development) required to comprise 15% of Title I funds; Section 406(a) of Title IV authorized farmer-to-farmer development assistance with discretionary funding level; Section 416 of Ag. Act of 1949	Under Title I, at least 10% of local currencies generated are to be lent to financial intermediaries in recipient countries for private enterprise development. Title II minimum tonnage increased to 1.9 mil. tons, of which not less than 1.425 mil. for nonemergency programs to be distributed through PVO's, cooperatives, & the WFP; at least 75% of nonemergency minimum must be processed, fortified, and/or bagged commodities. Title II authorization changed from calendar to fiscal yr. basis.

Title III share of Title I funds reduced to 10%; not less than one-tenth of 1% of P.L. 480 funds in FY 86-87 to be spent for Section 406(a); not less than 75,000 tons, but not more than 500,000, to be distributed through new Food for Progress program, to encourage market-oriented agricultural policy reform in recipient countries. Authorizes a Special Assistant to the President for Agricultural Trade & Food Aid. All commodities acquired by CCC can be distributed by Section 416 |

Provision	Old law	New law
Trade (cont.)	authorized overseas donations of CCC dairy products, wheat, & rice.	of the Ag. Act of 1949, with minimum grains, oilseeds, & dairy product levels specified.
Export transportation	Under cargo preference law, 50% of Government impelled exports must be carried on U.S. flag vessels, if available at reasonable rates. Included shipments under P.L. 480, & Sect. 416. Blended Credit was subject to cargo preference law.	Cargo preference does not apply to any commercial export activities of Sec. or CCC including exports under Blended Credit, short-term export credit sales, or barter agreements. Cargo preference does apply to "concessional sales," including shipments under P.L. 416 & 480 with 50% requirement increasing to 75% by 1988 & Dept. of Transportation financing increased ocean freight charges. Reverts to old law if DOT does not finance increased charges.

Conservation

Provision	Old law	New law
Sodbuster	No provision.	A producer who plants on highly erodible land, except land that was in set-aside or diversion program between 1981-85, will lose all Federal farm benefits on any land. For erodible land cultivated, diverted, or set aside after 1981, producer is exempt from loss of benefits until 1/1/90 or 2 yrs. after a soil survey unless producer is actively applying an approved conservation plan, then exempt until 1/1/95.
Swampbuster	No provision.	A producer who cultivates converted wetlands (wetlands drained, dredged, filled, or leveled in order to make production suitable) after 12/23/85 will lose all Federal farm benefits on any land.
Conservation reserve	No provision.	Retires up to 45 mil. acres that are highly erodible with a minimum total acreage in 1986 of 5 mil.; 1987, 15 mil.; 1988, 25 mil.; 1989, 35 mil.; & 1990, 40 mil. Program allows for contracts of 10-15 yrs. to retire cropland base or historical allotment. Producers submit bids for annual rental payments, with $50,000 cash or in-kind payment limit per person per yr. Sec. to pay 50% of cost of implementing conservation measures; haying & graz-

Provision Conservation (cont.)	Old law	New law
		ing not permitted unless area is subject to drought; if possible at least 5 mil. acres must be devoted to trees; reserve maximum is 25% of a county's cropland. This program may provide for permanent retirement of cropland base.

Credit

Emergency, operating, & ownership loans	Emergency loans to borrowers unable to get credit elsewhere made at subsidized rates; other borrowers charged market rate; FmHA authorized to make direct loans at reduced interest rate for farm ownership, operating purposes, & disaster relief; maximum repayment period for operating loans that were extended 7 yrs. could be extended to 15 yrs.; 20% of operating loans to low-income, limited-resource borrowers.	Emergency loans only to family farms & up to $500,000 per person; removes Sec. authority to make emergency loans to applicants who are able to obtain credit elsewhere; maximum interest rate for emergency loans is 8%. Sec. may not restrict eligibility for real estate & operating loans to borrowers of loans that are outstanding. Clear title & homestead provisions included. Restrictions on land sales in areas with depressed land prices.
Interest buydown	No provision.	Available only in FY 86-88; buydown for 3 yrs. on FmHa-guaranteed loans with Government giving up to 2 points if matched by lender.

Food Stamps

Authorization level	FY 85 = $11.7 bil. FY 86 = $11.871 bil. (President's budget projection).	FY 86 = $13.037 bil; FY 87 = $13.936 bil.; FY 88 = $14.154 bil; FY 89 = $14.695 bil.; FY 90 = $15.970 bil.
Sales tax	No provision; thus, States could impose a sales tax on food stamp purchases.	Prohibits sales taxes on food purchased with food stamps.
Earned income deduction	For determining eligibility, households could deduct 18% of earned income to compensate for taxes, union dues, & other work expenses.	Raises deduction to 20% on 5/1/86.

Provision **Food Stamps (cont.)**	**Old law**	**New law**
Dependent care & excess shelter deductions	A combined deduction allowed for actual dependent care costs &/or excess shelter cost (maximum in 1985, $139/mo.).	Separates the dependent care & excess shelter deductions. Raises excess shelter deduction to $147. Sets the maximum dependent care deduction at $160.
Work requirements	Persons between 18 & 60 who are physically & mentally fit required to register for work & accept suitable employment if offered. Exceptions include persons with dependents under age 6 & persons receiving unemployment compensation.	Requires all States to establish an employment & training program. Maximum cost to the State is $25/participant/month. Work registration suspended.
Asset limitations	Up to $1,500; $3,000 if two or more people & one was over 60.	Increased to $2,000 for individuals.
Puerto Rico nutrition assistance program	Omnibus Budget Reconciliation Act of 1981 provided for general nutrition assistance grant program in Puerto Rico & set funding at $825 million/yr.	Authorizes the following funding levels: FY 1986 = $825 mil; FY 1987 = $853 mil.; FY 1988 = $880 mil.; FY 1989 = $908 mil.; FY 1990 = $937 mil.
Temporary emergency food assistance program	Program expired on 9/30/85 & was extended through temporary legislation.	Extends program to 9/30/87.

reserve has the potential to reduce deficiency and storage payments too, although much will depend on the rental payment levels used to attract land into the reserve. Since the amount farmers will accept to idle acres varies greatly, it is an advantage that the conservation reserve can accept large acreages from those farmers who will rent for less.

By reducing benefits from cultivating highly erodible land, the conservation compliance provision encourages more land to enter the conservation reserve. The result is new assistance to owners of highly erodible land, but also new requirements that may alter the distribution of program benefits.

TRADE TITLE PROVIDES NEW TOOLS

For trade, the Food Security Act of 1985 aims to provide the tools for U.S. agriculture to recapture lost export markets and its share of world trade. The act provides a number of instruments to promote agricultural exports directly and others to combat unfair trade practices. The greatest impact on U.S. sales should come from reduced loan rates in the commodity titles. Competing exporters, however, may view the new bill as another broadside in a trade war.

The United States' primary short-term credit program (GSM-102) has been authorized at $5 billion a year, the same as the fiscal 1985 level. Before 1985, the GSM-102 credit program was a critical factor in U.S. ability to compete in world markets. However, the difference between U.S. price/credit and competitor price/credit offerings grew so large last year that only about 60 percent of the available GSM credit was used by importers.

With sharply lower U.S. prices, the GSM-102 program will regain much of its attractiveness. For example, $300 million of credit would have bought around 2 million tons of U.S. wheat in fiscal 1985. If the new 1986/87 wheat loan rate of only $2.40 a bushel is fully reflected in export prices, the volume of wheat that can be purchased with $300 million will rise to 2.7 to 2.8 million tons.

In addition to the GSM-102 program, the new act authorizes $500 million to $1 billion a year for an intermediate credit guarantee program, with a payback period of 3 to 10 years (the GSM-102 program requires payment in 3 years). This longer repayment period will be attractive to importers with hard currency or credit constraints. Also, the longer repayment allows importers to gamble on repaying loans in substantially less expensive dollars if the U.S. dollar declines over the loan period.

Since the current buyer's market will likely continue for some time and a number of countries will still have limited import funds, credit will continue to be a critical component of the U.S. sales pitch. The cargo preference exemption will also help. Credit customers will no longer have to bear all of the burden of the added cost of shipping their purchases via U.S. vessels. However, the percentage of food aid that must be carried by U.S. vessels will rise from its current 50 to 75 percent by 1988, with the Department of Transportation (DOT) picking up the added costs. If DOT lacks funds for the increased costs, then only 50 percent of these exports must go out on U.S. vessels.

Other promotion tools in the act, such as the targeted assistance and export enhancement programs, will not only provide funds to directly combat unfair trade practices, but also will give the Secretary additional ways to offset unfavorable movements in exchange, interest, or loan rates.

WHAT DOES THIS MEAN FOR U.S. EXPORTS?

It is difficult to determine how fast U.S. export recovery will take place. The degree of importers' sensitivity to changes in world prices is uncertain.

In a free market, a drop in world prices would lead to lower consumer prices and expanded consumption. However, many governments insulate their consumers and farmers from changes in world prices. Also, countries with limited hard currency or credit may use the savings from lower priced imports not for more food, but to purchase other imports or repay outstanding debts.

Still, the new farm legislation and the announcement of 1986/87 wheat and feed grain program provisions are causing concern among U.S. export competitors. Foreign producers benefited from the decline in U.S. market share. The additional export earnings provided critically needed hard currency to help repay debts and fund imports of agricultural and industrial products. Just like the United States during its boom export years, the competing exporters have come to depend on their earnings.

For example, between 1980/81 and 1984/85, the combined wheat production of Australia, Argentina, and Canada rose almost 15 million tons, with increased exports taking more than 12.5 million. The situation in the European Community was similar; wheat production was up 21 million tons, and net exports rose 5 million tons.

How competing exporters will react to the U.S. policy changes is unknown. Many countries may match the U.S. price declines in the short run. However, if the United States indicates through 1987/88 program provisions that it is committed to recapturing its dominant role in world markets, competitors may be forced to make substantial changes in their farm policies. Except possibly for the EC, no country has the budget to match the United States in a full-blown price war.

FOOD STAMP FUNDING EXPANDED

The 1985 farm bill continues the Food Stamp Program through September 30, 1990. Funding for Puerto Rico's block grant program is increased, and the

Temporary Emergency Food Assistance Program is reauthorized for 2 years. The title expands authorization for nutrition education programs and nutrition monitoring of the needy. In total, the 1985 act is expected to increase Federal expenditures for food assistance programs by approximately $1 billion over the next 5 years.

The provisions that will have the greatest cost impact are the increased allowances for assets, which will make about 200,000 more households eligible for food stamps, and the increased allowances for work-related expenses, shelter, and dependent care costs that can be deducted from household income to determine both eligibility and benefit levels. These amendments could increase Food Stamp Program costs nearly $500 million during 1986-90.

The provision to include Job Training Partnership Act earnings as part of countable income will reduce program costs over the next 5 years to $150 to $200 million. The required implementation of employment and training programs by States may increase program costs by as much as $100 million a year. However, if the programs are successful, the reduction in the number of food stamp participants and in benefit levels should be about equal to the added costs. [*Text and charts for this article were prepared by Mike Dicks, Tom Fulton, Lewrene Glaser, Masao Matsumoto, Herb Moses, Clay Ogg, Jerry Rector, Pat Singer, Terry Townsend, and Larry Traub.*]

NOTES

1. The minimum acreage to be placed into the conservation reserve is 5 million for crop year 1986, 10 million for 1987, 10 million for 1988, 10 million for 1989, and 5 million for 1990.

Agriculture's Problems Require "Macro" Solutions

John Lee*

The new farm legislation will be vitally important to American agriculture, perhaps for years to come. Resources throughout the agricultural community and beyond, into government, nonfarm industries, and public interest groups, were mobilized to prepare for and contribute to farm bill deliberations.

Why, then, do many agricultural economists continue to focus their attention elsewhere—on the health of the general economy and the policy decisions that affect it? Why are they suggesting that developments in these two areas could prove even more significant for agriculture than the 1985 farm bill?

The answer requires a basic understanding of *macroeconomic* policy and its impact on agriculture. Macro or general economic policies guide the actions taken by the federal government to shape the nation's economy. *Monetary policy* and *fiscal policy* are the two major components, and they are closely related.

Monetary policy deals with the supply and regulation of money and credit. Fiscal policy determines what the government spends and how it finances those expenditures.

A PRIMER ON MONETARY POLICY

As the economy grows, it needs more money for normal commercial transactions, capital investments, and other purposes. Monetary authorities, primarily

*John Lee is the administrator of USDA's Economic Research Service, a position he has held since October 1981. He grew up on a family farm in Pickens County, Alabama. Lee holds a Ph.D. degree in economics from Harvard University and has served as a USDA economist since 1962.

From *Farmline,* December-January 1986, pp. 4-7. Reprinted by permission.

the Board of Governors of the Federal Reserve Board (often called *the Fed*), control growth in the money supply. Briefly, they do this by buying and selling federal securities and by setting rules and regulations for the nation's banking system.

The Fed can fuel economic expansion by allowing the money supply to increase faster than real growth in economic activity. When more money is available relative to the normal needs of the economy, interest rates tend to fall just as the price of any good falls when supply grows faster than demand. When interest rates drop, businesses invest more, consumers buy more, and overall economic activity increases.

Unfortunately, inflation also increases because more dollars are available to buy the same supply of goods and services, thus bidding up their prices.

Conversely, the Fed can "cool" the economy by causing the money supply to expand more slowly than real growth in economic activity. This makes money scarcer relative to the need for it, and that drives up interest rates. Higher interest rates discourage investment, consumer spending, and overall economic activity. At the same time, people have fewer dollars to pay for the same stock of goods and services, so inflation slows.

The Fed must do a balancing act, constantly adjusting the growth rate of the money supply to assure adequate funds for sustainable economic growth without fueling inflation. The Fed's tendency to favor one side of this growth-inflation tradeoff over the other is what characterizes the nation's monetary policy in any given period.

A quick review of recent history may help explain. For several decades culminating in the 1970's, the Fed "targeted" interest rates, allowing inflation to adjust as needed. Low, stable interest rates were maintained by increasing the money supply, which, in turn, tended to push up inflation. Inflation rates began to climb in the late 1960's and early 1970's.

After a number of attempts to check accelerating price levels in the 1970's, runaway inflation finally prompted a major shift in Fed policy. Since 1979, the Fed's policy has been to hold money supply growth within a given range, providing enough money for high but sustainable economic growth while keeping inflation in check. Instead, interest rates are allowed to float up and down to reflect forces in financial markets.

This policy shift has been crucial for agriculture, affecting the availability and cost of credit, inflation rates, foreign demand, and economic growth here and abroad. More about that later.

A PRIMER ON FISCAL POLICY

Fiscal policy determines how much money the federal government collects and how much it spends. Spending in excess of revenues creates a deficit, and deficit spending can stimulate the economy by pumping more money in than taxes take out. This increases the demand for goods and services, encouraging production and new investments.

Several strategies can be employed to finance federal budget deficits: The government can borrow money from private sources, the Fed can increase the money supply to fund the deficit spending, or some combination of both methods can be used.

Financing the deficit by increasing the money supply was the predominant policy from World War II until the late 1970's. The money supply was increased enough to provide for normal business needs and to cover the federal deficit. This created no major problems as long as budget deficits were modest and tied mostly to cyclical downturns in the economy.

During the 1970's, however, budget deficits grew and became more persistent as rising tax revenues did not keep pace with more rapidly rising federal spending. The policy of financing the deficit by printing more money began to fuel rising inflation. This was the logical result of letting the money supply grow faster than real economic activity.

With the shift in monetary policy at the end of the decade came a parallel shift in fiscal policy. Instead of increasing the money supply to cover the deficit, the government opted to fund the deficit like you and I do—by borrowing money. This policy, pursued more or less since 1980, reduces inflationary pressures but increases competition in credit markets, pushing up interest rates.

AGRICULTURE IN DOUBLE JEOPARDY

In tandem, current fiscal and monetary policies have two striking consequences. First, they send conflicting signals to the economy, since rising deficits effectively put one foot on the accelerator while monetary restraint puts the other foot on the brake.

Second, and more important for agriculture, interest rates are driven up in two ways: by the fiscal policy of borrowing to finance the deficit, and by the monetary policy of allowing interest rates to float to allocate the more tightly controlled supply of money among prospective borrowers. The result is interest rates that, after adjustment for inflation, have been at historically high levels in the 1980's.

High interest rates are hardest on those sectors of the economy that are capital intensive and export oriented. Capital-intensive industries tend to depend very heavily on borrowed funds. Export-oriented industries are vulnerable to changes in foreign exchange rates, which are strongly influenced by real interest rates here and abroad.

Agriculture fits into both the vulnerable groups. It has the highest ratio of investment to sales of any major industry, making it one of the most capital-intensive sectors of the economy. It also has one of the highest ratios of exports to total production, putting it among the most export-dependent sectors.

We have just seen how large federal deficits and anti-inflationary monetary policy have combined to drive up interest rates. It is equally important, I think, to understand how interest rates and other effects of monetary and fiscal policies are channeled to the farm sector because of agriculture's links with the rest of the U.S. economy and the world economy.

These effects are difficult to trace through, but they can be grouped under three categories: effects on farm costs, effects on the demand for goods that farmers produce, and effects on asset values.

IMPACT ON FARM COSTS, LAND VALUES

Because farmers are heavy users of borrowed funds, rising interest costs have increased the costs of production in agriculture. In 1979, farmers' interest expenses amounted to $12 billion, or about 13 percent of all cash production expenses. By 1984, farmers paid more than $22 billion in interest on farm debt, or 19 percent of all costs. Interest had become the largest single cash cost of production in farming.

It is worth adding that when the average interest rate on outstanding farm debt rises by 1 percentage point, farm production expenses increase by about $2 billion.

The high cost of money has also helped to depress the value of farm assets, especially land. Other things being equal, the higher the interest rate, the less one can afford to pay for land.

The demand impacts of macroeconomic policies are just as important as the more obvious cost effects.

In the late 1970's, an overheated world economy produced galloping inflation, prompting the United States and other industrialized countries to adopt restrictive monetary policies. The less developed countries, meanwhile, were beginning to slow or trim their imports in response to mounting foreign debt problems. In 1980, the world was plunged into a severe recession.

It is against this backdrop of events that our domestic economic policies have had a series of negative effects on the farm economy.

High real interest rates in the United States, coupled with foreign perceptions that the United States was and is a safe haven in troubled times, attracted capital from abroad. The United States quickly became a magnet for foreign investment. Demand for dollars to make those investments caused the dollar's value to appreciate sharply in terms of other currencies. (At the same time, the large inflow of foreign capital masked some of the pressure on our own credit markets, probably slowing the rise in interest rates caused by federal borrowing.)

Some rules of thumb: Each $50 billion of structural deficit in the federal budget causes real interest rates to be 1 or 2 percentage points higher than they would otherwise be. Further, for each 1 percentage point increase in the gap between real interest rates in the United States and those in other countries, the value of the dollar rises 5 to 10 percent.

TRANSLATES INTO WEAKER DEMAND

This increase in the value of the dollar—which is perceived as an export price increase for American goods—translates directly into weaker demand for our farm products. The higher value of the dollar relative to other currencies makes U.S. export goods more expensive to foreign buyers, while foreign goods look cheaper to Americans. Hence, U.S. exports decline, and our imports from other nations surge. The lost exports end up as larger carryover stocks, which tend to depress farm prices and farm incomes. In other words, farmers end up selling a smaller volume, and often at a lower price.

There are other demand consequences, too, stemming from high real U.S. interest rates and the factors that cause them. As more foreign capital is banked in the United States, for instance, funds available abroad are reduced. Developing nations have less money to pay for imports and to invest in economic recovery and growth. Their potential to become better customers for U.S. farm products is directly tied to their economic growth. The drain of capital from these countries reduces both our near-term and long-term export prospects.

There is still more. The high cost of money and the attractive alternative of investing in dollar-denominated U.S. assets reduces the incentive of other nations to tie up money by holding commodity stocks. They do better by keeping their own food stocks at low levels, letting the United States shoulder the costs of stockholding.

Similarly, private U.S. firms facing high money costs also try to minimize nonessential stockholding, thus pushing the burden back to the farm level. This increases farm costs and reduces demand, the most obvious result of which is lower commodity prices.

A strong dollar has some redeeming features. Lower priced imports hold down U.S. inflation, and that helps hold down farmers' expenses. A 10-percent increase in the value of the dollar reduces the general inflation rate about 1 percent, and that could translate into a reduction of around $1.5 billion in farm production expenses.

Of course, cheap imports also cost us jobs. More than half the income of our farm operator households comes from nonfarm sources, primarily wages and salaries. Industries that provide many of the rural jobs in the Southeast and other areas are very vulnerable to foreign competition.

WHERE DO WE GO FROM HERE?

Adding up all the effects of macroeconomic policy on the farm sector, it's easy to see why many agricultural economists are concerned about the general economy. It is our view that macroeconomic developments are the principal source of the problems farmers face today.

As a society, we may have little difficulty agreeing on general economic goals, such as stimulating growth in the economy and reducing interest rates if we can avoid a new round of inflation. Similarly, few people would object to sharp cuts in the federal deficit if that could be accomplished without raising taxes or trimming programs.

In practice, however, economic decisions involve many tradeoffs and uncertainties. That leaves the future direction of fiscal, monetary, tax, and trade policies open to debate. Whether they participate in the debate or not, farmers have a vital stake in the outcome.

Factory Farming: An Imminent Clash Between Animal Rights Activists and Agribusiness

Jonny Frank*

I. INTRODUCTION

Although the animal rights movement is relatively old[1] it has, until recently, been largely unpublicized and unsupported. Indeed, the notion of rights for animals, both legal and nonlegal,[2] remains an unfamiliar concept to many people. Nevertheless, the animal rights movement is gaining momentum. Those people concerned with the plight of animals are publishing books[3] and articles,[4] instituting court actions,[5] drafting model statutes,[6] and lobbying for the enactment of legislative reforms.[7] In short, they are establishing a foundation for effectuating a fundamental change in our relationship with animals.

Contemporaneous with this heightened interest in animal rights stands the trend toward industrialization of animal husbandry to the food industry. The small farmer living an idyllic, pastoral life has become virtually nonexistent, being displaced by large conglomerates that conduct their farm operations like any other business.[8] These industrialized farming techniques are commonly referred to as "intensive farming" and "factory farming".[9] Although the phrases, "intensive farming" and "factory farming" are oftentimes used interchangeably,[10] the two are, in fact, quite different. Intensive farming involves increasing productivity through better management and breeding techniques but without significantly changing the pattern of life the animals lead.[11] Conversely, factory farming alters the pattern of the animal's life and results in undue physical pain and mental suffering.[12]

---

*Staff Member, BOSTON COLLEGE ENVIRONMENTAL AFFAIRS LAW REVIEW

From *Boston College Environmental Affairs Law Review*, 7, 1979, pp. 423-456. Reprinted with permission.

Until recently, animal welfare groups have avoided the controversial factory farming issue, focusing instead on more conventional issues such as pet overpopulation, abandonment or individual instances of animal cruelty.[13] This reluctance to deal with the plight of factory farm animals is now fading. The older and established humane societies, as well as a host of smaller and more radical groups, are confronting controversial issues and publicly campaigning against factory farming.[14] A clash between these animal rights activists and the powerful agribusiness corporations appears unavoidable.

This article examines those factors which contribute to the likelihood of such a confrontation, and offers strategies of reform for use by animal interest groups. The first part of the article describes many of the abuses that animals experience in factory farming prior to their transportation to market and slaughter. The second section presents a survey and critique of the federal and state legislation which protects these animals, emphasizing what little protection is, in fact, given to farm animals. The next section canvasses foreign laws as potential models for reform. The article concludes with several proposed strategies for change.

II. LIFE ON THE FARM

Factory farming,[15] characterized by overcrowding, restricted movement, unnatural diets and unanesthesized surgical procedures utilizes intensive farming procedures in such a way that results in severe suffering for the farm animal. The poultry industry uses factory farming techniques in nearly every phase of poultry production and, consequently, most vividly illustrates the abuses of factory farming. However, factory farming occurs in the raising of all farm animals— hogs, calves, dairy cows, cattle, and so forth. This section presents several examples of factory farming techniques and the cruelties they impose on farm animals.

A. Chickens

Two types of chickens are raised in factory farming systems: laying hens, which are grown for egg production but which are also subsequently used in soups, stews and pot pies; and broiler/table chickens, which are raised solely for consumption.[16] The methods of producing laying hens and broiler chickens share some, but not all, of the same features.[17]

Both broiler production and laying hen production begin at the primary breeder, a laboratory that develops the genetically different strains of chickens.[18] Broiler birds are bred to gain weight rapidly and have good body conformation, while laying hens are bred to lay thick shelled eggs with thick yellow yolks.[19]

The multiplier hatcher,[20] the second stage in the production of both types of birds, consists of large sheds containing ten to fourteen thousand chickens called breeders.[21] The breeders, a third strain of chicken, lay fertile eggs which hatch into laying or broiler chicks.[22] Breeders are used solely to sustain the population of laying hens and broiler chickens and, unlike the two other strains of chicken, are not retailed to the consumer. If the hatchery breeds laying hens, workers separate out and eliminate the male chicks at hatching[23] because they cannot lay eggs and thus lose their economic usefulness. These male chicks are either dumped alive into trash bags and left to suffocate or are drowned.[24] The dead chicks are then used in the manufacture of various animal feeds.[25]

The third phase of production entails the use of breeding farms[26] where the chicks are kept until maturity. The grower uses artificial lighting for unnaturally long or short periods of time in order to produce certain behavior in the birds. In broiler breeding farms, bright lights encourage the chicks to start feeding, while dimmed lights reduce the stress caused by overcrowding as the birds mature and increase in size.[27] In laying hen breeding farms, just the reverse occurs. Laying hens are kept in darkness or near darkness until they are ready to lay eggs, normally a period of approximately twenty weeks. Later, when the birds begin to lay eggs the lights are turned on, thereby conditioning the hens to lay eggs whenever the lights are on. Each week the lights are left on for progressively longer periods of time until, after forty weeks, they are on for seventeen hours per day. This lengthening of the bird's "day" increases egg-laying productivity and generates greater profits.[28] Such a regimen, however, takes its toll. While chickens raised under natural conditions can lay eggs for as long as twenty years, laying hens subject to these artificial conditions exhaust their laying capacity after only one or two years.[29]

After the breeding farm, broiling chickens are shipped to growing farms and placed in broiler sheds, while the laying hens are sent to laying farms and placed in battery cages.[30] These birds spend the rest of their lives in these surroundings and, under these conditions, encounter most of their suffering.

From ten to fifty thousand broilers live on the floor of each broiler shed.[31] Life in the broiler shed is completely automated in order to enhance the bird's growth. No natural light enters the shed; instead, an automatic mechanism adjusts artificial light depending on the need, either brightening the light to induce the birds to eat, or dimming it to reduce the effects of overcrowding. Hoppers suspended from the roof automatically dispense food and water. By the time the chicken is ready for slaughter, the overcrowding in the shed is so severe that only half a square foot of floor space remains for each bird, creating a high level of stress that manifests itself in outbreaks of fighting and cannibalism.[32] If a sudden change occurs in the shed because of a variation in the lighting or the entry of human intruders, the chickens panic and rush to one corner of the shed, piling on top of each other and suffocating those on the bottom.[33]

The most logical solution to these problems would, of course, entail relief from the crowded conditions. Such a solution, however, is less economical than the present growing techniques and therefore unacceptable to agribusiness.[34] In fact, growers use solutions that create even more suffering for the poultry. As a way of controlling the cannibalism that results from overcrowding, for example, farmers routinely include drugs in the chicken feed.[35] In addition, they remove the chickens' main defense weapon, the beaks. De-beaking is an extremely painful process, accomplished either with a guillotine-type device that chops off the beak,[36] or with a hot knife machine that burns it off.[37]

Laying hens live under even greater conditions of stress than broilers. The battery cages are even more crowded than broiler sheds, ranging in size from one to four and a half cubic feet, and in occupancy from four chickens in the smaller cages to nine chickens in the larger ones.[38] Cage life creates great physical discomfort for the animal. Cage floors are made of wire and while this facilitates cleaning, it runs counter to the instinctual need of hens to scratch dirt. Since this instinctual scratching also operates to wear down their nails, chickens confined in wire cages often grow toenails so long that they become entangled with the cage and are "literally grown fast to the cage."[39] Cage life also produces a condition known as "cage layer fatigue,"[40] symptomized by "brittle bones, inability to stand, and a pale, washed out appearance."[41] In addition, "breast blisters, foot pad lesions, feather follicle infection and feather loss all are commonly suffered by caged hens."[42] Studies show a ten to fifteen percent death rate among chickens raised under these conditions.[43] Some of these deaths result from fighting and cannibalism, and, as a result, growers subject laying hens to de-beaking, although the longer lifespan of laying hens means that the operation must often be performed twice.

Growers rationalize the use of battery cages by citing their alleged necessity for maintaining a reasonable price for eggs.[44] More humanely designed cages do exist, however, and they are just as efficient as battery cages. These alternative cages, about one cubic meter in size, have two tiers. The lower level contains nestboxes in which the birds lay their eggs and the second level contains perches, food and water. A six-month study that compared the new cage with the traditional battery cage found not only that egg production remained equivalent,[45] but also that the birds in the new experimental cages showed less pecking, pushing, and other problems caused by stress.[46] Unfortunately, without the impetus of legal compulsion, farmers have displayed no willingness to use these cages.

The chicken's suffering does not terminate at the farm. Broilers are loaded into trucks in a variety of inhumane ways: some farmers still catch birds by hand, others use bulldozer-like devices to force the birds into the trucks;[47] and, in Europe, a vacuum machine has been developed which actually sucks the birds through a large hose into waiting crates.[48] Laying hens receive somewhat better treatment: growers transport them to market in their cages. The slaughter of both laying hens and broilers, however, is unnecessarily brutal: the birds are unloaded from the trucks and hung upside down on a conveyor belt as they await slaughter.[49]

Factory farm operations have become widespread in the poultry industry with ninety-eight percent of all broilers raised by such systems.[50] Yet these factory farm operations are by no means exclusive to the poultry industry. Agribusinesses are utilizing similar confinement systems in the production of larger farm animals such as hogs, calves, and cattle.

B. Hogs

In recent years, hog farming has developed "total confinement" systems[51] which range from a two-phase breeding/growing system to more elaborate multiphase operations. In the breeding phase, the pregnant sow generally remains in an individual stall until about a week before she is ready to give birth.[52] She is then moved to a farrowing stall where she gives birth and nurses her piglets for about a week. In order to restrict the sow's movement, the breeding and farrowing pens are kept quite small; typically, the pens permit the animal to stand up and lie down, but prohibit the sow from turning around. Many farms have begun to use iron frame devices known as "iron maidens"[53] which prevent the sow from moving at all. In effect, she becomes a "living reproduction machine."

The United States Department of Agriculture supports the use of farrowing pens as a safety device, reasoning that the young piglet would have "little chance of surviving if its 500 pound mother accidentally rolled over it."[54] However, the Department fails to recognize that the sow's confinement to such a small area is the true cause of such a danger. Moreover, the piglet which the Department seeks to protect in fact suffers abuse just like its mother: within a day or two of birth, the young piglet has its ears notched, its teeth clipped, its tail docked and, if male, is castrated as well.[55]

In a two-phase system the farmer transfers the piglets when they are five or six weeks old to a "finishing" pen where they are fattened for the next thirteen to fifteen weeks before being sent to market. In a multiphase system, the pig first goes through a nursery phase[56] before being sent to the finishing pen.

Although they vary in size, finishing pens allow no more than six square feet per pig.[57] While some pens are outdoors and have cement floors, the more modern ones are indoors and have either slatted floors or sloping concrete floors to facilitate cleaning.[58] Such floors, besides being quite uncomfortable, also damage the hogs' feet and legs since they are unsuited for such hard surfaces.[58] Hogs raised in dirt pens, on the other hand, show only minor damage.[60]

Although the overcrowding of hogs does not reach as severe a level as that of chickens, it is high enough to produce stressful behavior. For example, the hogs bite each other's tails, a phenomenon the farmers have tried to control with chemical food additives[61] and tail-docking. Stress also manifests itself as a physical condition known as the "porcine stress syndrome,"[62] noticeable by such symptoms as "rigidity, blotchy skin, panting, anxiety, and often sudden death."[63]

Hogs possess high degrees of intelligence, remarkably similar to those of dogs.[64] If farmers raised dogs in the same manner in which they raise hogs, prosecutions for cruelty to animals would surely result. Yet no such prosecutions are imminent for pork producers. On the contrary, the government endorses current growing techniques and, in fact, actively supports research to develop systems which would "offer the potential for greatly increased animal capacity in confinement facilities."[65]

C. Calves

Veal production has earned its reputation as being "the most morally repugnant" factory farm operation, "comparable only with barbarities like the force-feeding of geese through a funnel that produces the deformed livers made into paté de foie gras."[66] The origins of the veal industry lie in dairy farming, where a farmer would slaughter unwanted bull calves, prior to weaning, for use by his own family.[67] Veal's pink color and extremely tender quality made its sale to consumers quite attractive, although each young calf had insufficient meat to make such efforts profitable. However, the demand for veal spurred the development of a system that fattened the calf but simultaneously maintained its premature condition by denying the calf any exercise, maintaining it in semi-darkness and providing a diet designed to make it anemic.[68]

In modern husbandry systems, the calf spends its entire life in a tiny stall in which it can neither turn around nor lie down. Instead, the calf must lie in an uncomfortable hunched position on either a cement or slatted floor.[69] No straw is provided for cushioning because straw contains iron which, if ingested, would cure the anemia necessary to create veal's pinkish tone.[70] In addition, the separation of the calf from its mother causes psychological harm.[71] The cumulative effect of these conditions creates great stress, making the calf susceptible to salmonella, diarrhea and other infections.[72] To prevent these diseases farmers ordinarily add antibiotics and other drugs to the calf's feed.[73]

Animal welfare groups have been researching more humane alternatives for veal production without impairing the quality of the meat.[74] One system would permit the calves to exercise, sit on straw and be fed milk through teats on automatic milk machines.[75] Unfortunately, farmers have not as yet demonstrated any willingness to utilize these alternative production systems.

D. Dairy Cows

The plight of the veal calf's dairy cow mother is little better than that of her offspring. Only a few small dairy farms conform to the traditional pastoral scene, permitting their cows to graze in outdoor pastures during good weather. Large agribusinesses implementing total confinement systems are rapidly displacing these small farms. Dairy operations use two kinds of confinement systems: "freestall" holding barns and "tie-stall" holding barns. In freestall holding barns, the cows can move throughout a limited area within the barn, although they must walk on slippery, slatted floors.[76] In tie-stall holding barns, a tether confines the cow within a narrow stall.[77] No reports have yet been published about the effect of these systems, although it is likely that the same problems associated with stress in other animals exist in the case of dairy cows.

E. Cattle

Ironically, while those who become vegetarians because they abhor the treatment of animals tend to eliminate "red-meat" from their diets first, cattle, as compared with other farm animals, endure the least severe treatment. The high cost of grain makes it more profitable to graze cattle on open fields during their first two years of life.[78] Nevertheless, beef production does not lack its share of abuses; indeed, cattlemen have begun to adopt many of the procedures utilized in the production of other animals. The most notable changes in cattle raising have occurred in the feed lot, where cattle are placed for fattening for their final six months before slaughter. Although feed lots in general still consist of open, outdoor lots, an unfortunate trend has begun toward total confinement buildings.[79] While the space allocations are not as inadequate in these indoor lots as in other confinement systems,[80] their floors are often inches deep in a soupy manure mixture which densely cakes the animals' coats.

Cattle must endure other abuses such as hot iron branding[81] and castration. The castration process has been described as follows:

> The procedure is to pin the animal down, take a knife and slit the scrotum, exposing the testicles. You then grab each testicle in turn and pull on it, breaking the cord that attaches it; on older animals it may be necessary to cut the cord.[82]

Cattlemen rationalize this procedure by stating that steers gain weight more rapidly than bulls; in actuality castration simply makes them put on more fat.[83]

In sum, factory farming is enormously abusive. Chickens, hogs, calves and cattle are all forced to live under abnormal, stressful conditions. Agribusiness, concerned solely with ensuring that its final market goods are not injured, is unsympathetic to the plight of farm animals. Thus, the life of a farm animal does not resemble the lazy, serene existence described in story books; instead it is a horror for which we as consumers must bear the ultimate responsibility.

III. LEGISLATION

Legislators approach the problem of animal protection through criminal anti-cruelty statutes and regulatory statutes. Anti-cruelty statutes seek to curb individual instances of cruelty to animals. Regulatory statutes, on the other hand, address specific animal-related activities, such as hunting, selling, and trapping, and, in some instances, seek to protect a species from extinction. An examination of federal and state legislation demonstrates that none of the abuses occasioned by the factory farming of animals are presently illegal or regulated. The law has apparently ignored factory-farmed animals.

A. Federal Legislation

Regulatory statutes provide the main source of federal protection for animals. Some legislation seeks to conserve the existing stocks of a given species,[84] while other legislation protects an animal after it has left the farm.[85] No statute, however, regulates farm animal treatment during the rearing process.

The Bureau of Animal Industry in the Department of Agriculture was originally responsible for the protection of farm animals. Established in 1884, a stated purpose of the Bureau was "to investigate and report upon the condition of the domestic animals and live poultry in the United States, *their protection and use,* and also inquire into and report on the causes of contagious, infectious and communicable diseases. . . ."[86] However, the Bureau's role in investigating and reporting upon the protection and use of farm animals appears to have been discarded in the transfer of the Bureau's research function to the Agricultural Research Service in 1947.[87] The Agricultural Research Service's reports indicate no concern for the humane treatment of farm animals. Rather, their research is solely aimed toward the "efficient production of safe, high quality protein."[88] The only other federal regulatory legislation which is even remotely concerned with the conditions of farm animals is the National Agricultural Research, Extension and Teaching Policy Act of 1977.[89] This Act was enacted by Congress to coordinate national agricultural research. Although the Act includes a section on animal health[90] it fails to mention any concern for the humane treatment of animals.[91] Thus, no federal regulatory programs exist to control the abuses inflicted upon farm animals.

Moreover, no federal anti-cruelty statute exists to fill the void. The Animal Welfare Act of 1970[92] provides, *inter alia,* for the humane marking and identification of animals,[93] humane standards with respect to handling[94] and housing,[95] and investigations and inspections of animal conditions by the Secretary of Agriculture.[96] However, the Act expressly excludes farm animals from its coverage.[97] The legislative history of the Act gives no explanation for the exclusion of farm animals, although it probably stems from the fact that the 1970 Act was an amendment to the Laboratory Animal Welfare Act[98] and thus farm animals were outside the scope of Congressional concern at the time.

Although no federal legislation specifically protects farm animals, Congress has not altogether avoided the issue. A bill before the last few sessions of Congress proposed the establishment of a commission to study the treatment of animals in intensive farming.[99] The commission would consist of eleven members, five members representing animal welfare and humane societies, five representing medical schools, veterinary medicine, and animal husbandry, and one possessing administrative or judicial ability. The scope of the commission's investigatory functions would not be limited solely to farm animals, but would also include laboratory research experimentations, domestic pet growth rates and the effectiveness of existing laws. In addition, the commission would also "evaluate and recommend practiced and economical alternatives to present husbandry methods and evaluate the effectiveness of public and private programs with respect to the development of such alternatives."[100]

The identification of economic alternatives is particularly important to animal welfare reform. While ample evidence exists concerning the current treatment of animals in factory farm systems, less data is available about alternative procedures. Certainly, a government report suggesting practical alternatives to factory farming would bolster the animal rights movement. Unfortunately, the proposed bill which would establish such a commission has never reached the floor of either house of Congress.[101] Thus, at the present time, no federal law offers any protection for farm animals; consequently, state statutes present the only possible source of protection.

B. State Legislation

Although a few state statutes regulate the treatment of animals generally, [102] none specifically regulate the treatment of farm animals. This leaves state anti-cruelty laws as the only source of state protection for farm animals. While the first anti-cruelty statute appeared in 1638,[103] such laws did not become widespread until the mid-19th century.[104] Today, virtually every state has an anti-cruelty statute.[105] However, an analysis of this body of legislation demonstrates that these statutes provide virtually no real protection for the modern farm animal.

1. Construction

a. Definition of Animal. The threshold issue posed by state anti-cruelty statutes concerns whether farm animals are included within their scope. Obviously, if they are excluded, such statutes can have no beneficial effect on the raising of farm animals.

Most state statutes define animals in very broad terms, similar to Florida's definition of animal as "every living dumb creature."[106] While in theory such broad definitions would seem to encompass intensively farmed animals, judges have used this vagueness as a basis for refusing enforcement and as a means of circumventing the statute.[107] In one case involving a cruelty prosecution for cockfighting,[108] the court held that birds were not within the purview of a statute which prohibited the wounding of "an animal,"[109] noting that, although birds are, biologically speaking, animals, there was no clear legislative intent to include them within the statute. To hold otherwise, the court stated, would "render [the statute] vague, indefinite and uncertain and therefore in violation of the due process clause. . . ."[110]

In some states, the anti-cruelty statutes specifically exclude farm animals. For example, in Georgia the anti-cruelty statute provides that "this section does not apply to the killing of animals raised for the purpose of providing food."[111] In other states, farm animals, although not specifically excluded from protection, are indirectly excluded by provisions limiting the application of the statute. For example, the Illinois Humane Care for Animals Act[112] excludes from its prohibitions "normal, good husbandry practices utilized by any person in the production of food. . . ."[113] Although there are no published court opinions interpreting "good husbandry practices," it seems very doubtful that intensive farming procedures developed by state agriculture research stations[114] and endorsed by professional farming associations would be considered poor husbandry practices.[115]

b. Definition of Cruelty. The second issue of statutory construction concerns the definition of cruelty. Cruelty is typically defined as "every act, omission, or neglect whereby unnecessary or unjustifiable pain, suffering, or death shall be caused or permitted."[116] The crucial portion of this definition is the phrase "unnecessary or unjustifiable," since it makes the success of an anti-cruelty prosecution depend upon a showing that the contested factory farm practices are indeed unnecessary.

The case law provides little clarification as to what acts are unnecessary or unjustifiable. However, those cases that do address the issue of the necessity of abusive farm techniques, although they are quite old and do not involve factory farming,[117] nevertheless do offer a few tentative interpretations. In general some benefit must result to either the animal or to the community to justify painful farm procedures. Factory farming, by definition, provides no benefit to the animal; therefore the issue turns on whether an economic savings to the farmer is a benefit to the community. The cases split on this issue.[118]

Whether factory farm techniques are indeed unnecessary or unjustifiable has created a controversial and emotionally charged debate raising economic and moral considerations. Proponents of factory farming assert that the price of food would be astronomical if factory farm systems were banned.[119] The history of industrialization and mass production results in an almost automatic, although unjustified acceptance of this premise by the general public. Yet strong arguments support the conclusion that factory farming is unnecessary and unjustifiable. First, the major costs of food production occur after the animal is slaughtered, with packaging, shipping, and marketing representing two-thirds of the retail cost.[120] Savings in the growing of animals thus have a minimal impact on the actual cost to the consumer. Second, no definitive proof exists that the abusive factory farmer insures any savings at all in the raising of animals. In fact, one study of egg production found that the stress produced by the overcrowded conditions to which chickens are subject actually decreased the net income per bird![121] Third, efficient humane alternatives are available if factory farmers were willing to modify their systems; no such inclination is evident. Chicken farmers have, for example, failed to utilize the improved cage for laying hens.[122] Finally, apart from these economic aspects, the moral question remains concerning the extent to which increased profits justify accompanying animal abuse.

Convincing a court that an abusive practice is unnecessary solves only a threshold issue. A second problem exists in those states that define cruelty as the unnecessary infliction of *physical* pain, suffering, or death.[123] Factory farming not only entails instances of physical abuse, but also includes the infliction of mental abuse, such as the stress level in broiling sheds or the separation of the calf from its mother. If this issue ever arose in litigation, agribusiness interests would probably argue that the cruelty statutes are limited to physical abuse and that the law should not recognize an animal's "feelings." On the other hand, animal welfare groups would be likely to maintain that the statute creates a distinction between pain and suffering, with pain relating to physical pain and suffering correlating with mental suffering. Even though some judicial precedent does exist for legal recognition of an animal's "feelings,"[124] no reported cases have resulted in convictions under the cruelty statutes for causing emotional or mental deprivation. Thus, the question whether the mental abuse inflicted upon an animal comes within the definition of "cruel," remains open.

Moreover, even demonstrating that a particular farming activity is unnecessary and that non-physical abuse falls within the statute may be insufficient to support a cruelty conviction. Many anti-cruelty statutes are too specific in delineating what acts are prohibited, containing long lists of particular proscribed acts.[125] Supporters insist that such statutes are easier for courts to interpret and enforce.[126] Courts, however, tend to interpret such lists quite narrowly.[127] Therefore, although these statutes may be useful in attacking ordinary forms of cruelty, they lack the flexibility necessary for application to factory farm practices which are ordinarily not included among the statute's proscription. On the other hand, statutes which are overly broad in their prohibitions present other difficult enforcement problems.[128] In either event, the factory farm animal remains defenseless.

Excessive specificity or excessive generality do not present the only legislative deficiencies of anti-cruelty statutes. State statutes simply fail, either narrowly or broadly, to proscribe specific factory farm abuses. For example, all anti-cruelty statutes fail to include overcrowding of farm animals as a forbidden activity. Although one case[129] resulted in a successful prosecution for overcrowding under a broad anti-cruelty statute, the case involved dogs, not farm animals. A court most likely would decline to extend such a precedent to the overcrowding of farm animals in the absence of specific statutory prescriptions, especially since the two situations are distinguishable on the basis of economic necessity. No economic necessity exists to keep dogs in an overcrowded condition, while agribusiness may arguably present evidence of such a necessity in factory farming. Moreover, since the dogs in the above case died from the overcrowded conditions, there was a much stronger presumption of cruelty than would exist under merely stressful conditions. In reality, life under the stressful conditions of factory farming produces more severe results for the animal than death.[130] Nevertheless, prosecutions based on the overcrowding of farm animals, absent a statutory prohibition of overcrowding, seem unlikely.

Even if a statute purports to proscribe a given factory farming abuse, adequate enforcement[131] is often lacking. For example, some state statutes seem to make certain factory farm practices illegal by requiring that exercise be provided for confined animals.[132] Factory farming practices in the poultry, beef, veal, and pork industries thus could all be challenged under such provisions. Unfortunately, no attempt to make use of these statutes in prosecuting factory farmers has ever been made.

Another example of inadequate enforcement of anti-cruelty laws concerns the neglect of injured animals under factory farming procedures. Since such farming procedures permit one person to maintain thousands of animals,[133] injured or dead animals invariably go unnoticed for long periods of time. Some statues specifically proscribe such neglect of sick, or disabled animals. For example, one such statute penalizes the owner of an animal if "any maimed, sick, infirm, or disabled animal shall fail to receive proper food or shelter from said owner or person in charge of the same for more than five consecutive hours. . . ."[134] In interpreting this provision, courts must determine whether shelter will be limited to protection from the weather or whether it also encompasses protection from other animals due to such behavior as chicken cannibalism or hog tailbiting. A very limited interpretation might limit shelter only to protection from the weather. However, if the purpose of the regulation is to help an injured animal to recuperate, then shelter from other animals would be equally as important as shelter from the weather. No evidence yet exists indicating which interpretation courts will follow. Moreover, due to the lax enforcement of the neglect statute, it now appears unlikely a court will ever be forced to make such a determination.

In sum, the construction of state anti-cruelty statutes illustrates how ineffective they have been in stopping factory farm abuses. In the first instance, such statutes might specifically exclude farm animals from the definition of "animal." Second, the legal definition of "cruelty" requires a showing both that the abusive practices are "unnecessary or unjustifiable" and, in those statutes which delineate what acts are cruel, that the activity is one of a number of enumerated abuses. Yet, even where a particular statute impliedly proscribes certain factory farming abuses, enforcement procedures against the violators create another serious obstacle.

2. Enforcement

Enforcement of anti-cruelty laws operates through either public or private programs. Public enforcement ranges from enforcement by policy departments[135] to enforcement by specialized administrative agencies.[136] Private enforcement programs grant police power to local humane societies and allow court actions by private citizens.[137] Most state enforcement programs primarily rely on criminal prosecutions,[138] although private civil actions also are sometimes involved.[139] While the impotence of these several enforcement programs ultimately results from the substantive deficiency of the laws to be enforced, the weak enforcement structure itself is instrumental.

Many states do not assign responsibility for enforcement of the anti-cruelty statutes to any particular agency, relying instead on the local police or sheriff. Since this approach has failed to adequately prevent conventional animal cruelty offenses,[140] it seems equally inadequate for preventing intensive farming abuses. Due to the increased incidence of other types of crimes, police officials simply are not equipped with the resources necessary to actively enforce animal protection statutes, but only respond to warrants sworn out by others.[141]

Another public enforcement scheme places statutory responsibility under the state departments of agriculture.[142] However, such an approach does not effectively protect factory farm animals. State departments of agriculture, often staffed by farmers, usually sympathize with farming interests.[143] Consequently, such departments are naturally antagonistic toward attempts to regulate modern farm procedures. In addition, even if a department did want to regulate intensive farm practices, it might lack the necessary legal tools. For example, one state statute provides a department with the limited power to formulate rules and regulations for preventing the inhumane treatment of animals used in the operation of "creameries, butter and cheese factories . . ."[144] but not for other farming enterprises;[145] the agency thus could not make regulations to generally protect farm animals even if it was politically persuaded to do so. Therefore, the basically ineffective anti-cruelty statutes severely limit the enforcement powers of state agricultural agencies.

Other states have created specialized bureaus of animal protection to perform such duties as "secure[ing] the enforcement of the law for the prevention of the wrongs to animals; aid[ing] agents in the enforcement of the laws for the prevention of wrongs to animals; and promote[ing] the growth of education and sentiment favorable to the protection of animals."[146] Such an independent bureau could be more effective in protecting farm animals, although the influence of politics and agribusiness might also restrict its effectiveness in arresting factory farm abuses.[147]

Private enforcement programs which grant police powers to local humane societies (SPCAs)[148] present more viable prospects for successfully challenging factory farm methods. Unlike state departments of agriculture or bureaus of animal protection, SPCAs are not indifferent to the plight of animals. Indeed, they exist solely to protect animals. The general trend of increasing interest in the abuses of factory farming should spur those SPCAs with police powers to more forcefully attack this problem.

Unfortunately, local SPCAs have generally avoided controversial areas like factory farming,[149] abdicating the responsibilities of enforcement to concerned private citizens. However, since cruelty to animals constitutes a criminal act, enforcement at the behest of private citizens remains a virtually futile gesture. Because a private citizen cannot make arrests unless the offense is committed in his presence,[150] such citizens' arrests for animal cruelty seldom, if ever, occur. Normally, private citizens contact the local police or SPCA and file a complaint, shifting enforcement responsibility back upon the very institutions whose inaction prompted the private citizen to act. Under some statutes, if the complainant receives an inadequate response from these institutions, he may petition a magistrate to issue a search warrant authorizing the appropriate officer to investigate.[151] This procedure vests a large amount of discretion in the magistrate, who may be hesitant to issue such an order. Moreover, the private citizen must undertake so much affirmative action that it is likely that few would actually persevere to the conclusion.

These obstacles to effective criminal enforcement by private citizens become less important with the availability of civil actions. One state statute embodies a relatively progressive enforcement scheme which does provide such a cause of action.[152] The statute states that an action may be commenced by any "real party in interest as plaintiff,"[153] with "real party" being defined to include "any 'person' . . . even though such person does not have a possessory or ownership right in an animal. . . ."[154] Moreover, the statute provides for the issuance of preliminary and permanent injunctions by the superior court against the owner of an abused animal.[155] However, no one has taken advantage of this private enforcement scheme. This lack of enforcement becomes even more discouraging when one realizes that this type of statute represents the exception among state legislation. Most statutes create problems of standing to use which generally preclude citizens from bringing private causes of action.[156]

In sum, none of these various enforcement plans can adequately implement cruelty statutes to protect animals from the brutality of factory farming. Traditional police protection is inadequate because of the priorities placed on other crimes. State departments of agriculture and state bureaus of animal protection remain ineffective due to the traditional agribusiness influence over those groups. Human societies, although the logical choice to enforce anti-cruelty statutes, have historically avoided such controversial issues. Of course, the private citizen may act, but traditional notions of standing and the current nonrecognition of legal rights for animals generally renders the private citizen powerless as well.

Moreover, even if there were effective enforcement agencies, our country lacks workable anti-cruelty laws for them to enforce. At the federal level, some regulatory statutes protect non-farm animals, but none protect farm animals. State anti-cruelty statutes offer little more protection, since they too are not intended, constructed or enforced to protect farm animals.

Fortunately, the bleak legal status of farm animals in the United States does not prevail throughout the world. Whereas the United States has just begun to recognize the injustice of factory farming, other countries have actively attacked the problem through legislative reform and governmental commissions. Although the vast size of agribusiness in the United States makes reform in this country particularly difficult, much of the activity in foreign countries offers an excellent model for reform.

IV. MODELS OF REFORM: FOREIGN APPROACHES

In 1965, in response to the public outcry which followed the publication of a book depicting the deplorable condition of farm animals,[157] England conducted perhaps the largest government investigation into the abuses of intensive farming. A committee consisting of experts in veterinary science, animal husbandry and agriculture compiled a report at the conclusion of the investigation[158] which not only reported on the treatment of animals in intensive farm operations, but also proposed reforms. The committee's proposals included such recommendations as: (1) minimum space allowances for chickens and a prohibition of debeaking; (2) minimum space allowances for pigs and a prohibition of routine taildocking; (3) prohibition of the confinement of sows; (4) freedom of movement and a diet of iron and roughage for calves; and (5) a general demand for better stockmanship.[159] Although these proposals did lead to "Codes of Practice" being issued by the Minister of Agriculture, many animal welfare activists have criticized the Codes as adopting too few of the suggestions of the Committee report and for watering down those which were adopted.[160] For example, the Codes sharply reduce the space allowances for poultry, permit debeaking, allow slotted floors for cattle and continue the abusive practices of the veal trade.[161] The most widespread criticism of the Codes is that they are merely government recommendations and do not have the force of law.[162] Nevertheless, they do represent an important breakthrough in government regulation of intensive farming.

Other countries have been more effective in enacting reform legislation. In 1976, the French legislature enacted a Law on the Protection of Nature[163] which, among other things, permits the State Council to take measures in order to protect domestic animals from maltreatment and the "sufferings resulting from the manipulations inherent in the various rearing methods and methods of transport and slaughter."[164]

By referendum vote in December, 1978, an overwhelming majority of the Swiss electorate accepted a new federal law that (1) requires the Federal Council to (a) regulate minimum size and construction requirements of animal enclosures, (b) set standards for the keeping of piglets in battery cages, and (c) limit the keeping of farm animals in total darkness; (2) prohibits the keeping of calves on grid floors; (3) prohibits the keeping of poultry in battery cages; and (4) requires that surgical procedures on animals be done by a veterinarian under general or local anesthesia.[165] Although this provides an excellent framework, the actual effectiveness of the law depends on the detailed regulations which are currently being prepared by the federal veterinary office.[166]

In West Germany, the German Animal Protection Act of 1972[167] provides that:

> Any person who is keeping an animal or who is looking after it:
> (1) shall give the animal adequate food and care suitable for its species; and he shall provide accommodation *which takes account of its natural behavior*;
> (2) shall not permanently so restrict the needs of an animal of that species for movement and exercise that the animal is exposed to avoidable pain, suffering or injury.[168]

The Act's importance results from the fact that it is the first piece of legislation to explicitly recognize behavioral distress.[169] West German law also authorizes the Minister of Food, Forestry and Agriculture to regulate tetherings, cage size, feeding equipment, lighting, temperature, ventilation and care and supervision by the farmer.[170]

In Denmark, the caging of laying hens has been banned since 1950.[171] Moreover, Danish law forbids force-feeding, castration of poultry and tethering so as to cause discomfort or pain. The laws of Norway and Luxembourg contain similar clauses.[172] Also, the 1965 Animal Welfare Act of Luxembourg prohibits "the housing of domestic . . . animals . . . in such a manner that they suffer from the lack of space in the stall or enclosure in which they are kept or from inadequate ventilation, lighting or protection from the elements."[173]

In Sweden, the Swedish Animal Protection Act of 1944[174] provides that "animals shall be treated well and as far as possible protected from suffering. The . . . animal housing shall provide adequate space and shall be maintained at a satisfactory level of cleanliness."[175] In addition, the law sets minimum space requirements for calves, hogs and chickens, and forbids the transport of calves under two weeks of age.

European countries[176] have led the factory farm reform movement, but such reform is more easily accomplished in these smaller nations. Europeans traditionally have had a more humane regard for animals than Americans.[177] Moreover, agribusiness in Europe has not attained as great an influence in decision making.[178] In light of the different situation in America, reform in the United States must be very well planned for it to be successful.

V. STRATEGIES FOR CHANGE: A THREE PRONG ATTACK

The preceding sections of this article have demonstrated that intensive husbandry systems abuse farm animals and that the existing anti-cruelty statutes are an ineffective means of protection. This section addresses those steps which can be taken to improve the existing situation.

A three part approach to the problem is helpful. The first part of this approach consists of a model statute which creates an administrative bureau to regulate factory farming since criminal anti-cruelty statues alone cannot adequately regulate an entire industry. Unfortunately, the present political climate is not receptive to the enactment of such legislation. The second part addresses those actions which animal rights groups can take to create a politically sympathetic mood for the future. This involves educating the consumer and identifying alternative husbandry techniques. The third part suggests that, during the interim, animal rights activists should institute court actions challenging factory farm practices.

A. The Future: Increased Regulation of Intensive Farming

Animals would be better protected by regulatory statutes than by criminal anti-cruelty laws. The Committee for Humane Legislation has drafted a model statute which would create a "State Department of Animal Protection."[179] Such an agency would have "jurisdiction over all matters relating to the preservation and protection of animal life."[180] Although writers have applauded this plan as providing an excellent administrative framework within which to attack problems,[181] the proposed statute does not specifically address the problem of intensive farming. Therefore, the author proposes an alternative Model Act (see Appendix). The Model Act would create a Bureau of Farm Animal Protection whose duties would include: (1) investigation of the treatment of farm animals; (2) research into more humane alternative farming methods; (3) promulgation of rules and regulations for the protection of farm animals; and (4) enforcement of such rules and regulations. This Model Act either could be combined with the plan suggested by the Committee for Humane Legislation[182] or could be enacted independently. Moreover, either the states or Congress could enact the Act. Because of the national expanse of agribusiness, the program would be more effective at the federal level, but animal protection historically has been a matter of state concern,[183] and local governments can more easily resolve enforcement problems. Ideally, of course, the statute would become both a federal and state law.

The Model Act begins with a statement of public policy that recognizes the concept of legal rights for animals and the abuses of factory farming.[184] Subsequent sections establish a Bureau of Farm Animal Protection which is supervised and controlled by a Board of Farm Animal Protection consisting of members representing the interests of animal welfare societies, veterinary medicine and animal husbandry.[185] The Board has the powers and duties to (1) investigate the treatment of farm animals;[186] (2) conduct research and develop alternative farming methods;[187] (3) analyze the merits of the contention that factory farming is essential to the economy;[188] (4) publish annual reports of its investigations and research;[189] and (5) establish rules and regulations to protect animals from pain and suffering.[190] The Act also establishes the position of Director as the executive and administrative head of the Bureau.[191] The Director (1) issues licenses;[192] (2)

inspects and reports on the treatment of farm animals;[193] (3) investigates all allegations of animal mistreatment; (4) issues cease and desist orders to persons engaging in activities likely to result in irreversible or irreparable damage to an animal;[195] and (5) petitions for custody of an animal to protect it from neglect or cruelty.[196] In addition to criminal penalties,[197] the Act authorizes private actions to be brought on behalf of the injured animal.[198] In the event that civil damages are awarded, the judge may order the award to be used either for the rehabilitation of the injured animal, for research into more humane farming practices or for both.[199]

Admittedly, no political realist could believe that this proposed statute would be enacted today. Therefore, animal rights groups must formulate presently viable strategies for reform. Such activists must seek to create a congenial political climate; and in the interim, should challenge the most atrocious factory farm methods through civil and criminal court actions, and through civil disobedience if necessary.

B. Planning for the Future: Creating a Political Base

The self-interest of agribusiness is not the sole cause for the paltry protections of farm animals. Consumer ignorance of the manner in which animals are raised in food production shares equal responsibility for this sad situation. Therefore, reform will only result from the education of the public who, as consumers and voters, are the generators of legislative change. One author has suggested that Americans will remain apathetic as long as the abused animal tastes good,[200] but this view overlooks the tradition of American responsiveness to publicized animal cruelty. For example, the publication of a 1966 *Life* magazine article about the sale of stolen animals to medical research laboratories[201] spurred more mail to Congress than the issues of civil rights and Vietnam, and more mail to *Life* than any other article in the history of the magazine.[202] This vigorous outcry reveals an unmistakable sensitivity to the plight of animals which animal rights groups could draw upon to effectuate legislative reforms.

Consumer education is made more difficult, however, because agribusiness spends huge sums to advertise the pastoral myth of farm animal life. For example, industry supplies children with coloring books which "depict cows in a cozy barn, one after one in a row"[203] and chickens, "dressed in hats and aprons in a nice clean house with lots of fresh air."[204] The National Livestock and Meat Board, an industry lobby, distributes filmstrips, pamphlets, charts and other classroom materials across the country.[205] These programs, combined with such usual media influences as cartoons, movies and novels, instill false deeply-ingrained notions about farm life. Consumer education programs must combat these misconceptions and expose the actual abuses of farm practices. One such consumer program is already being planned. The Humane Education Center is currently being constructed on a farm in Massachusetts by the Massachusetts

SPCA and will have exhibits demonstrating the true life on the factory farm.[206]

A necessary second step in creating a useful political base entails developing and promoting practical alternatives to factory farming.[207] Although Americans might sympathize with animals, they are not yet willing to adopt a vegetarian lifestyle. Concern about rising food costs persists and will fuel the debate over the economic necessity of factory farming. Practical alternatives to the factory farm would surely demonstrate that abusive husbandry procedures are not necessary, and would also help to dispel the public's inaccurate perceptions of the lives of farm animals.[208] Most importantly, the alternative procedures would benefit animals that would otherwise suffer terrible abuse.

C. The Present: Using Courts to Challenge Abuse

Although a fundamental change cannot occur in the absence of massive legislative action, animal activists must continue to judicially challenge animal abuse while concurrently working for statutory changes. Private citizens must undertake private civil actions and must pressure District Attorneys and SPCAs to criminally prosecute offenders of anti-cruelty laws. If prosecutors do not respond to such pressure and prosecute violators on their own initiative, citizens should obtain court orders requiring them to do so. Although the success of such actions appears doubtful, they nevertheless would at least publicize the abuse of farm animals. Perhaps more importantly, these challenges could force courts to reinterpret state anti-cruelty statutes.

Another judicial approach to enforce anti-cruelty statutes would permit courts to utilize equitable remedies as well as traditional legal sanctions,[209] so that the violation of a criminal statute would provide a basis for injunctive relief against the wrongdoer. Such equitable relief was unsuccessfully sought in a New York case[210] where an individual requested injunctive relief against state officials for allegedly cruel pre-slaughter handling of animals. The court dismissed the suit, holding that the plaintiff had no standing because he had not demonstrated any "personal or property rights of his at stake."[211] Nevertheless, later New York cases relaxed the standing requirement and suggested that equitable suits remain possible. In the landmark decision of *Boryszenski v. Brydges*,[212] the New York Court of Appeals expanded standing to permit suits where "the failure to accord . . . standing would be in effect to erect an impenetrable barrier to any judicial scrutiny of legislative action."[213] The ultimate effect of *Boryszenski* remains uncertain. In *Jones v. Beame*,[214] various individuals and animal rights organizations sued the City of New York requesting a declaratory judgment that the city was operating its zoos in violation of the state anti-cruelty law and seeking an injunction to (1) restrain the sale of animals from city zoos; (2) close city zoos; and (3) transfer all animals to the Bronx Zoo.[215] The lower court rejected the city's claim that the plaintiffs had no standing and that a criminal allegation does not support the imposition of a civil remedy, using *Boryszenski* to hold that "'statutes which on their face provide penal actions also imply a private right of action.'"[216] The Appellate Division reversed, holding that the plaintiffs lacked standing because the suit interposed the courts into the management of public enterprises.[217] However, the court noted that, "while plaintiffs do not have standing to maintain their action for declaratory judgment, they may be able to seek enforcement of the criminal sanction for violation of the [state anti-cruelty] law."[218] The Court of Appeals affirmed the Appellate Division,[219] although their decision focused on the political question issue rather than on the issue of standing.[220] Thus, although the plaintiffs were not successful in this particular case, they were not discounted as plaintiffs altogether. The Appellate Division, without any disagreement by the Court of Appeals, preserved their option to seek an injunction against violation of the anti-cruelty laws.

Civil disobedience has emerged as another weapon with which to protest animal abuse. A clandestine radical group in England known as the Animal Liberation Front (ALF) has made the most widespread use of this form of protest.[221] The ALF attacks all forms of animal abuse through direct, and sometimes violent action, such as raiding kennels, releasing animals from fur farms and research laboratories, wrecking circus tents and ruining the offices of breeders of laboratory animals.[222] The group attacks factory farming by rescuing abused farm animals and burning empty buildings.[223] In February, 1978, five ALF members were tried and acquitted on charges of stealing twelve chickens from a poultry farm.[224] Their acquittal resulted largely from a showing that the animals were severely overcrowded according to the standards established in the Welfare Codes.

The Greenpeace Foundation, probably the best-known American group to use civil disobedience tactics, seeks to halt whale and seal hunts by physically placing its members between the hunters and the hunted.[225] Although no group has yet undertaken such direct action against American factory farms, this activity likely will occur as anger about factory farm abuse heightens.

In summary, this section has offered a three prong approach to solving the abuses of factory farming: (1) a future phase, containing major legislative programs to regulate all intensive farming; (2) a planning phase, propounding consumer education and practical alternatives to factory farming as means of creating the climate to enact legislative reforms; and (3) the present phase, consisting of court actions and, if necessary, civil disobedience to challenge factory farm abuse.

VI. CONCLUSION

The magnitude of animal abuse is overwhelming, and our legal system, both conceptually and structurally, fails to offer any protection. The problem of factory farming illustrates this dilemma. The first part of this article describes many of the abuses inflicted upon animals in factory farming prior to their transportation to market and slaughter. Sadly, an even greater use of such factory farm methods seems likely in the future. The survey of federal and state legislation in the second part of the article demonstrates that no meaningful legal protections exist to counteract this trend. However, a small but growing animal rights movement has established itself and has already won successes in such areas as regulation of animal slaughter,[226] wildlife conservation[227] and marine animal protection.[228] Yet the power and wealth of agribusiness interests present formidable opponents. Indeed, nothing short of a well-planned, well-coordinated effort stands any chance of success.

NOTES

1. *See generally* G. CARSON, MEN, BEASTS, and GODS (1972).
2. Rights for animals emanate from a variety of sources. Some believe that humans have a moral obligation to recognize animal rights. *See, e.g.*, S. CLARK, THE MORAL STATUS OF ANIMALS (1977). Others feel that our legal system should include legal rights for animals. *See, e.g.*, Burr, *Toward Legal Rights for Animals* 4 ENV. AFF. 205 (1975). This article assumes an acceptance of the notion of rights for animals, be it legal or philosophical. A discussion of the merits of that position is beyond the scope of this article.
3. *See, e.g.*, J. McCOY, IN DEFENCE OF ANIMALS (1978); S. CLARK, THE MORAL STATUS OF ANIMALS (1977); P. SINGER, ANIMAL LIBERATION (1975); C. STONE, SHOULD TREES HAVE STANDING? TOWARD LEGAL RIGHTS FOR NATURAL OBJECTS (1972).
4. *See, e.g.*, Dichter, *Legal Rights for Animals*, 7 B.C. ENV. AFF. L. REV. 147 (1979); Tischler, *Rights for Nonhuman Animals: A Guardianship Model for Dogs and Cats*, 14 SAN DIEGO L. REV. 484 (1977).
5. *See, e.g.*, Jones v. Beame, 56 App. Div.2d 778, 392 N.Y.S.2d 444 (1977).
6. *See, e.g.*, Committee For Humane Legislation, Inc., Model State Animal Protection Statutes (undated) and Burr, *supra* note 2, at 232.
7. *See, e.g.*, the efforts of the Society For Animal Protection Legislation, P.O. Box 3719, Georgetown Station, Washington, D.C. 20007.
8. Approximately 1,000 small farmers go out of business each week. J. HIGHTOWER, EAT YOUR HEART OUT 155 (1975).
9. Harrison, *Animals in Factory Farms*, ANIMAL WELFARE INST. INFORMATION REPORT 2, col. 1 (June, 1977) [hereinafter cited as AWI REPORT].
10. *See, e.g.*, M HUTCHINGS, MAN'S DOMINION 96 (1970).
11. Harrison, *On Factory Farming*, in ANIMALS, MEN AND MORALS 14 (Stanley & Rosalind Godlovitch eds. 1970).
12. See Section II, *infra*.
13. *See, e.g.*, C. STEVENS, LABORATORY ANIMAL WELFARE, ANIMALS AND THEIR LEGAL RIGHTS 55-58 (1970).
14. For example, the Humane Society of the United States (HSUS) recently published a report entitled *HSUS Intensifies Campaign to Eliminate Cruelty on 'Factory Farms.'* A copy of the report can be obtained from HSUS National Headquarters located at 2100 L. St., N.W., Washington, D.C. 20037.
15. This section purports only to acquaint the reader with the suffering of animals on factory farms. For a more thorough study, *see* R. HARRISON, ANIMAL MACHINES (1964) and P. SINGER, *supra* note 3. Two new books on factory farming are scheduled for

publication in the fall of 1979, one by Michael Fox and another by James Mason. Much of the information in this section is based on Mr. Mason's manuscript.

16. P. SINGER, *supra* note 3, at 100.

17. Thomsen, *The Poultry and Egg Industry,* 41 REPORT TO HUMANITARIANS 1 (1977).

18. J. Mason, Animal Factories (unpublished manuscript).

19. Thomsen, *supra* note 17, at 4.

20. J. Mason, *supra* note 18, at 19.

21. *Id.*

22. *Id.*

23. The modernization of the process used to separate the male chicks illustrates how intensive farming, unlike factory farming, can benefit the animal. The procedure formerly used was known as "vent sexing." Under this procedure, males were separated from females by examining the chicks' "vents" or anuses. *Id.* at 20. This process has been replaced in intensive farms by feather and color sexing. This procedure relies on sex-linked feather and color traits to produce visible marks on the birds to distinguish males from females. *Id.*

24. Thomsen, *supra* note 17, at 5.

25. J. Mason, *supra* note 18, at 20.

26. *Id.* at 24.

27. *Id.*

28. *Id.* at 22.

29. *Id.*

30. There are several reasons why broilers are not raised in cages, including the fact that chickens raised in cages develop sores which reduce their value, and that the labor needed to remove the chickens from their cages increases costs. There has been an increasing trend, however, to use cages for broilers as well because many more caged chickens can be put in one building. The labor problem has been solved through cages which are transported directly to the slaughterhouse. UNIVERSITY OF DELAWARE AGRICULTURAL EXPERIMENT STATION, (Newark, Delaware), PROGRESS REPORT, (April-September, 1970).

31. Cook. *How Chicken on Sunday Became an Anyday Treat,* THE 1975 YEARBOOK OF AGRICULTURE 125; P. SINGER, *supra* note 3, at 101.

32. P. SINGER, *supra* note 3, at 101-02.

33. This phenomenon is called the "piling" effect. *Id.* at 105.

34. J. Mason, *supra* note 18, at 136.

35. According to the United States Department of Agriculture:

> A constant problem in broiler production is stress. Stress includes such things as extremes in temperature, disease, crowding and poor management. One or more of these is almost invariably present in broiler production, and stress slows growth in the broiler . . . [S]tress is overcome by adding antibiotics to the broiler's feed. Feed manufacturers now routinely include antibiotics in broiler foods, and broilers grow faster than ever.

Cook, *supra* note 31, at 130.

36. P. SINGER, *supra* note 3 at 105.

37. J. Mason, *supra* note 18, at 4.

38. The dimensions of battery cages vary from cages as small as 12 cubic inches to cages 18 inches wide by 24 inches long by 18 inches high. An area of 20 inches by 18 inches is the equivalent to a single page of The New York Times. Using this guideline, the crowding in cages translates to an average of seven to eight chickens spending their entire lives on a single page of The New York Times. P. SINGER, *supra* note 3, at 113.

39. *Id.* at 111, *quoting from* the Poultry Tribune, February, 1974.

40. J. MASON, FACTORY FARMING 5 (1976).

41. *Id.*
42. *Id.*
43. Ostrender & Young, *Effects of Density on Caged Layers,* 3 NEW YORK FOOD AND LIFE SCIENCES 6 (1970)
44. J. Mason, *supra* note 18, at 137.
45. Bareham, *A Comparison of the Behavior and Production of Laying Hens In a New and Conventional Battery Cage,* ANIMALS & FOOD PRODUCTION (1977).
46. *Id.*
47. Cook, *supra* note 31, at 131.
48. P. SINGER, *supra* note 3, at 106.
49. Thomsen, *supra* note 17, at 6.
50. J. Mason, *supra* note 18, at 27.
51. It was estimated at a Swine Facilities Symposium conducted in Des Moines, Iowa, in 1975, that, by 1985, 70 percent of all hogs raised in the corn belt states would be grown in confinement systems. FARM JOURNAL 33 (December, 1975); NATIONAL HOG FARMER 5 (August, 1975).
52. J. Mason, *supra* note 18, at 32; P. SINGER, *supra* note 3, at 125.
53. P. SINGER, *supra* note 3, at 125.
54. Steyn, *Streamlining the Hog, An Abused Individual,* THE 1975 YEARBOOK OF AGRICULTURE 136 (1975).
55. J. Mason, *supra* note 18, at 33.
56. The nursery phase allows the farmer to re-breed the sow immediately after birth. Within a day or two after birth, farmers separate the piglets from the mother sow and place them in individual cages. A mechanical feeder travels back and forth on rails in front of these cages dispensing a liquid diet to the newly born. In other systems, the pigs are placed in slatted-floor pens containing about 25 piglets in an eight or ten foot square area. *Id.* at 34.
57. *Id.*
58. *Id.*
59. P. SINGER, *supra* note 3, at 122.
60. J. Mason, *supra* note 18, at 92.
61. *Id.* at 121-27.
62. P. SINGER, *supra* note 3, at 129 n.38.
63. *Id.*
64. J. Mason, *supra* note 18, at 26.
65. U.S. DEP'T OF AGRICULTURE, LIVESTOCK AND VETERINARY SCIENCES ANNUAL REPORT OF THE NATIONAL RESEARCH PROGRAMS 83 (1976).
66. P. SINGER *supra* note 3, at 127.
67. *Id.*
68. Goodman, *Veal Calves and Factory Farming,* REPORT TO HUMANITARIANS 3 (1978). The University of Massachusetts reports that "the health of the veal can best be described as weak, anemic and susceptible to disease." COOPERATION EXTENSION SERVICE, UNIVERSITY OF MASSACHUSETTS, RAISING VEAL CALVES, No. 106.
69. P. SINGER, *supra* note 3, at 130.
70. *Id.*
71. *Id.* at 130. Mason noted in his visits to calf barns that the calves would attempt to "suckle a finger, hand or part of our clothing. The farmer explained that they always do this because, 'they want their mothers, I guess.'" J. Mason, *supra* note 18, at 43.
72. J. MASON, FACTORY FARMING 14 (1976).
73. M. HUTCHINGS, MAN'S DOMINION 98 (1970).
74. An English organization, the Universities Federation for Animal Welfare, has been the

most active group in the field. They can be contacted at 8 Hamilton Close, Potters Bar, Herts, England EN6 3 Q D.

75. AWI REPORT, *supra* note 9, at 3.

76. J. MASON, *supra* note 18, at 40.

77. *Id.*

78. E. LAPPÉ, FOOD FIRST. (1977).

79. J. MASON, *supra* note 18, at 46.

80. An average of 20 square feet is allotted for each animal. *Id.* at 46.

81. Nebraska, for example, requires that all cattle be branded by a hot iron. NEB. REV. STAT. §54.101-.01 (1978 Supp.).

82. P. SINGER, *supra* note 3, at 152.

83. *Id.*

84. *E.g.,* the Horse Protection Act, 15 U.S.C. §§1821 *et seq.* (1976); the Endangered Species Act, 16 U.S.C. §§1531 *et seq.* (1976); and the Marine Mammal Protection Act, 16 U.S.C. §§ 1361 *et seq.* (1976).

85. Two statutes, the Twenty-Eight Hour Law, 45 U.S.C. §§ 71 *et seq.* (1976) (prohibiting the shipping of an animal on a railroad for more than twenty-eight hours without food, water and rest); and the Humane Slaughter Act, 7 U.S.C. §§ 1901 *et seq.* (1976) provide some regulation and protection after the animal has left the farm.

86. 7 U.S.C. § 391 (1976) (emphasis added).

87. 5 U.S.C. app. Reorg. Plan of 1947, no. 1, Part III (1976).

88. U.S. DEP'T OF AGRICULTURE, LIVESTOCK AND VETERINARY SCIENCES ANNUAL REPORT OF NATIONAL RESEARCH PROGRAMS 1 (1976).

89. 7 U.S.C.S. §§ 3102 *et seq.* (1979).

90. 7 U.S.C.S. §§ 3191-3201 (1979).

91. A stated purpose of the Act is "to promote the general welfare through the improved health and productivity of domestic livestock, poultry, aquatic animals, and other income producing animals . . . to minimize livestock and poultry losses due to transportation and handling . . . and . . . to improve animal health." 7 U.S.C.S. § 3191 (1979). Although this purpose may benefit animals indirectly, economic concerns are clearly the motivating force.

92. 7 U.S.C. §§ 2131 *et seq.* (1976).

93. *Id.* § 2141.

94. *Id.* § 2143.

95. *Id.* § 2131.

96. *Id.* § 2146.

97. *Id.* § 2132(g). The Act defines an animal as "any live or dead dog, cat, monkey . . . but such term excludes . . . farm animals, such as, but not limited to livestock or poultry, used or intended for use as food or fiber. . . ." *Id.*

98. Pub. L. No. 89-544, 80 Stat. 350 (1966).

99. *See, e.g.,* H.R. 1112, 94th Cong., 1st Sess. (1976).

100. H.R. 10522 § 2b, 95th Cong., 2d Sess. (1978).

101. Letter from Congressman Robert Drinan to author (October 13, 1978).

102. *See, e.g.,* Colorado Nongame and Endangered Species Act, COLO. REV. STAT. § 33-8-101 (1973).

103. In 1638, the General Court of Massachusetts adopted a general legal code entitled "The Bodies of Liberties." The ninety-second section provided: "No man shall exercise any tirrany or crueltie towards any bruite creature which are usuallie kept for men's use." LEAVITT, ANIMALS AND THEIR LEGAL RIGHTS 3 (1970). However, this law was far ahead of its time. It wasn't until nearly 200 years later that normally progressive England passed its first anti-cruelty statute. G. CARSON, MEN, BEASTS, AND GODS 116 (1972).

104. *See* E. LEAVITT, *supra* note 103, at 71, for a chart indicating the chronological enactment of anti-cruelty laws in the various states.

105. The typical anti-cruelty law provides:

> Cruelty to animals. Any person who overdrives, drives when overloaded, overworks, tortures, deprives of necessary sustenance, mutilates or cruelly beats or kills or unjustifiably injures any animal, or who, having impounded or confined any animal, fails to give such animal proper care or neglects to cage or restrain any such animal from doing injury to itself or to another animal or fails to supply any such animal with wholesome air, food and water, or unjustifiably administers any poisonous or noxious drug or substance to any domestic animal or unjustifiably exposes any such drug or substance, with intent that the same shall be taken by an animal, or causes it to be done, or, having charge or custody of any animal, inflicts cruelty upon it or fails to provide it with proper food, drink or protection from the weather or abandons it or carries it or causes it to be carried in a cruel manner, or sets on foot, instigates, promotes or carries on or performs any act as assistant, umpire or principal in, or is a witness of, or in any way aids in or engages in the furtherance of, any fight between cocks or other birds, dogs or other animals, premeditated by any person owning, or having custody of, such birds or animals, or fights with or baits, harrasses or worries any animal for the purpose of making it perform for amusement, diversion or exhibition, shall be fined not more than two hundred and fifty dollars or impoisoned not more than one year or both.

CONN. GEN. STAT. § 53-247 (1979).

106. FLA. STAT. § 828.02 (1976). In South Carolina, animal is defined to include "all brute creatures." S.C. CODE § 47-1-10 (1976); in North Carolina, animal is defined as "every useful living creature." N.C. GEN. STAT. § 19A-1 (1978); in Nebraska, animal is limited to those "enumerated as domesticated animals." NEB. REV. STAT, § 28-553 (1978 Supp.) *See* E. LEAVITT, *supra* note 103, at 22, for a table indicating kinds of animals protected under the different state anti-cruelty laws (distinguishing by states that define animals as "any animal," "owned animals," and "domestic animals.").

107. Friend, *Animal Cruelty Laws: The Case For Reform*, 8 U. RICH. L. REV. 201 (1973).

108. State v. Stockton, 85 Ariz. 153, 333 P.2d 735 (1958)

109. ARIZ. REV. STAT. § 13-951 (1976).

110. State v. Stockton, 85 Ariz. 153, 155, 333 P.2d 735, 736 (1958). *Accord,* State ex rel. Miller v. Cloibourne, 211 Kan. 264, 505 P.2d 732 (1973).

111. GA. CODE ANN. § 26-280 (1974).

112. ILL. ANN. STAT. ch. 8, § 702.01 (Smith-Hurd 1975). Unlike the Federal Animals Welfare Act which excludes farm animals by definition, this act includes all animals other than man.

113. *Id.* § 713.

114. For an insight into the contributions of state agriculture experiment stations, *see* U.S. DEP'T OF AGRICULTURE, THE 1975 YEARBOOK OF AGRICULTURE (1975).

115. There is precedent in English law for a court rejecting a customary farming practice. In Waters v. Braithwaite, 30 Times L. 107 (Div. Ct.) (Eng. 1913), the court held that a practice of keeping cows unmilked to show prospective buyers that the cows were good milkers was cruel regardless of whether the custom was similarly practiced by all farmers in the country.

116. *See, e.g.,* N.D. CENT. CODE § 36-21.1-01 (1976).

117. In People ex rel. Freel v. Downs, 136 N.Y.S. 440, 26 N.Y. Crim. 327 (Mag. Ct. 1917), a case involving the cruel transport of turtles, the court noted that the pain inflicted upon animals used for food consumption is "justifiable and necessary"; but, in State v. Critchter, 4 Ohio Dec. 481, 11 Ohio Dec. Report 782, 29 WL Bulls (1892), the court upheld a cruelty conviction for the painful dehorning of cattle. The court noted that either

the animal or the community must benefit to justify painful suffering but rejected the argument that an economic savings to the farmer benefitted the community. In Davis v. Society for Prevention of Cruelty, 16 Abb. Pr. (n.s.) 73 (N.Y. 1874) the court dissolved an injunction which had enjoined the ASPCA from interfering with a slaughterhouse. The court held that the issue was not whether the mode of slaughtering was "the best and most expedient, but whether . . . 'wanton acts of cruelty are allowed and practiced.'" *Id.* at 78.

118. *Compare* People ex rel. Freel v. Downs, 136 N.Y.S. 440, 26 N.Y. Crim. 327 (Mag. Ct. 1917) *with* State v. Critchter, 4 Ohio Dec. 481, 11 Ohio Dec. Report 782, 29 WL Bulls (1892).

119. Defenders of factory farming also rationalize factory farming as a cure for the world food shortage. M. HUTCHINGS, MAN'S DOMINION 98 (1970). However, animal protein is a very inefficient source of protein; it is much more effective to use plant protein directly rather than converting it into animal protein. *See* LAPPÉ, DIET FOR A SMALL PLANET (1975) and LAPPÉ, FOOD FIRST (1977).

120. J. HIGHTOWER, EAT YOUR HEART OUT—HOW FOOD PROFITEERS VICTIMIZE THE CONSUMER 53 (1975).

121. Crober, *Social and Economic Aspects of Commercial Poultry Production*, ANIMALS & FOOD PRODUCTION 27 (1977).

122. See text at note 45, *supra*.

123. *See, e.g.*, LA. REV. STAT. ANN. § 14:102 (West 1969) (emphasis added).

124. *See* Hunt v. State, 3 Ind. App. 383, 385, 29 N.E. 933, 934 (1892), where the court noted that "to justify a conviction there must be a . . . disregard of the rights and feelings of the brute creation." *See also* Stephens v. State, 65 Miss. 329, 3 So. 458 (1888), and State v. Karstendiek, 49 La. Ann. 1621, 22 So. 845 (1897).

125. For example, Maine defines cruelty as acts of any person who:

> cruelly overdrives, overloads, or overworks, who torments, tortures, maims, wounds or deprives of necessary sustenance, or who cruelly beats, mutilates or kills any horse or other animal or causes the same to be done, or having the charge or custody thereof, as owner or otherwise, unnecessarily fails to provide such animal with proper food, drink, shelter and protection from the weather.

ME. REV. STAT. tit. 17, 1091 (1964).

126. *See* Burr, *supra* note 2, at 215.

127. *Id.*

128. Broad statutes leave a large amount of discretion to the judge and jury. This might prove to benefit animal welfare interests when the judge and jury are sympathetic; however, any such advantage vanishes whenever a judge or jury that is unsympathetic to the plight of animals handles the case. *See, e.g.*, State v. Buford, 65 N.M. 51, 331 P.2d 110 (1958). *See also* Annot., *Cruelty to Animals*, 82 A.L.R.2d 794 (1962).

129. McClosky v. State, 222 Ind. 514. 53 N.E.2d 1012 (1944).

130. Although a dead animal appears gruesome, it can feel no pain, whereas those animals living under conditions described in Section II, *supra*, most certainly do.

131. See text at Section III (B)(2) *infra*, for a discussion of the enforcement structure of anti-cruelty laws. The enforcement problem referred to here does not lie so much in enforcement mechanisms, but in the absence of any enforcement attempts whatsoever.

132. Minnesota's anti-cruelty statute provides that "no person shall keep any cow or other animal in any enclosure without wholesome exercise and change of air." MINN. STAT. ANN. § 346.21(3) (1974). *See also* OHIO REV. CODE ANN. § 959.13(A) (Baldwin 1978) and FLA. STAT. §828.13 (1976). Kansas has a similar provision. KAN. STAT. § 21-4310(d) (1974); however, farm animals are excluded from that provision. *Id.* § 21-4310(f).

133. The United States Department of Agriculture reports that "using a modern feeding

system for broilers, one man can take care of 60,000 to 75,000 broilers." U.S. DEP'T OF AGRICULTURE, THE 1970 YEARBOOK OF AGRICULTURE xxxiii (1970).

134. D.C. CODE § 22-811 (1967).

135. If the statute does not specifically assign responsibility for enforcement of the anti-cruelty law, the local police department will enforce the statutes under its general authority to enforce criminal laws.

136. *See, e.g.,* COLO. REV. STAT. § 35-42-102 (1978).

137. *See, e.g.,* FLA. STAT. § 828.03 (1976).

138. For example, enforcement in Connecticut relies solely on criminal prosecutions. CONN. GEN. STAT. § 53-247 (1979).

139. *See, e.g.,* N.C. GEN. STAT. §§ 19A-1 *et seq.* (1978).

140. Friend, *supra* note 107, at 216.

141. *Id.* at 217.

142. For example, Utah provides that "the department (of agriculture) shall enforce the law of this state relating to the inhumane and cruel treatment of livestock." UTAH CODE ANN. § 4-1-14 (1974).

143. The enabling statute of the Massachusetts Department of Agriculture, for example, requires that four out of the seven members of the Board of Agriculture be farmers. MASS. GEN. LAWS ANN. ch. 20, § 1.

144. UTAH CODE ANN. § 4-1-15 (1974).

145. *Id.*

146. COLO. REV. STAT. § 35-42-102 (1973).

147. Agribusiness is politically well-connected. For example, former Secretary of Agriculture Earl Butz served on the board of Ralston-Purina prior to becoming Secretary of Agriculture. Similarly, former Undersecretary of Agriculture Phil Campbell is a consultant for Goldkist, one of the South's largest broiler integrators and former Assistant Secretary of Agriculture Richard Lying is now President of the American Meat Institute. J. MASON, *supra* note 18, at 40.

148. *See, e.g.,* FLA. STAT. § 828.03 (1976).

149. *See, e.g.,* C. STEVENS, LABORATORY ANIMAL WELFARE. ANIMALS AND THEIR LEGAL RIGHTS 55-58 (1970).

150. WHARTON'S CRIM. PROCEDURE § 63 (12th ed. 1974).

151. *See, e.g.,* MICH. STAT. ANN. § 28.163 (1978).

152. N.C. GEN. STAT. §§ 19A-1 *et seq.* (1978).

153. *Id.* § 19A-2.

154. *Id.*

155. *Id.* §§ 19A-3; 19A-4.

156. The complex standing issues are beyond the scope of this article. For a thorough discussion *see* C. STONE, SHOULD TREES HAVE STANDING? TOWARD LEGAL RIGHTS FOR NATURAL OBJECTS (1974), *also appearing in its entirety in* 45 S. CAL. L. REV. 450 (1972); Dichter, *Legal Rights of Animals,* 7 B.C. ENV. AFF. 147 (1979); and Burr, *supra* note 2.

157. R. HARRISON, ANIMAL MACHINES (1964).

158. Command Paper 2836 (London: Her Majesty's Stationery Office 1965) [hereinafter called Branbell Report]

159. *Id.* For a detailed account of the report, *see* P. SINGER, *supra* note 3, at 139-52.

160. *Id.* at 150.

161. Agriculture (Miscellaneous Provisions) Act of 1968, § 3(4).

162. *See, e.g.,* Harrison, *On Factory Farming,* in ANIMALS, MEN AND MORALS 18 (Stanley & Rosalind Godlovitch eds. 1971).

163. (1976) J.O. No. 76629.

164. *Id.*

165. Letter from Claude M. Beck to the author (January 7, 1979). A copy of the referendum is on file at the Boston College Environmental Affairs Law Review Office.
166. *Id.*
167. Law of 24 July 1972, BGBL 1. (p) 1277, *cited in* Taylor, *Animal Welfare Legislation in Europe,* ANIMALS AND THE LAW 33 (1975).
168. *Id.* (emphasis added).
169. AWI REPORT, *supra* note 9, at 3. Recognizing an animal's mental suffering in addition to its physical pain is fundamental to the whole notion of animal rights.
170. J. MASON, *supra* note 18, at 98-99.
171. *Id.*
172. AWI REPORT, *supra* note 9, at 3.
173. Law of 26 Feb. 1965 of the Protection of Animals, Memorial 1965, p. 193.
174. AWI REPORT, *supra* note 9, at 3.
175. *Id.*
176. In addition to legislation passed by individual countries, the Council of Europe (which includes all the countries in the European Economic Community (EEC) as well as Austria, Cyprus, Greece, Iceland, Norway, Sweden, Switzerland and Turkey) published in 1976 the European Convention for the Protection of Animals Kept for Farming Purposes. Article 4 of that Convention is particularly noteworthy. It provides:

> 1. The freedom of movement appropriate to an animal, having regard to its species and in accordance with established experience and scientific knowledge, shall not be restricted in such manner as to cause it unnecessary suffering or injury.
> 2. Where an animal is continuously or regularly tethered or confined, it shall be given the space appropriate to its physiological and ethological needs in accordance with established experience and scientific knowledge.

COUNCIL OF EUROPE, EXPLANATORY REPORT ON THE EUROPEAN CONVENTION ON THE PROTECTION OF ANIMALS KEPT FOR FARMING PURPOSES 12 (1976).
177. For example, European countries have pioneered animal welfare legislation since the inception of the humane movement in the mid-nineteenth century. *See generally* G. CARSON, MEN, BEASTS, AND GODS (1972).
178. Telephone interview with Nancy Payton, Legislative Assistant, Massachusetts Society for the Prevention of Cruelty to Animals (April 18, 1979).
179. Committee for Humane Legislation, Inc., Model State Animal Protection Statutes (undated). Copies are available from the Committee for Humane Legislation, Inc., 11 West 60th Street, New York, N.Y. 10023.
180. *Id.*
181. *See, e.g.,* Burr, *supra* note 2, at 232.
182. The Bureau of Farm Animal Protection could be a subdivision of the State Department of Animal Protection proposed by the Committee for Humane Legislation.
183. Geer v. Connecticut, 161 U.S. 519 (1896).
184. *See* Model Farm Animal Protection Act § 101 at Appendix, *infra.*
185. *Id.* § 103.
186. *Id.* § 105(a).
187. *Id.* § 105(b).
188. *Id.* 105(c).
189. *Id.* 105(d).
190. *Id.* 105(e). The Act specifically mandates (1) the prohibition of the keeping of any animal without the opportunity for exercise; (2) the prohibition of any environment that produces an inordinate amount of stress; (3) the prohibition of painful surgical procedures; and (4) a licensing system for all farms. *Id.*

191. *Id.* §§ 106, 107.
192. *Id.* § 107(a).
193. *Id.* § 107(b).
194. *Id.* § 107(c).
195. *Id.* § 107(d).
196. *Id.* § 107(e).
197. *Id.* § 108.
198. *Id.* § 109.
199. *Id.*
200. Friend, *supra* note 107, at 209.
201. Wayman & Stan, *Concentration Camps for Dogs,* LIFE, February 4, 1966.
202. E. LEAVITT, *supra* note 103, at 49.
203. J. MASON, *supra* note 18, at 22, *quoting from* THE DAIRY COW AND HER MARVELOUS MILK (1976).
204. *Id., quoting* THE CHICKEN AND THE INCREDIBLE EDIBLE EGG (1975).
205. *Id.*
206. Telephone interview with Nancy Payton, Legislative Assistant, Massachusetts Society for the Prevention of Cruelty to Animals (March 5, 1979).
207. *See, e.g.,* the efforts of Universities Federation for Animal Welfare, 8 Hamilton Close, Potters Bar, Herts, England and the Farm and Food Society, 4 Willfield Way, London NW 11 7XT.
208. Marketing food products advertised as humanely raised should spur consumers to inquire into the treatment of animals in products not so advertised.
209. Burr, *supra* note 2, at 229.
210. Walz v. Baum, 42 App. Div. 2d 643 (N.Y. 1973).
211. *Id.* at 644.
212. 37 N.Y.2d 361 (1975) (granting standing to a taxpayer in his suit attacking the constitutionality of a state legislative and executive retirement plan).
213. *Id.* at 364.
214. 86 Misc.2d 832 (1976), *rev'd* 56 App. Div. 2d 778 (N.Y. 1977), *aff'd* 45 N.Y.2d 402 (1978).
215. *Id.* at 834. The Bronx Zoo is a private zoo operated by the New York Zoological Society.
216. *Id.* at 835, *quoting* Boryszenski v. Brydges, 37 N.Y.2d 361 (1975), *quoting* Barnes v. Peat, 69 Misc.2d 1068, 1070 (1972).
217. Jones v. Beame, 56 App. Div. 2d 778, 779 (N.Y. 1977).
218. *Id.*
219. Jones v. Beame, 45 N.Y.2d 402 (1978).
220. *Id.* at 452. "[I]f anyone has standing to litigate these issues, plaintiffs do. The difficulty is not, however, whether plaintiffs are the wrong ones to present and litigate the issues; the point is that the courts are the wrong forum for the resolution of these disputes." *Id.*
221. For a general description of ALF activities, see New Musical Express, November 12, 1977, at 13 *et seq.*
222. *Id.*
223. *Id.*
224. JOURNAL OF COMPASSION IN WORLD FARMING SOCIETY, Ag. No. 48 (1978).
225. To contact the Greenpeace Foundation, write to Greenpeace Foundation, 240 Fort Mason, San Francisco, California 94123.
226. *See, e.g.,* The Humane Slaughter Act, 7 U.S.C. §§ 1901 *et seq.* (1976).
227. *See, e.g.,* The Endangered Species Act, 16 U.S.C. §§ 1531 *et seq.* (1976).
228. *See, e.g.,* The Marine Mammal Protection Act, 16 U.S.C. §§ 1361 *et seq.* (1976).

II
Foreign Effects of American Agricultural Policy

Statement of Lester R. Brown, President, Worldwatch Institute, Washington, D.C.

Lester Brown

Mr. BROWN. Thank you, Mr. Chairman.

Like those who have preceded me this morning, I would like to commend you as chairman of the Select Committee on Hunger for focusing on population growth and its relationship to the problem of malnutrition. If those who have been concerned with hunger in the past had paid more attention to population, there would not be so many starving people in the world today.

In the interest of time, I would like to submit as testimony excerpts from our report, "State of The World 1985," dealing with these issues, that was released a couple of months ago.

Chairman LELAND. Please know that your full testimony will be entered into the record. We appreciate your summary of the testimony.

Mr. BROWN. Thank you.

What I would like to do is look very quickly at the relationship between population and a number of key resources including cropland, water, fertilizer, oil, technology, and even the relationship between population and climate.

Looking first at cropland trends, we see that the growth in cropland has slowed markedly over the past generation. I am going to refer to some of the charts in the testimony. I assume that the committee members have copies of this. On page 24 of "State of the World 1985" we have adapted some data from the U.S. Department of Agriculture, including their projections of world cropland growth over the rest of this century. What we see is that growth in cropland, which was averaging about 1 percent per year for the world as a whole during the 1950's, has slowed dramatically. The Department of Agriculture is projecting that, from 1980 until 2000, world cropland area will grow by only 4 percent. And

---

Lester Brown, "Testimony," *Population Growth and Hunger,* Hearing before Select Committee on Hunger, U.S. House of Representatives, June 6, 1984, pp. 13-19.

this is during a period when population will grow by 40 percent. So, you can get a sense of how rapidly the population-land ratio for the world as a whole is going to be declining between now and the end of the century.

A third of the people in the world now live in countries where the cropland area is actually declining, countries like China and Italy, just to cite two examples. The reasons for the shrinkage in the cropland area in those countries where it is declining are, one, severe degradation to the point where the land is no longer agriculturally viable. A second reason is urban expansion, and that is a problem throughout the world. And a third, that does not get much attention, is village expansion.

There has been a fairly detailed study in Bangladesh, for example, of the relationship between the size of villages and the size of the population. It is almost a 1-to-1 relationship. In a society where the structural materials do not permit multistory buildings, as population and housing expand, they take up more and more land. In Bangladesh, which is basically a country of rice fields, the expansion of villages is at the expense of cropland.

One of the countries that is most concerned with the loss of cropland at the national policy level is China. As you know, most of China's billion people are in an area about 1,000 miles wide on the eastern coast of the country, an area roughly the size of the United States east of the Mississippi. Almost all of the industrial growth in China has been concentrated in this area. You have to build the factories where the people are, and the people are located near the good cropland.

The Chinese, when I was in Beijing just over a year ago, were having a subcabinet meeting on the problem of peasant housing. As liberalization of agriculture in China has proceeded, the peasants have begun to earn quite a bit of money. The first thing they do is build a new house when they get enough money. When you get a large fraction of a population of 1 billion building new houses, you can chew up a lot of cropland in a short period of time. So, they are actually trying to develop incentives to get peasants to build two-story houses instead of one-story houses, just to save that cropland.

Another example of the level of concern with cropland in China shows up in the burial practices. The Chinese Government is now actively encouraging cremation, which is a new procedure in China. Traditionally, there have always been the burial mounds. Given the ancestor worship, this has been an important part of Chinese culture. And that is changing now. They are actively and publicly promoting cremation as a way of conserving cropland.

The second resource very much influencing the food prospect is water. The world irrigated area between 1950 and 1980 nearly tripled, an enormous growth (See table on p. 28 SOTW 1985). Up until 1950, there were only 94 million hectares of irrigated land in the world. By 1982, that had nearly tripled, to 261 million hectares, an explosive growth. But that growth, too, is slowing and will not be expanding nearly as much as we move toward the end of the century.

As with cropland, we now have a few countries, including our own, where the irrigated area is now declining. In the United States the irrigated area, which grew rapidly from the end of World War II up through 1978, turned downward after 1978 and has declined by about 3 percent nationwide since then. There are two principal reasons: One is the depletion of the Ogallala aquifer in the southern plains, including importantly the State of Texas; the second is the loss of irrigation water to urban and industrial development, the Sun Belt phenomenon, if you will. Texas and Florida have each lost about a fifth of their irrigated area over the last 5 years or so. So, we are facing a very new situation here, where urban development is siphoning water away from agriculture.

A third resource that we need to be concerned with is fertilizer. World fertilizer use has increased nine-fold since 1950. It is probably the best single indicator we have of the growing energy intensity of world agriculture. As the population-land ratio declines, we compensate, or at least attempt to compensate for that decline by substituting fertilizer for cropland.

On average in 1950, we used 5 kilograms of fertilizer per person; this is for the world as a whole. By 1980, that had reached 25 kilograms. We are clearly in a situation now where further increases in world food output depend directly on the growing use of fertilizer and therefore the growing energy intensity of world food production.

On page 30, [SOTW 1985] there is a figure that shows rather graphically the relationship between cropland area per person, it shows it declining steadily since 1950, down by more than a third, and, at the same time, the way in which fertilizer use has increased in order to offset the effect of that decline.

Another issue—and this was touched on by Congressman Porter in what I thought was an outstanding statement—is technology. We look at technology with some hope, and justifiably. But in agriculture there has been a tendency to overestimate the contribution of the new biotechnologies that are unfolding so rapidly: Recombinant DNA, tissue culture, cloning, et cetera.

There is no question but that these new technologies are going to play a role. But I think they should be seen as a new tool in the researcher's tool kit and not as a quick solution to the problem of world hunger. They will permit researchers to achieve research goals faster in some cases and in some cases at less cost. But we have to remember that we are still dependent on the process of photosynthesis to convert solar energy into biochemical energy, into forms that we can use. And the basic chemistry of this process imposes the ultimate constraint on food production.

If we look at some of the trends in grain production in the United States, for example, turning to page 34, we can see both the potential and the limitations. This graph on page 34 shows the U.S. grain sorghum yield from 1950 through 1984. Grain sorghum, as you know, is our second leading feedgrain now after corn. Most of it is grown in the Southern Plains. During the 7 years between 1955 and 1966, our sorghum yields tripled, a dramatic increase. Three things were involved: The hybridization of sorghum, expanding irrigation of sorghum, and the intensive use of fertilizer.

Since 1966, sorghum yields have not increased at all. They have fluctuated but not increased. As we begin to lose the irrigation resources of the Ogallala aquifer in the Southern Plains, it is quite possible that at the end of century U.S. sorghum yields will be less than they are today.

And in country after country, we are beginning to face this S-shaped curve in yield, that is, a period of rapid increase followed by a leveling off. We see it in corn yields on page 35 of SOTW 1985, for example, where U.S. corn yields between 1950 and the early 1980's nearly tripled and then since have increased very little. We can look at rice yields in Japan on the same page and see exactly the same S-shaped curve.

One of the questions that ties food and population together is the question of food security and what is happening to food security. If we look at page 37, we can see the change over the past generation. During the period from 1950 to 1973, world food output increased, in per capita terms, about 1 percent per year. That is, food production exceeded population growth from 1950 to 1973 by nearly 30 percent. So, this was a period when the rising tide of food production was raising nutritional levels throughout the world. There were very few countries in which nutrition did not improve between 1950 and 1973. That was a unique historical period.

Since then, there has been very little increase in per-capita grain production for the world as a whole. It is a combination of both supply-side constraints and limited growth in demand.

One of the reasons that grain production growth has slowed from something like 3 percent before 1973 to roughly 2 percent since then has been rising production costs, particularly those inputs that involve the use of energy.

On the demand side, per capita income for the world as a whole has not increased very much at all since 1973. That is, world economic growth has been keeping up with population and gaining a little, but not very much. So, per capita income has not increased very much. And when per capita income is not increasing, per capita food consumption does not increase much.

Perhaps the most disturbing development on the population front recently has been the growing realization that population growth may now be inducing climate change in some parts of the world, most importantly Africa. Almost all of the land-use changes associated with population growth such as deforestation, either to clear land for agriculture or because of a firewood shortage, or overgrazing, or clearing land for agriculture, all of these changes have the effect of increasing rainfall runoff and reducing the amount that is retained and evaporated into the atmosphere to recharge clouds.

If I can use a very rudimentary meteorological model, I would simply point out that there is a complementary relationship between trees and clouds. Trees take liquid water from under the soil and convert it into water vapor through transpiration. That water vapor enters the atmosphere and collects in the form of clouds. Clouds take that water vapor and under the right conditions convert it into liquid form. It becomes rainfall. So, you have this complementary relationship in the hydrological cycle between trees and clouds. When you take the trees out of that system, as is happening all across Africa now, that cycle is affected.

We do not yet have the sophisticated meteorological models incorporating the changes in land use over the past generation such as deforestation and the changes in rainfall patterns. But there is now a growing number of meteorologists who think that the scale of human-induced land-use changes in Africa are now large enough to be affecting climate, specifically, to be reducing rainfall. If that is happening, then we have before us a challenge in Africa that has no historical precedent.

I could go into more detail on what is happening in Africa, but I understand that the committee has hearings scheduled sometime next month on this, so I will pass in the interest of time.

The final two points deal with population, population policy specifically.

The demographic transition, which is a device used by demographers to explain changing rates of population growth, is useful in looking at what is happening in the world today. As you know, there are three stages in the demographic transition. In the first, you have the very traditional societies, premodern, that have high birth rates and high death rates and very little population growth because birth and death are in balance at a high level.

In the middle stage, death rates come down, but birth rates remain high; and you get rapid population growth. That is where you get the 3-percent rate of population growth. That is where a good part of the Third World, almost all of Africa, is today.

Then the third stage, you get birth rates coming down to come into balance with death rates, and again you have population stability. Much of Western Europe has reached that point. There is very little population growth in Western Europe because births and deaths are in balance but at a very low level.

Historically, we have always thought of the demographic transition as being a progressive thing. Countries went from stage 1 to stage 2 and then eventually to stage 3 as living conditions and access to family planning services improved. What is beginning to happen now is that some countries in the middle stage are getting trapped there over an extended period of time, long enough that rapid population growth is beginning to undermine the resource base through soil erosion, deforestation, desertification, et cetera. And per capita food consumption is beginning to decline, as it has been in Africa now for a decade and a half. And countries are losing the demographic momentum that would have carried them into the final stage, as the industrial world has done, for example, and as China is doing. They are beginning to fall back toward the first stage as death rates rise.

The most recent tabulation, for example, by African governments indicate at least 1 million lives lost to starvation just over the past year. That number is increasing.

The real risk is that those countries that are in the middle stage, that have the 3-percent rates of population growth, which is twentyfold per century, are going to lose momentum and not make it into the final stage and begin to fall back toward the first. There is evidence that that is now happening in Africa. This is the first time that this has happened, historically.

This is one reason why it is so important that the groups that are providing family planning services, such as the International Planned Parenthood Federation and the U.N. Fund for Population Activities, be able to help these countries now. There has been a sea change in Africa in interest in family planning services and the population issue over the last 18 or 24 months.

I was in Zimbabwe last month and learned that the Government of Zimbabwe had underestimated the growth in demand for family planning services and for contraceptives and, as a result, was almost out of contraceptives. The supply of pills was down to a 2-week supply, for example. They requested an emergency air shipment of contraceptives from the U.S. AID mission in Zimbabwe. Now, in a continent where we have been hearing about emergency food shipments, I think that was a refreshing development. But there are some changes.

I think it is terribly important, as the Congressmen who appeared on the panel before me have indicated, that we respond to these needs. It is literally becoming a matter of life or death.

The final point is that I think in many situations governments have failed to understand the gravity of the population problem and have waited too long in trying to get the brakes on population growth. This is exactly what happened in China, where for ideological reasons, for at least a couple of decades they ignored the population problems, believing that more people was a good thing, and ignoring the possible negative consequences of unlimited population growth.

The result was that the Chinese by the late 1970's found that they had to choose between an increase in population of several hundred million that would undermine and reduce their living standards, or they would have to launch a very aggressive family planning program, which took the form of the one-child family.

In looking at other parts of the Third World and at Africa in particular, I sense that many countries are waiting too long. The alternative to the China model of sharply reducing birth rates, with a one-child family program, is probably the Ethiopian model, where agricultural support systems collapse and death rates rise. As a result of having waited too long, I think many governments are now going to have to choose between either the China model, slamming on the population brakes, or the Ethiopian model of watching death rates rise. I think that is the real choice.

That is why the hearings that you are holding are so terribly important and why I commend you strongly for doing so.

[Excerpt from State of the World—1985 submitted by Mr. Brown appears at the conclusion of the hearing, see p. 59.]

Chairman LELAND. All the plaudits for this hearing really go to our colleague, Peter Kostmayer. I yield to him now for questions he may have. I will hold my questions.

Mr. KOSTMAYER. Thank you, Mr. Chairman, very much.

I appreciate, Mr. Brown, your very exhaustive testimony and your important work in this area and especially the linkage between the factors you talked about in such an expert way and the problems of population. I think, as I am sure you do, that we are headed for really serious problems if this country, the leader of the free world, reduces substantially, as we are about to, our funding to international organizations and agencies which participate in voluntary family planning around the world. I think it would be a major mistake, and I am sure we will see the consequences not only in population growth but in all of the other factors which are linked to population.

I thank you for your testimony and for your important work in this area.

Mr. BROWN. Thank you.

Mr. KOSTMAYER. I wish I knew one-tenth as much as you about anything.

Mr. BROWN. How do I respond to that, Mr. Chairman?

Chairman LELAND. Just smile.

You spoke of cropland shrinkage. Is there any method to restore the lands that have been severely degraded by the process that you alluded to?

Mr. BROWN. It is technically possible to restore lands that have been degraded to the point that they lose much of their productivity, but it becomes very costly. In northern Ethiopia, for example, where I was in late April, there are, in the highlands of Ethiopia, where the land is often very steep, there are areas where the soil is gone entirely; there is only rock left. So, you can create soil out of rock. I mean, soil is just rock that has been broken down through weathering. You can put pieces of rock in a machine and pulverize it, and you can make soil. But it is a very energy-intensive process. It is a lot cheaper to keep what you have rather than to have to try and create soil where none is.

Realistically, once the soil is lost through erosion, and you are down to bare rock, agriculture is finished.

Prepared Statement of Robert Taft, Jr.

Robert Taft Jr.*

Congressman Leland, distinguished members of Congress, I am pleased to be invited here to testify before the House Select Committee on Hunger.

I am a member of the board of directors of the Population Crisis Committee. PCC is a private non-profit organization which has, since its establishment in 1965, been a leader among population organizations in efforts to strengthen political and financial support for family planning overseas. Our work involves high-level advocacy at home and abroad to increase government commitment and also selective support of innovative private family planning programs in developing countries. It is perhaps important to state that we receive no U.S. government money for any part of our programs. Thus, while we may express strong opinions about the direction of U.S. population assistance, these comments are not motivated by any financial interest in the program. It is also important to affirm that PCC does not advocate the use of abortion as a method of family planning.

PCC welcomes the opportunity to share with the Select Committee on Hunger our growing concern over the future of U.S. assisted international family planning programs and the potentially devastating impact that a reduced U.S. commitment to efforts to reduce rapid population growth might have on the prospects for long-term development in the Third World, including developments that would face the problems of food production and hunger.

Unless Congress intervenes directly to challenge certain aspects of the Administration's management of U.S. population assistance, the overseas family planning infrastructure which has been painstakingly built over the last two decades will be dismantled. The process is already well underway.

The origins of the current policy crisis date back to the International

---

*Former U.S. Senator, Population Crisis Committee.

Robert Taft, "Testimony," *Population Growth and Hunger*. Hearing before Select Committee on Hunger, U.S. House of Representatives, June 6, 1984, pp. 103-118.

Conference on Population held last August in Mexico City. In preparation for U.S. participation in the conference, the White House issued a policy statement on U.S. population assistance which was a dramatic reversal of longstanding bipartisan policy on the subject.

The draft White House policy statement made some incredible statements. It argued that population growth "is, of itself, a neutral phenomenon," that in fact "population growth has been an essential element in economic progress." It characterized the efforts of Third World countries to moderate population growth rates as "an overreaction." Arguing that the post-war population boom need not have become a crisis, it blamed the problems associated with current population pressures abroad on mismanagement by Third World countries of their economies, in particular, government control and interference in the form of price fixing and confiscatory taxes. Finally, it argued that economic freedom, leading to economic growth, would in and of itself lead to population stabilization. By proposing free enterprise as the solution both to the problems created by rapid population growth and to population growth itself, the paper implicitly rejected the importance of direct interventions to bring down birthrates through organized family planning services.

In addition to these spurious pronouncements on population growth, the paper set forth specific new restrictions on eligibility for U.S. population assistance, designed to impose the Administration's views about abortion on family planning programs around the world. The paper stated that the United States "does not consider abortion an acceptable element of family planning programs and will not contribute to those of which it is a part. Nor will it any longer contribute directly or indirectly to family planning programs funded by governments or private organizations that advocate abortion as an instrument of population control."

Over the summer, public reaction to the White House draft poured in from across the country. In June, July and August of 1984 no less then 244 editorials and Op-Ed pieces opposed the Mexico City policy statement. Only 37 supported the proposed policy changes. A Gallup poll showed that fully 71 percent of those who expressed an opinion rejected the new abortion restriction and 90 percent rejected the arguments about population growth and economic development.

In an effort to diffuse a growing public relations fiasco, the Administration moved on July 13 to issue a revised policy paper for the Mexico City Conference, which it characterized as a "compromise." The sections dealing with the relationship between population growth and economic development remained unchanged. The single compromise related to the new abortion restrictions. Governments which include abortion in family planning programs are exempted from the new abortion provisions so long as they maintain segregated accounts for U.S. funds. But multilateral organizations and nongovernmental groups are to be rendered ineligible for further U.S. assistance if they "perform or actively promote abortion," regardless of the source of funding for abortion activities. The way in which these terms are now defined poses a serious threat to continued Agency for International Development (AID) support of those nongovernmental organizations most active in the expansion of family planning services worldwide.

The policy that the United States delegation took to the Mexico City Population conference was blatantly self-contradictory—it pledged continued U.S. population assistance, but at the same time rejected the need for it.

AID is now in the process of attempting to implement the new Mexico City population policy, and the agency continues to profess a continued strong commitment to international family planning. But any illusions that the Administration would temper the implementation of its new policy so as to avoid damage to ongoing family planning programs were shattered by the withdrawal of U.S. support to the International Planned Parenthood Federation (IPPF) last December. More recently, AID has withheld $10 million out of the $46 million U.S. contribution to the United Nations Fund for Population Activities (UNFPA), the amount earmarked by Congress last year, because of concerns over UNFPA's assistance to programs in China. Future U.S. contributions to UNFPA now appear increasingly vulnerable to attacks by anti-family planning groups.

Unfortunately, the attack on family planning programs has not stopped with UNFPA and IPPF. Since February, AID officials have taken steps to move against the large U.S. nongovernmental family planning organizations (NGOs) which constitute the remaining major channels of population assistance other than direct support to governments. The potential impact on international family planning programs of a withdrawal of U.S. funds to both IPPF and UNFPA, combined with ineligibility of large numbers of foreign NGOs to receive AID funds through U.S.-based intermediaries, is enormous.

In a large number of countries receiving support through NGOs, abortion is legal for reasons other than a threat to the life of the woman. In 35 countries receiving AID assistance in FY 1984, representing 1.5 billion people or over 70 percent of the population in all countries receiving assistance, the availability of abortion is permitted for non-life-threatening conditions. In some countries, the legal status of abortion is similar to that in the United States. However, the list of 35 countries also includes major Catholic countries like Brazil and Mexico where abortion is partially restricted as well as important pro-Western aid-recipients like Kenya, Morocco and Thailand. Six out of 10 countries on AID's priority list for population assistance fall into this category. Most medical institutions and health providers in these countries—the backbone of AID-supported family planning programs—would lose eligibility for support, since under AID's proposed language they are performing or promoting abortion "as a method of family planning." Their loss of eligibility would represent a major longterm setback to ongoing family planning programs.

In terms of the impact on the major channels of population assistance, a planned $17 million grant of cash and commodities to the International Planned

Parenthood Federation (IPPF) has already been withdrawn. All technical assistance, training and research programs carried out by U.S. universities are threatened because universities cannot, according to their legal advisors, accept responsibility for policing the Administration's new restrictions. The major U.S.-based NGO intermediaries, have also indicated that they may be unable to reach accommodation with AID on the new contractual language. Out in the field, foreign organizations are indicating that they cannot agree to some or all of the provisions, including organizations with no current involvement in abortion. Some $140 million in current programs may be at stake.

As ineligibility eliminates current NGO intermediaries, AID will be forced to allocate increasing amounts of population funds to generally less effective government programs. Ironically, less effective family planning programs that reach fewer couples will result in unwanted pregnancies which in turn will lead to more maternal deaths in childbirth, infant deaths and an *increased* number of abortions. Closely-spaced births and frequent childbearing are major contributors to high rates of infant and maternal mortality in the Third World. Large families adversely affect maternal and child nutrition, birth weight and limit immunity against disease. Family planning alone could reduce infant and maternal mortality by half by helping couples space births and avoid high-risk pregnancies. Researchers at Johns Hopkins University estimate that 5.8 million infant and maternal deaths could be prevented annually if ideal child spacing and avoidance of pregnancy by very young and older women were universally achieved. Unfortunately, only one-third of the 500 million couples in developing countries, excluding China, have access to family planning services. By lowering the cost-effectiveness of family planning efforts, the new population policy will reduce access to family planning services and increase the number of couples resorting to abortion.

Besides the disastrous practical impact the implementation of the new policy will have on international family planning programs, serious questions of principle are raised by the Administration's new policy. We believe the committee should recognize several broad concerns shared by many in the international family planning field, including general issues of foreign assistance policy.

First, implementation of the Administration's new policy suggests to people in developing nations that the U.S. government now seeks to manipulate the population policies of their countries by imposing conditions on its assistance to indigenous nongovernmental organizations potentially at odds with law and policy in the aid-recipient country. This represents a precedent-setting break with the longstanding principles of non-interference and voluntarism associated with U.S. population assistance programs. Bedrock principles of U.S. population assistance since the inception of the program 20 years ago have been that population assistance is never to be imposed on disinterested developing country governments, that other forms of development assistance such as PL 480 are not conditioned on acceptance of a particular population policy, and that U.S.-

supported programs respect local cultural and religious values. Implementation of the policy attempts to make U.S. private sector institutions and their indigenous subgrantees in developing countries tools of the Administration's anti-abortion campaign. Such misuse of private sector institutions tarnishes the image of all U.S. foreign assistance programs and in particular of population assistance.

Second, in implementing its new policy, the Administration has taken care to protect the constitutional rights of U.S.-based organizations to engage in legal abortion-related activities with funds received from sources other than AID. The decision not to apply the new abortion restrictions to U.S. organizations is obviously based on the Administration's recognition that U.S. courts could be expected to overturn such a policy on both statutory and constitutional grounds. The message of the new policy is that the Administration is prepared to punish the citizens of other countries by denying funds for much needed family planning services because of the availability of a medical procedure which is legal and widely performed in our own country.

While such a clear double standard may be permissible in a strict constitutional sense, it exceeds the statutory provisions of the Foreign Assistance Act and runs directly counter to important principles of current U.S. foreign policy. The U.S. has a longstanding commitment to both the spread of democratic institutions and the respect for national sovereignty. Although the Administration has recognized the inherent national sovereignty of other nations in its decision not to impose the new abortion restrictions on government-to-government programs, it has failed to recognize that national sovereignty extends to foreign nongovernmental organizations which operate under laws and policies of their own countries and which often receive funding for family planning from their own and other donor governments. Our critics around the world are likely to exploit a policy which imposes restrictions on the activities of LDC institutions and citizens which would be unacceptable—even unconstitutional—in the U.S.

Third, the new population policy runs directly counter to one of the centerpieces and broad policy themes of the Reagan Administration's agenda—support for the private sector. The private sector can be an extremely powerful and dynamic force for change in the developing world, and we fully support efforts to expand private sector initiatives in family planning. However, one must question the sincerity of the Administration's promotion of the private sector when the existence and effectiveness of innovative and creative private institutions is threatened for reasons of political expediency.

The organizations threatened are some of the most cost-effective and innovative institutions in the U.S. foreign assistance program. They are also the repository of most of the world's technical expertise on family planning—an essential resource that cannot be easily replaced. The organizations play a critical institution-building role, especially important in the developing countries which are plagued by a lack of infrastructure and trained manpower. By virtue of long experience, they pioneer new strategies and invent innovative solutions to problems that are tailored to local conditions.

If the Administration is sincere in its commitment to expand access to voluntary family planning services worldwide, it cannot realistically accomplish that goal without the private sector and multilateral organizations. Currently, AID government-to-government population assistance reaches less than 30 countries. In contrast, NGO programs reach 90 countries, and UNFPA programs reach 120 countries. (See Table 1.) There are no bilateral population programs (but large NGO programs) in key countries such as Mexico, Brazil and Nigeria where direct government-to-government support would be politically unacceptable to those countries. The small number of bilateral programs, combined with problems of political sensitivity which would be engendered by direct U.S. population assistance in a number of countries important to U.S. national security, make private, nongovernmental funding channels not just cost-effective, but essential.

The declarations of the International Conference on Population in Mexico City indicate that world leaders have come to recognize the serious consequences of excessive population growth. Many of the leaders of developing nations now understand fully the intensity of the problem and the urgency of immediate action to confront it.

In the long run, sustained fertility declines depend on indirect development measures such as raising the status of women, improving child survival and increasing economic opportunities for the poor majority. These efforts increase the impact of direct interventions to lower birthrates through family planning and are desirable on their own merits. Although socioeconomic development does not affect fertility directly or immediately, it can have an enormous impact on levels of contraceptive prevalence, acceptance of small family ideals, and women's perception of alternative roles to childbearing. Without these changes, it will be extremely difficult for most countries to attain population stabilization even if family planning efforts are greatly expanded.

But it should be noted that the bulk of U.S. development assistance is devoted to these types of social and economic programs, in particular to programs which have the effect of further reducing death rates. Only a small proportion is committed to population and family planning measures designed to affect birthrates. In FY 1984 and FY 1985, AID spent over seven times the amount expended for population assistance on efforts to improve health and nutrition through bilateral and multilateral assistance and PL-480 title II. During the period FY 1962 to FY 1984 AID expended $2.4 billion on international family planning and $30.4 billion, or roughly 12 times the amount, on PL-480 assistance. These figures include the U.S. contributions to the UNFPA—the only multilateral agency with any major focus on population programs. The figures do not include our contributions to the multilateral development banks and other agencies which are heavily involved in agricultural development, health and nutrition, but for the most part support few if any family planning programs. (See Table 2.) Commendable efforts to improve health and nutrition and accompanying reduction in mortality rates and increased life expectancy must be balanced with increased efforts to reduce fertility rates. Otherwise, our well-meaning assistance will simply complicate the long-range problems in developing countries.

PCC applauds the efforts of the Select Committee on Hunger to discover the best strategies for alleviating hunger through long-term development. Such an endeavor is especially important in the wake of the recent food crisis in Africa. Realistically, the food crisis will not be resolved without resolution of the population crisis. Unfortunately, most African governments were reluctant until recently to establish and maintain effective family planning programs. But foreign aid donors might have prevented some of the tragedy in Africa. Too little of their investment in Africa has gone for family planning. The 400 million Africans living in sub-Saharan countries require $600 million to $800 million per year to ensure access to good voluntary family planning services. The donor community has been providing only about 10% of the needed amount.

Donors provided about $1 billion worth of food aid for Africa in 1984, and at least $500 million more is needed for the present emergency. It is likely that a decade of adequate investment in family planning would have been much more cost-effective and would have gone a long way toward alleviation of the human misery now occurring.

Every year donor nations provide developing countries with foreign aid totaling about $11 a person. Of that amount only 14 cents goes for population planning and programs. Without substantial increases in funds for family planning programs the developing world is doomed to repeat, perhaps several times, the tragedy in Africa.

Studies show that most couples in the developing world wish to plan when to have children and how many to have. World Fertility Survey data from 29 developing countries in Asia and Latin America indicated that almost half of married women of reproductive age (15-49) want no more children, and one-third did not want or plan their last pregnancy. The approximately 40 million pregnancies terminated worldwide by abortion each year, the majority illegal, indicate unmet demand for effective family planning services. Family planning programs can substantially reduce reliance on abortion to regulate fertility. Family planning programs can help in acceptance of such plans, especially where the problem is most severe.

However, current world efforts are inadequate. Family planning information and services are not readily available to roughly two-thirds of Third World couples (outside of China). As a result, contraception is used by an average of only *21 percent of couples in these countries*. Third World access to and use of contraception must increase three to four-fold to reach all couples who need family planning services. This will require annual worldwide expenditures of $4 billion to $8 billion, or between $10 and $20 per couple of reproductive age living in developing countries.

Economic conditions in the less-developed countries make the initiation of new family planning programs difficult. Decreased foreign exchange earnings and increased costs for imports and debt services have left many countries in serious economic straits. Even so, many have substantially increased spending on population programs. Countries like India and Indonesia now cover most of the cost of their own programs. Nevertheless, requests from developing nations for population assistance substantially exceed funds available from AID, UNFPA and IPPF. Approved but not funded UNFPA programs total at least $250 million this year. AID and IPPF together need an additional $120 million per year to meet current backlogs.

A minimal budget to serve 400 million couples with basic services would require an increase of aid from the U.S. and other donors from $450 million to at least $2 billion, with developing nations (excluding China) themselves increasing their budgetary allocations to family planning from $650 million to at least $4 billion. Even these figures do not take into account the fact that the number of reproductive age couples will continue to expand (by 40% by the end of the century). Most of these future parents are already born. To meet the U.S. share of these requirements and help initiate new programs, an increase in the AID budget for population assistance from $290 million to $450 million is needed immediately.

The increased awareness and receptivity to family planning programs worldwide are largely the result of U.S. leadership over the past 20 years. We are still the most important technical and financial resource around the globe, and this kind of leadership remains clearly in the national interest. The new Mexico City population policy calls into question the leadership role the U.S. has played in expanding the availability of voluntary family planning services worldwide over the last two decades. It is overwhelmingly clear that the U.S. must continue its leadership role not only in financial aid, but in urging developing world governments to give higher priority to family planning.

Congress must directly challenge the implementation of the Administration's new Mexico City population policy by addressing the issue this year. Failure to do so may result in a dismantling of the vast network of multilateral and nongovernmental organizations, both at home and abroad, that have paved the way for government acceptance of the necessity of family planning services around the world.

Table 1

POPULATION ASSISTANCE PROVIDED BY AID BILATERAL PROGRAMS, IPPF, OTHER NGOs & UNFPA BY REGION
(in millions of dollars)

	Bilateral (proposed FY 1986)	IPPF (actual FY 1984)	Other Centrally Funded NGOs*	UNFPA
Africa				
Total Number of Countries	8	28	26	42
Total Funding Levels	$23.9	$10.2	$6.9	$33.7
Latin America and the Caribbean				
Total Number of Countries	11	34	21	32
Total Funding Levels	$25.5	$13.9	$12.7	$17.5
Asia and the Pacific				
Total Number of Countries	4	19	12	31
Total Funding Levels	$43.3	$11.7	$5.9	$57.2
Near East				
Total Number of Countries	2	13	6	10
Total Funding Levels	$6.0	$2.7	$5.2	$12.3

*Includes only field expenditures associated with the programs of nongovernmental organizations centrally-funded by AID's Office of Population in FY 1984. An estimated $20 million in additional NGO programs are included under the bilateral programs. These would also be affected by the new policy. Total allocations to NGOs in FY 1984 represented 48 percent of the AID population budget.

Table 2
RELATIVE PRIORITIES IN U.S. FOREIGN ASSISTANCE
(millions of dollars)

	FY 1984 actual	FY 1985 estimate	FY 1986 proposed
EFFORTS TO IMPROVE HEALTH & NUTRITION	1695.9	2184.5	1620.8
Bilateral Assistance	851.4	1038.0	943.8
Agriculture, Rural Development & Nutrition	723.2	769.7	797.4
Health	128.2	243.3	146.4
Child Survival Fund	-	25.0	-
P.L.-480—Title II	740.0	1001.0	650.0
*Multilateral Assistance**	104.5	145.5	27.0
EFFORTS TO LOWER BIRTHRATES	242.4	287.1	250.0
Bilateral & Multilateral Assistance Population Planning	242.4	287.1	250.0

*Multilateral assistance includes only U.S. voluntary contributions to the following organizations: United Nations Children's Fund (UNICEF), Food & Agriculture Organization/World Food Programme (FAO/WFP), and International Fund for Agricultural Development (IFAD). Total multilateral funding levels do not include U.S. voluntary contributions to the international financial institutions (IFIs), such as the World Bank, the International Development Association (IDA), and the regional multilateral development banks (MDBs). The IFIs devote an extremely small percentage of their total expenditures on population assistance and spend in excess of one quarter of their budgets on agriculture and rural development activities.

The Future Productive Capacity of U.S. Agriculture: Economic, Technological, Resource, and Institutional Determinants

Clark Edwards and David H. Harrington*

During the late 1970s it appeared that U.S. agriculture might not develop the capacity to meet the domestic and foreign demands then in prospect. Domestic demands rose at a steady pace during the decade while exports burgeoned at 8% per year. Projections of those trends led onlookers to conclude that the pace was unsustainable and that food prices could increase dramatically. Then export demand slackened. The value of exports fell 21% during 1981-82; about half was the result of reduced shipments and the remainder the result of lower prices received. The concern about agricultural capacity turned from how to deal with prospective shortages to how to deal with the accumulating surpluses. During such turbulent times, it is difficult to focus on long-run trends.

Is U.S. agriculture likely to have the capacity to meet the demands to be placed on it during the next two or three decades? The question is ambiguous. First of all, capacity for what? Certainly we can meet the growth in domestic food demand. We can do so with fewer and fewer agricultural resources each year. One can imagine domestic biomass demands (for gasohol, for example) that could strain capacity, but such demands do not appear very likely to materialize. It is growth in export markets that raises issues about capacity. If exports resume the rate of growth of the 1970s for an extended period, capacity could become

---

*Clark Edwards and David H. Harrington are economists with the Economic Research Service, U.S. Department of Agriculture.

From *American Journal of Agricultural Economics*, December 1984, pp. 585-591. Reprinted with permission.

strained; but if export markets stagnate, U.S. agriculture will experience excess capacity. Second, capacity at what price? It is conventional to assume that U.S. agriculture could produce at almost any level if the prices received were high enough. At historical prices, U.S. agriculture has usually found itself in the position of having some idle resources; output could have been increased at then-present prices. Third, there is ambiguity about capacity with respect to viewpoint. The greater the capacity the more food there can be for hungry people to eat. But the smaller the capacity the easier it is to maintain prices and farmer income.

U.S. agriculture, according to our research, is likely to have ample capacity to meet not only the export demands most likely to be placed on it but more, should it materialize. Projected demands can be met at present, or even decreasing, real prices received by farmers. Agriculture has the resilience to adjust efficiently to a wide range of market demands; however, prospective shifts in demand can have important implications for the redistribution of income among not only consumers and farmers but also marketing firms, input suppliers, and U.S. trading partners.

U.S. AGRICULTURAL SUPPLY RESPONSE TO EXPORT GROWTH

Imagine two or three decades of growth in food production and consumption such that there is little change in real food prices. Consumers, would spend smaller shares of their increasing real incomes for increasing quantities of food per capita and farmers would maintain or improve their earnings. On which side of this hypothetical trend line is food production and consumption likely to fall: toward higher real food prices of benefit to farmers or toward lower real food prices of benefit to consumers?

To assess this question, we first looked at world trends. We found that neither extreme abundance nor extreme scarcity is very likely. The past few decades have been close to the middle but show a tendency toward the scenario of plenty. Real food prices have been trending downward over the decades and per capita production has been rising. We found no reason for calling for a change in these trends. And we found that food prices have returned to their earlier level of volatility after an interlude of relative stability during the 1950s and 1960s. We concluded that U.S. agriculture will be exporting into markets characterized by prices that show short-run volatility around a long-run, moderate downtrend.

To help assess the U.S. supply response to changes in world food markets, we simulated growth from 1982 to 2000 for alternative levels of exports based on the structure of U.S. commodity markets for major crop and livestock products over the last decade or so. If exports of the seven crops were to grow at 3% per year over the next two decades, we estimate that production would expand to satisfy both domestic and foreign demands with little change in consumer's real food prices. There would be little or no need for price and income support if present farm programs are continued. This scenario implies less than a 10% increase in cropland use over the next two decades, with most of the added acreage used for soybeans. Export markets grow faster than domestic markets, and the proportion of cropland harvested for export would rise from 40% in 1982 to 50% in 2000. Expectations are for export growth close to this 3% scenario. This suggests that domestic agriculture will become increasingly dependent on foreign markets. And it implies that real food prices could be little changed or moderately lower, not only because of prospective growth in domestic capacity relative to demands but also because of the need to keep prices of export products competitive in world markets.

If exports were to grow only about 2% per year for the next two decades, the forthcoming U.S. food supply would be large relative to domestic plus export demand. This would result in lower real food prices than under the 3% scenario. Domestic consumers would spend a smaller share of disposable income for slightly more food and the marketing sector would expand to handle the increased volume. Farmers would produce less wheat, corn, soybeans, and cotton and nearly the same amount of livestock products compared to the faster growth scenario. Real prices received by farmers would decrease for all commodities. If advanced technology continues to be adopted, then many resources now available to agriculture would not be required. For example, less cropland would be used in 2010 than in 1982. Export growth of 2% or less per year is unlikely for the long term. Were it to occur, it implies plentiful food supplies for domestic consumers; but in the absence of farm income and price programs, there would be depressed farm incomes, capital losses, and a reallocation of resources out of agriculture in search of better economic opportunities in the nonfarm sector of the economy.

If, instead, exports rise at an annual rate of 4% or 5% per year, the domestic plus foreign demand would be large relative to supply. Real food prices would increase. Domestic consumers would pay a larger share of disposable personal income for a smaller quantity of food than under the 3% scenario. Consumption of most livestock products would decrease but more wheat products would be consumed. More resources would be required and higher prices would be paid for them. Acreage planted would increase about 22% above the 1982 level under the 5% scenario and land values would increase. The proportion of acreage harvested for export would rise to around two-thirds of harvested acreage by 2000. Export growth of 5% or more per year is not expected for the long term. Were it to occur, it implies higher real food costs to domestic consumers and reduced consumption of livestock products relative to crop products. Livestock growers would sell fewer products at higher prices; crop growers more at higher prices. Farm income would be high enough to eliminate most payments and supports if present farm programs are continued. However, the gains in farm income are mostly for crop enterprises. Livestock enterprises face higher feed costs which induce a reduction in livestock production and, despite higher prices received, may result in a reduction in livestock income.

Resource availabilities, prospective advances in technology, and the institutions reflected in the structure of these simulations appear to be adequate to support domestic markets which grow in line with past trends, plus export markets which grow at between 2% and 5% per year. If export growth is below that range, the agricultural sector could again become a severely disadvantaged and depressed industry. If export growth is above that range, various structural and distributional problems could beset agriculture long before natural resource availability becomes limiting. Rapid growth presses against institutional arrangements before it presses against physical capacity. Export growth within that range implies continued internationalization of U.S. agriculture. Fluctuations within the range are considered likely. This raises considerations of how to maintain balance between consumer and farmer interests, between livestock and crop growers, and/or between land owners and land users as relative prices change for individual commodities and resources.

U.S. AGRICULTURAL SUPPLY RESPONSE TO PRICE VOLATILITY

Price volatility has characterized U.S. agriculture throughout this century; the major exception was during the 1950s and 1960s when massive government intervention stabilized domestic farm prices above world price and therefore above prices that would have existed in the absence of commodity programs. The price volatility of the 1970s was of the same relative magnitude as the volatility of the first half of this century. Forty years ago when T.W. Schultz spoke of agriculture in an unstable economy, he identified unbalanced economic expansion and business fluctuations in the domestic nonfarm sector as the major sources of agricultural instability. The price volatility experienced by farmers during the 1970s appears to be mostly of foreign rather than domestic origin. World production did not appear to be less stable than formerly, but prices became more volatile. Insular trade policies during the 1970s of both grain importing and exporting countries were major contributors to the recent price volatility as were floating exchange rates and other nonagricultural policies of various governments.

Farmers who are risk averse treat increasing price uncertainty similarly to an increase in the cost of production or to a decrease in the price received. They cope with uncertainty by physical and financial diversification, flexibility, reluctance to borrow and invest, off-farm employment, and similar actions that may reduce farm production efficiency. Price uncertainty and income variability affect the physical organization and financial structure of individual farm businesses. An increase in the variation in world food prices reduces the U.S. supply of cash crops by risk-averse farmers. The accompanying higher prices lead to a reduction in the quantity of crop products used in food, feed, and export markets. Income to crop enterprises improves, but the reduced demands for farm resource decreases the income to resources suppliers. Higher feed costs reduce income to the livestock enterprise. An increase in world price volatility decreases production and thereby results in what appears in descriptive statistics to be a reduction in agricultural capacity. However, the decrease is not large and the prospect of high risk is not expected to limit the ability of U.S. agriculture to meet prospective domestic and export demands.

THE IMPLICATIONS FOR RESOURCE USE IN U.S. AGRICULTURE

The analysis of supply response in the commodity markets indicates that we will have the capacity to meet the market demands likely to be placed on U.S. agriculture in coming decades. The commodity supply response—and the capacity of U.S. agriculture—depends on the changes in technology, resource availability, regional location, and institutional arrangements. Let us look at some of these. Cross-sectional simulations using linear programming constraints helped us assess the allocation of resources among alternative uses. The framework incorporated additional livestock and crop enterprises relative to the time-series simulations and recognized regional location. The analysis was comparative statics; that is, the time path between two periods was not examined. The time-series simulations focused on commodity markets; however, they included estimates of cropland requirements.

Technology

Total resource use in U.S. agriculture is about the same now as it was in the 1930s but production has doubled. An increase in productivity through adoption of new technology tends to increase the level of farm output and reduce the demands for traditional farm inputs. The increased availability of food products at lower prices benefits consumers, trading partners, and the domestic marketing sector. It also benefits agriculture despite its tendency to reduce net income because it keeps agriculture competitive with other sources of food, such as imports. If technology were the same now as it was in the 1930s, the cost of production would be higher and U.S. agriculture would be priced out of domestic as well as world markets.

During the 1970s, the growth in productivity appeared to slow. This slowdown occurred during a decade in which total output was expanding to fill export markets. The slowdown raised questions whether technological advance in agriculture was approaching a limit at the same time that cropland harvested was approaching its historical high. However, the slowdown was not substantiated for various disaggregations of the aggregate measure. For example, trends for corn yields did not change in either the Corn Belt or the South, but an increase in corn acreage in the lower-yielding South resulted in a reduction in the weighted-average national corn yield. And trends in livestock and crop productivity were little changed, but an increase in purchased inputs for the rapidly expanding crop enterprise changed the weighted average ratio of crop plus livestock outputs to all inputs. Therefore, what appeared to be a change in productivity may instead have been regional and commodity shifts in production.

Prospects for further technical change in U.S. agriculture include genetic engineering and a new generation of more specialized and computerized machinery. Other prospects include remote machinery monitors, controls, and robotics; reduced-tillage and no-till practices; varieties which are more pest resistant, higher yielding, and capable of being grown in new geographic locations; varieties with shorter growing seasons; fertilizer and pesticide encapsulation; crop hormone changes; drought resistant and salt tolerant crops; nitrogen fixation by grass crops; biological pest controls and vaccines; control of animal reproduction; more efficient animal feed conversions; and alternative ways to satisfy human nutrition requirements. Improvements in information flows and decision making by farmers will also increase efficiency.

If the growth in productivity were to continue for the next thirty years at the 1.9% per year pace shown in the past thirty, total farm output can increase by 70% from the present level. With domestic markets likely to increase by well under 1% per year, a 1.9% per year increase in productivity from existing resources would support a 3% per year increase in exports. Current projections are for average annual increases of less than 3% for the coming decade. In addition, rate of adoption of technology may increase. Therefore, as long as markets grow close to the projected trends or slower, technology is not likely to become limiting. The question is what happens if exports grow faster, say at 4% or 5% per year, or at the 8% rate observed during the 1970s. Then, of course, technology could become limiting unless other changes are made. However, when this happened during the 1970s, the commodity and regional mix changed and resources were reallocated in response to changing resource price ratios. These resilient adaptations by agriculture enabled it to meet the expanding market demands despite the apparent decrease in the growth rate of the ratio of output to input. Technological advance is not likely to be a limiting factor in the ability of a flexible, resilient agriculture—which has opportunities for substitutions among resources, commodities, and regions—to meet the domestic and foreign demands likely to be placed on it during the next two or three decades.

Land

An unused potential to convert other lands into cropland has always been available to U.S. agriculture. During the past half century there was not sufficient economic incentive to use this potential. Quite the contrary, more often the problem was how much land to idle under supply management programs to limit price-depressing surplus production. The 1982 Natural Resources Inventories (NRI) estimate that there was 421.4 million acres of cropland in the United States compared to 413.3 million acres in 1977. An additional 35.3 million acres (8.3% of the total) is considered to have a high potential of conversion to cropland. Yet an additional 117 million acres (27.9% of the total) is considered to have a medium potential. Allowing for various institutional, economic, and physical constraints on conversion, cropland might be increased by 17% before conversion difficulties and accompanying high conversion costs are encountered. That is, some 70 million acres of cropland might be added on a cost-effective basis if it is needed.

If U.S. exports were to increase around 3% per year until 2000 (to a level 70% above the 1982 level) and if yields continue to increase in line with the past trend, the time-series analysis suggests that about 10% more crop acres will be required. Export growth of only 2% per year (to a level 40% above the 1982 level) can be met with about the same amount of crop acres used in 1982. Present expectations are for export growth within these ranges. If, instead, exports were to grow at an annual rate of 5% per year to 2000 (to a level of 140% above the 1982 level) 22% additional cropland will be required. This would stretch land use to a level only moderately above the readily convertible level of 17% and well below the high plus medium conversion potential. Using the cross-sectional simulation, it was estimated that if exports were to increase 90% from the present level, using present technology, about 40 million more acres would be required after all resource and regional adjustments to the change were completed, well under the 70 million considered to be readily convertible. When adoption of technology was allowed for, it was found that exports could double during the next few decades and domestic plus export needs could be met using less cropland than is being used now.

Water

The number of acres irrigated doubled during the past three decades, mostly during the later years. This growth supported considerable expansion in agricultural production. While there could be increases in output from additional supplemental irrigation in humid areas, there is little prospect for further expansion in the arid regions. It is more likely that we can find additional irrigable land beyond the 50.8 million acres now in use than it is that we can increase the quantity of water to a major extent from the 93.1 million acre-feet now in use.

When crop exports are increased, most of the added production is on dryland; therefore, a limit to the possibilities for irrigation need not limit the capacity of U.S. agriculture to meet growing export market demands for major crops. A 90% increase in exports, assuming yields constant, would require 25% more dryland and 7% more irrigated land after all adjustments were completed, according to our cross-sectional simulations. Additional soybeans and cotton would be irrigated for small increases in exports. But only for the high export scenarios, under which resources were relatively scarce and agriculture was approaching its capacity, would inducements be sufficient to irrigate substantial amounts of additional corn and wheat.

The output of irrigated crops from present water supplies can be increased in various ways. More efficient application systems are being developed and present systems can be used more effectively. Adoption of improved management facilities and practices can increase the effective supply of water sufficiently to meet the additional water requirements associated with a 90% increase in exports. Tight world food supplies and consequently higher prices received by farmers would increase the prices that farmers are willing to pay to irrigate but would not greatly increase the quantity used. The availability of irrigation water is not likely to limit the ability of U.S. agriculture to meet export demands during the next two or there decades.

Purchased Farm Inputs

Farmers are using more purchased inputs and less labor on the same amount of land than they used to. Nearly three-fourths of cash receipts are used for the purchase of farm inputs now compared with around one-third three decades ago. The productivity increases of recent decades are highly correlated with the increases in expenditures by farmers for purchased farm inputs. The availability of inputs and service from the nonfarm sector of the economy during the next two or three decades will be more important in determining the capacity of agriculture relative to market demands for food than the availability of natural resources and labor. Backward linkages from farmers to the nonfarm sector are primarily for machinery, materials, chemicals, energy, and various services such as transportation, real estate, and financial services. These linkages are a little stronger for crops than for livestock and therefore are responsive to changes in the export markets for crops.

The U.S. food system, from production to consumption, uses approximately 13% of the nation's energy. Until the early 1970s it was customary to assume that energy would continue to be plentiful and cheap. Since the energy crunch of 1973, this is no longer a safe assumption. The real price of world oil likely will increase over the next two or three decades. As petroleum prices increase two adjustments can be expected. First, users of oil will shift some of their demand for energy to other sources, such as electricity (increasingly from coal) and natural gas. Second, over the longer run, users will continue to invest in energy-conserving devices and practices, thereby substituting relatively less expensive capital and labor for the more expensive fuels. Energy supply disruptions can cause temporary changes in food production but are not expected to limit U.S. agriculture's ability to meet the domestic and foreign demands likely to be placed on it during the next two or three decades.

Prices that sellers of farm inputs are willing to accept are affected by opportunities to sell the same or related goods and services to the nonfarm sector.

Manufacturers, for example, set prices of farm machinery with recognition of opportunities for sales of other equipment they manufacture to construction firms. Prices in the farm input markets, therefore, are influenced not only by the demand for farm products but also by the prices of nonfarm producer goods and services. The nonfarm sector is expected to have the capacity to supply farms with the quantities of inputs needed to meet growing domestic and foreign demands for food; the real prices farmers pay for purchased farm inputs may increase, particularly for energy intensive inputs.

CONCLUSION

Farm policies likely will cope over the next two or three decades with a continuation in the long-run trend of a declining ratio of prices received by farmers to prices paid and with continued price variability of foreign origin. U.S. agriculture has shown a resiliency for adapting to these trends by making appropriate commodity, resource, and regional substitutions, adopting new technology, and changing its structure and its institutional relationships. The basis for domestic farm income support and price stabilization policies is changing, primarily because of increased reliance of U.S. farmers on export markets which are volatile and which are expected to continue to grow more slowly than the domestic potential to fill them.

There are three reasons for anticipating a probable long-run decline in real prices received by U.S. farmers. First, the trend since 1860 has been in that direction, and nothing in the present situation points to a new and compelling reason for concluding that a change has or is about to take place. Second, U.S. agricultural capacity is growing faster than the markets are expected to grow. This implies a domestic propensity to produce more than will clear the market at current real prices. This force for decreasing real prices need not be strong, but it is in the direction of reinforcing the other two forces. Third, world agricultural capacity is growing faster than world markets are growing. If U.S. farmers are to expand their markets by means of exports, then their real prices received for exported commodities will have to gradually decrease to remain competitive.

Price volatility returned during the 1970s to the level of the first half of the century. The relative stability of the 1950s and 1960s was attributable to U.S. price support policies which maintained domestic prices above world levels and permitted accumulation of burdensome carry-over stocks. Except for the war years, volatility earlier in this century was attributed to domestic sources including weather and instabilities in urban markets. The important source of volatility now appears to have shifted to foreign origin, particularly to policy changes of major governments. This includes decisions to import to stabilize domestic supplies, instead of "tightening the belt" regardless of the destabilizing impact on others, and embargos for political or diplomatic purposes. Prices seem unlikely to return to the unusual, relative stability of the 1950s and 1960s.

The estimated domestic agricultural supply response to a range of alternative world food conditions suggests that there will not be a physical capacity problem in meeting food demands in coming decades. It appears that U.S. agriculture can produce enough to meet domestic and export demands for food, even at moderately decreasing real prices. This requires that current efforts continue which conserve and develop natural resources, discover new technologies, promote efficient regional relocations of enterprises, and maintain an increasing supply of purchased farm inputs. Temporary strains are anticipated again, perhaps even as severe as those of the 1970s.

While physical limits on capacity are not anticipated, there may be institutional ones. Another doubling of exports within the short period of one decade such as was experienced during the 1970s, will again put the agricultural structure and its related markets under strain. Other events which are not considered agricultural can limit the demand for farm products and agriculture's supply response. These include high interest rates, credit rationing, and a substantial strengthening of the dollar against the currencies of countries which import U.S. farm products.

Changes in relative prices induce shifts in the distribution of income. Therefore, in view of the prospective continuance of price volatility, programs are likely to be considered which share the risk while at the same time maintaining agriculture's flexibility and resiliency in adjusting to change. How farm programs are financed and operated when world food markets are scarce or volatile compared to when they are plentiful or stable affects the distribution of food and income among domestic consumers, the marketing sector, farmers, input suppliers, and U.S. trading partners. The equity of such redistributions of income during times of short-run stress could prove to be of more concern for policy makers than will the long-run limits to U.S. agricultural capacity.

The Future of Food and Agriculture Policy

C.W. McMillan*

"Nothing is more terrible than activity without insight," said Thomas Carlyle, a 19th century historian. That still holds true today, but today there is also a new emphasis on *mutual* insight, where government and industry plan together.

This is especially important in the area of food and agriculture policy. Agriculture is America's biggest business, with assets topping one trillon dollars.[1] Agriculture-related jobs employ over twenty-two million people—one-fifth of the nation's workforce.[2] Farm products generate more than twenty percent of this country's gross national product.[3]

It is just as important to realize that agriculture is a global industry. The days are long gone when farmers fed only their counties, their states, or their country. The agricultural market is worldwide, and very competitive.

Many decisions about agriculture and agriculture policy are made from year to year, and even from day to day. They must be. First, farm production is inherently unstable and unpredictable; it is at the mercy of floods, droughts, frosts, pests, and other natural disasters. Second, the demand for farm products is relatively inelastic. This situation causes farm incomes to fluctuate widely in response to small changes in the quantities sold.

But these short-run decisions are not applied in a vacuum, so they should not be made in a vacuum. This is where joint long-range planning has value, as it provides for control, but still permits flexibility. At the same time, it has to treat the causes of our agricultural problems, and not merely the symptoms. These

*Mr. McMillan is the Assistant Secretary for Marketing and Inspection Services of the U.S. Department of Agriculture. Mr. McMillan presented this paper to the Food and Drug Law Institute's Food Update '84 conference in Orlando, Fla. (May 1984).

From *Food, Drug, Cosmetic Law Journal,* 40, 1985, pp. 77-84. Reprinted with permission.

problems do not respond to adhesive bandages; they need a good strong dose of vaccine.

THE 1985 FARM BILL

The four-year, omnibus farm bill is a perfect vehicle to provide that vaccine. Although the 1981 farm bill will not expire until next year's crops are in, work is beginning now on the 1985 bill.

The farm bill has always been an important piece of legislation, but this year it is especially critical. In the past few years, we have experienced the largest surpluses in history, the largest acreage reduction ever, and the worst drought in fifty years. Those problems may be behind us, but they have not disappeared. Today, food and agriculture policy stands at a watershed, and it is up to industry and government to shape its future.

The present administration has already taken some important steps in that direction. A few months ago, President Reagan instructed the Cabinet Council on Food and Agriculture to conduct a comprehensive assessment of current food and agriculture programs. Secretary Block, the head of the council, set up a working group to carry out this charge.

Deputy Secretary Lyng chairs the working group, which includes high-level officials from the Office of the U.S. Trade Representative, the Office of Management and Budget, the Council of Economic Advisors, the White House Office of Policy Development, and the Departments of State, Treasury, and Commerce.

The working group's mandate is threefold. First, they are reviewing and assessing the current programs. Second, they are initiating a policy dialogue with interested parties outside the government. As part of that effort, the Secretary and other members of the working group recently held two "listening sessions," one in Illinois and one in California, where public comments on the issues were aired. Finally, when the group is satisfied that every stone has been turned, a list of food and agriculture policy opinions will be prepared.

This is not something the working group can do alone, and they are not set up that way. They need the involvement of everyone who has a stake in agriculture: producers, consumers, suppliers, processors, distributors, and retailers.

The U.S. Department of Agriculture (USDA) and the agriculture industry have some concerns about future policy decisions. For one, the agriculture industry does not want domestic agriculture thrown into disarray. Throwing out all the existing programs would do that. Many of the producers do not want to jeopardize their ready supply of imported raw materials. Rampant trade wars, resulting from disorganized trade and production policy, would do this. First, a discussion of the previous programs, followed by the views of the Secretary of USDA.

PROBLEMS OF THE PAST

When the 1981 farm bill was being deliberated, many experts believed that the issue for the 1980s was managing food scarcity, not surpluses. This world view was taken against the backdrop of the 1970s, when farm policy was geared toward expansion. During this inflationary period, U.S. farm exports almost tripled in response to heightened world demand.[4] Farm production assets *more* than tripled in this time of heavy investment.[5]

By the end of the 1970s, world food shortages had U.S. agricultural interests convinced that there would not be enough. We saw ourselves as the only country that could fill the world's needs. At the same time, the dollar was weak, inflation was running at double-digit rates, and world oil prices shot up. This trade situation made our products easily affordable. It is not surprising that forecasts of continued strong export demand, rising production costs, and full production seemed perfectly reasonable only a few short years ago.

As a result of this situation, U.S. farmers went into high gear. The volume of exports increased from 60 million tons to 164 million tons.[6] The U.S. became the low-priced food supplier to the world.

As the decade ended, however, international food trade changed. The world entered a period of decreased demand marked by heavy debts and high unemployment. Meanwhile, the world also experienced unusually good weather in the 1981 and 1982 growing seasons, resulting in record crops at home and good crops abroad. The large surpluses clung to the market until 1983, reducing prices and incomes for farmers.

It did not take long to discover that the traditional commodity programs were insufficient to deal with the huge surpluses on hand. A special program was needed to specifically address the immediate needs of agriculture. That program was Payment In Kind, (PIK), a stopgap measure that used government stocks and secured loans as payment for the acreage taken out of production.[7]

The PIK program was designed to reduce acreage and potential production, while maintaining adequate supplies and putting farmers on firmer financial footing, and the program met those goals. This program was followed by the worst drought in half a century, which reduced crops even more than initially expected. Due to the fact that most wheat types were mature prior to the drought, the farmers experienced record wheat yields, which sharply reduced the effectiveness of PIK in reducing excessive wheat supplies.

FOCUS FOR THE FUTURE

In light of the surpluses, PIK, and the drought, USDA learned an important lesson about food and agriculture policy. It is, while one can anticipate and plan for the future, one cannot predict it. Therefore, agricultural policy must be flexible enough to bend with the circumstances, and strong enough to endure.

It is clear that the rigid price supports in the 1981 farm bill have worked against us in the highly competitive world market. It is also clear that the escalating target prices have escalated too high, so high that they induce increased production both here and abroad.

There is another important problem with the current policy. USDA has been at odds with itself on the goal of agricultural efficiency. On the one hand, through its agricultural research and extension activities, USDA contributes substantially to the productive efficiency of farmers. USDA also makes major contributions to orderly and efficient marketing of agricultural commodities.

On the other hand, USDA implements programs designed to lower our productive capacity. USDA does it at great expense, when budget deficits are a concern to everyone. Even here USDA is inconsistent. Target and loan prices above market clearing levels are telling producers in this country and others to expand production. This happens at the same time PIK and other acreage reduction programs are telling American farmers to cut back.

More clearly, the situation is that for more than two and a half years, the United States has been struggling with farm legislation that was designed for economic conditions that never materialized. If an appropriate policy is not developed as part of the 1985 farm bill, there could be irreparable damage to our farm and agribusiness economies, and to the economic standing of the country.

To get U.S. agriculture back on course, some fundamental issues must be examined in the coming months: the size and distribution of benefits, acreage reduction programs, commodity loan rates, and farmer-owned reserve. Further, there are the broader issues of agricultural trade policy and macroeconomic policy. The following discussion focuses on these topics, especially those that transcend the daily business of production.

First, one important point must be made. USDA can carve an improved food and agriculture policy from what it has learned from the past, but it must not start from scratch. If USDA shifts farm programs to where they can more accurately respond to the marketplace, and if it is done in increments, farmers only stand to benefit, and so does the U.S. economy.

THE SIZE AND DISTRIBUTION OF BENEFITS

Farm program costs are high. Federal budget deficits are high. It is in the public's interest to continue to support agriculture, but there is a cost. Today there is a tension between the high costs of current farm programs and the goal of supporting a reasonable level of income protection for the farm sector. As a result, some important questions will be evaluated in the farm bill debate:

—Who should receive this support and by what means?

—Should there be a payment limitation or should producers be provided income protection in direct proportion to their output?

—Should recipients be required to take certain actions regarding sound soil and water conservation practices?

Whatever the size or distribution of future farm program benefits, income transfer to the farm sector should not disrupt resource allocations or distort market signals. As our recent experience demonstrates, this will only lead to high program costs, large surpluses, and low prices.

A review of recent commodity programs suggests that limited acreage reduction programs are largely ineffective,[8] especially if there is unusually good weather that leads to record yields. But weather is not the only factor.

First, producers do not take their most productive land out of production; they start with the most unproductive land.

Second, the effectiveness of recent programs has been restricted because the payment limitation precludes some of the larger farms from participation.

Third, it appears that some of the more efficient producers outside the programs expand their own production, knowing that the government will try to support prices by whatever means necessary.

Finally, while the United States tries to reduce production through acreage reduction programs, our foreign competitors continue to expand production.[9] Some competitors export their surplus commodities and processed farm products using massive subsidies; others defend very high internal farm prices and inefficient production through import barriers.[10]

So maybe the question is not, "What kind of acreage reduction programs should we have?" but rather the more realistic question, "Are such programs truly in the best interests of agriculture?"

The soybean and peanut markets offer an answer and an example of the long-term effects of reducing supply and increasing price. In 1930, America harvested equal amounts of peanuts and soybeans—1.1 million acres each. Since that time, peanuts have operated continuously under a program of rigid production controls, artificially high prices, and little regard for world markets. Soybeans took the opposite approach: no production controls, minimal price supports, and total exposure to world market conditions.

By 1980, there was a harvest of 1.4 million acres of peanuts, only a nominal increase from fifty years before. In contrast, about 68 million acres of soybeans were harvested, 61.9 times the production in 1930. In dollar terms, the farmer's value of production for peanuts was about $500 million, the value for soybeans was $13.5 billion. The increased value of soybean production was 27 times the value of the peanut production.

This administration has advocated for some time that current loan rates and target prices are not in the best long-term interests of agriculture because they are so out of line with market realities. If USDA lowered the loan rates, we would reduce the incentives for major U.S. competitors to expand agricultural production.

Loan rates cannot and should not be above market clearing levels. They also should not be at the level where inefficient producers are sheltered. Most importantly, the level of loan rates should not be set at rigid, anticipatory levels in legislation.

FARMER-OWNED RESERVE

When farmers produce for a reserve and the production is locked up, it hangs over the market and depresses prices for years to come. The economic losses for our farmers are great.

What is the appropriate role of the reserve, and for what crops? Should it be used to enhance income over the long run? Does a reserve contribute to economic efficiency by reducing market extremes? Is there a real need for an open-ended government-sponsored reserve? If not, how much is enough?

More information is needed about the appropriate size of the reserve and the level for the release price, as well as the makeup, stability, and total amount of storage incentives. And again, like any good long-range policy, the rules that are developed for the reserve should be strong, yet flexible.

AGRICULTURAL TRADE POLICY

The global marketplace is extremely competitive and it can be extremely rewarding. It offers the best way for American agriculture to achieve solid, sustainable, long-term growth.

The United States is the world's leading exporter of agricultural products. We provide about 80% of the international corn trade, 55% of the coarse grain, 60% of all soybeans, and 40% of all wheat.[11] Besides business, this world trade also buys us economic strength: every $1 billion in agricultural trade creates at least an additional $1 billion in U.S. economic activity.[12] Moreover, our agricultural trade reduces our overall trade deficit by about $20 billion each year.[13]

Despite USDA efforts, exports have dropped from a $43.8 billion high in 1981 to $34.8 billion in 1983. Even with current forecasting calling for $37.5 billion this year, the increase will be due more to high prices than to greater volume.

In light of the important role our foreign customers play, there appears to be a growing interest in developing a more formal agricultural trade policy, a policy that would be closely aligned with our domestic farm policy. There are some who think that unless such a policy is adopted, policies to reduce agricultural output on a permanent basis will be seriously considered and perhaps even enacted into law. Some elements of the debate include:

More Effective General Agreement on Tariff and Trade (GATT)

In 1975, a complaint was submitted to GATT concerning unfair subsidization of wheat flour. Today, there has yet to be any conclusive action on this case. to many critics this is but one example of the ineffective system set up for settling international trade disputes. The critics contend that GATT must be made more effective and more responsive if we are ever to achieve free world trade.

Export Credits

Many importing countries are experiencing enormous debt burdens. The short-term liquidity problems in international capital markets severely restrict their ability to import. Some authorities contend that increased import financing would permit the import of food into those countries, as well as bridge the foreign exchange gap and allow nonfood imports vital to economic recovery. In turn, the larger exports of U.S. products and the greater economic growth in importing countries would ease the U.S. trade deficit problem.

Whether these particular issues are debated or not, Secretary Block has set four goals for U.S. agriculture in the world market. The first goal involves capitalizing on the potential growth markets of the developing world. This can only be done by expanding the domestic economies of these less developed countries. Although they receive nearly half of all U.S. exports, the United States is still reaching only a small share in view of the tremendous market out there.

To encourage more growth, USDA is helping build economic and political stability through the Food for Peace program. USDA has sent thousands of U.S. agriculturalists abroad to share our farming technology and has implemented a very successful program of blended export credit and commercial credit guaran-tees. But these nations need more than credit. They need to be free from the protectionist barriers that discriminate against them. And that is USDA's second goal: to eliminate trade barriers.

A third goal is to secure access to foreign markets. The new long-term agreement with the Soviet Union is a concrete example of that. This action has reestablished the United States as the top exporter of grain to that country. USDA is now pressing the Japanese for more access to their important market.

Finally, domestic farm policy must be designed to ensure that U.S. farm products will be competitive in world markets. This refers back to the earlier discussion about the need for a strong and flexible 1985 farm bill. The ultimate question is, should price support policies be geared to the market? Or should they be insulated? This will be a pivotal point in the policy debate.

MACROECONOMICS

Another important consideration is macroeconomics, which has nothing to do directly with food and agriculture, but can critically influence both. Macroeconomic trade developments have had a tremendous impact on the economic conditions of U.S. agriculture.

Today we are experiencing an unprecedented decline in agricultural export volume.[14] The causes are many, but the increased value of the dollar has had a very significant effect by simply making our products too expensive in terms of foreign currencies. A large part of this problem stems from our inability to bring the budget deficit under control.

It is not a simple problem, and it will not go away soon. The U.S. economy is recovering, but there is an inherent lag in the spread of this good fortune to our most important markets with growth potential. Furthermore, the strength of the dollar is likely to persist as long as a large number of countries experience economic and political stability problems.

As a direct result, appropriate monetary and fiscal policies are probably as important as the 1985 farm bill itself when it comes to the long-run health of U.S. agriculture.

CONCLUSION

Today, agriculture is the most efficient industry in America, and the healthiest. But under current laws and policies, agriculture is at odds with itself, pitting productivity against overproduction, and government support against spiraling program costs.

It is time for some insight into the problem, and USDA thinks the best way to plan future policy is to plan with everyone affected by that policy. Following these suggestions, together we can build a stronger, more flexible food and agriculture policy that can meet the challenges of the 1980s and beyond.

NOTES

1. U.S. DEPARTMENT OF AGRICULTURE, 1984 FACT BOOK OF U.S. AGRICULTURE, Miscellaneous Publication No. 1063, 1 (1983).

2. *Id.*

3. ECONOMIC RESEARCH SERVICE, U.S. DEPARTMENT OF AGRICULTURE, ECONOMIC INDICATORS OF THE FARM SECTOR: FARM SECTOR REVIEW 67-68 (1983).

4. U.S. DEPARTMENT OF AGRICULTURE, AGRICULTURAL STATISTICS 517 (1983).

5. *Id.* at 389.

6. Foreign Agriculture Service, U.S. Department of Agriculture, Foreign Agricultural Trade of the United States for Fiscal Year 1970 1 (1970); World Agricultural Outlook Board, U.S. Department of Agriculture, Outlook for U.S. Agricultural Exports, Table 1 (Aug. 20, 1984).

7. Typically, the approach to reducing surplus government stocks is to pay farmers cash to divert land from crop production to a conservation use. With PIK, the government pays farmers with some of the surplus stocks. The purpose of the program is to reduce surpluses without creating additional cash outlays by the government.

8. Remarks prepared for delivery by William G. Lesher, Assistant Secretary for Economics, U.S. Department of Agriculture, at the Conference on Alternative Agricultural and Food Policies and the 1985 Farm Bill, sponsored by th Giannini Foundation and Resources for the Future, Berkeley, Calif., June 11, 1984.

9. Johnson, *The Performance of Past Policies: A Critique,* Univ. of Chi., Office of Agricultural Economics Research (May 14, 1984).

10. For example, subsidized Japanese rice sales reduced U.S. export revenues in 1980 by an estimated $20 million. The Japanese rice policy reduced import demand for U.S. wheat by an estimated $30 million in 1980. Also, Japan primarily uses quotas, licensing, and health standards to control meat imports. Their health regulations are similar to those for other importing nations, but are used as general trade restrictions. Paarlberg and Sharples, *Japanese and European Community Agricultural Trade Policies: Some U.S. Strategies,* U.S. Department of Agriculture, Economic Research Service, Foreign Agricultural Economic Report No. 2042, 5 (Aug. 1984).

11. World Outlook Board, U.S. Department of Agriculture, *supra* note 6, Tables 5, 6, and 7.

12. U.S. Department of Agriculture, Agriculture's Role in the Economy of the United States, Economics and Statistics Service Staff Report, No. ARESS 810407 (April 1981).

13. Economic Report of the President, 98th Cong., 2d Sess. 329 (Feb. 1984).

14. World Outlook Board, U.S. Department of Agriculture, *supra* note 6, Table 1.

A Review of Selected Studies on World Hunger

INTERNATIONAL HUNGER: EXTENT OF HUNGER

Defining World Hunger

The popular press often portrays international hunger as being a result of acute crises such as severe droughts and civil wars. While these natural and political crises do exacerbate existing food shortages, natural disasters and political crises are not the major causes of hunger in developing nations. Instead, the central world hunger problem is a chronic condition affecting poor populations world-wide.

The nutrition science literature defines hunger in developing countries as the condition in which a person consumes too few calories to be able to meet the body's minimum daily requirements, technically identified as undernutrition. Protein deficiency, once thought to be a major hunger indicator is now thought to be secondary to calorie deficiency because diets adequate in calories generally also meet protein requirements. Put simply, hungry people are those whose diets lack sufficient calories because they are not getting enough food. The Food and Agriculture Organization/World Health Organization (FAO/WHO) calorie standard is the most widely accepted basis for evaluating the extent of undernutrition.

Magnitude of the Hunger Problem

According to the Food and Agriculture Organization (FAO) of the United Nations, one in four people in the developing countries is undernourished. Food and development agencies have calculated the number of hungry persons worldwide to be from 450 million to 1.3 billion. Despite this variability in numbers, there is no question that hunger is a major problem placing hundreds of millions of persons at risk of disease and death. (*194, 227, 230, 246, 250*)

"A Review of Selected Studies on World Hunger," Staff Report, Select Committee on Hunger, U.S. House of Representatives, September 1985, pp. 21-36.

Populations at Greatest Risk

The major reports agree on populations that are at greatest risk of hunger. The 1980 report of the President's Commission on World Hunger summarized these reports stating that 75 percent of the world's chronically undernourished live in India, Southeast Asia, and sub-Saharan Africa. (*227*)

According to the 1980 FAO report, Dimensions of Need, people in twelve nations are suffering "from undernourishment on a vast scale." With estimates of the number of their undernourished in millions the twelve nations are: India, 201; Indonesia, 33; Bangladesh, 27; Nigeria, 14; Brazil, Ethiopia and Pakistan, 12 each; the Philippines, 10; Afghanistan, 6; and Burma, Colombia, and Thailand, 5 each. The FAO has determined that, in 1984-85, 24 countries in sub-Saharan Africa experienced a food crisis due to the growing gap between their minimum food needs and the food supply that is available. (*194*)

Within each nation, women, infants, and children are those most affected by hunger. Infants and children are very vulnerable to the negative health impacts of inadequate food intake because of their critical nutrient needs for growth and development. The paramount importance of proper nutrition for women during pregnancy and lactation is also widely recognized.

According to the National Research Council, women's social roles in developing countries place them at more serious nutritional risk: "In communities where women carry heavy economic responsibilities, often as the sole or primary supporter of their children, neither pregnancy or lactation can be allowed to disrupt the pattern of work. Under such circumstances, when food availability is constrained, the physiological burden of pregnancy and lactation is immense." (*353*)

Not only are women, infants, and children among those most physiologically vulnerable to the damaging effects of hunger, they make up the majority of the hungry worldwide. The World Bank Development Report, 1982 and the report of the President's Commission on World Hunger have reported that infants and children make up more than one-half of the world's hungry. (*227, 246*) That women are also disproportionately affected by hunger is noted by the World Food Council which states that the bulk of the undernourished tend to be families of landless laborers headed by women. Women, infants, and children living in rural areas are disproportionately affected by hunger. (*250*)

Measuring Hunger

The discrepancy among published estimates of the number of hungry persons worldwide partially reflects the use of different indicators of hunger. Those reports that discuss hunger as a result of inadequate food supply measure the gaps between per capita calorie needs versus per capita food supply (production, imports and air combined). Recent World Bank studies of the extent of world hunger employ poverty indicators to measure the availability of food in households. A third category of reports on hunger measure the consequences rather than the causes of hunger. Falling into this category are the health and nutrition studies which document the prevalence of hunger related disease and death.

Food Supply

The U.S. Department of Agriculture (USDA) reports annually on the food supply in developing countries receiving U.S. food aid. They estimate food aid needs by calculating expected per capita food supply. They compare this expected supply to past supply to determine status quo food deficits; they also calculate nutrition based food deficits comparing supply to food actually needed to furnish the population with adequate calories (in grain weight equivalents). Using this methodology USDA reported in 1984 that developing countries experienced a drop from the previous year in per capita food supply. This, they deduced, resulted in a drop in food availability compared to food needed—an indicator of increasing hunger in developing countries. (*189*) Their region and country specific analyses identified the African continent (excluding South Africa), as having the worst declines in per capita food production, with the Sudano-Sahelian countries most drastically affected by food shortages resulting from a severe long-lasting drought in that area. (*187*)

The International Food Policy Research Institute (IFPRI) identifies a similar gap between food available and food needed. In Closing The Cereals Gap With Trade and Food Aid, their 1984 report, IFPRI calculated that 42 million metric tons of additional food aid (compared to 1980-81 actual food aid) would be required to bring the diets of those in developing countries up to FAO/WHO minimum nutritional standards, the most widely accepted international standards. (*202*)

The FAO also employs food supply needs as a measurement of the extent of hunger. Comparing per capita food supply to minimum per capita caloric requirements, FAO has concluded that worldwide there are approximately 450 million hungry persons. (*194*)

Food supply studies of hunger and food aid needs are useful indicators of the magnitude of the gap between food supply and minimal nutritional needs. They are also useful in locating regions and nations where that gap is the widest. However, neither USDA, IFPRI, nor FAO studies of a country's food needs adjust their per capita figures to reflect food available specifically to poor households—the group in each country most likely to be without enough food. To more accurately assess food available to those in poverty, several World Bank hunger and poverty assessment reports suggest adjusting each nation's per capita food supply figures to reflect income distribution. (*230*)

Poverty Measures

During the 1970's the World Food Council was estimating the extent of hunger by calculating food supply and food aid needs. At its 1984 10th anniversary session, the Council concluded that food supply and hunger should be viewed as different problems with related, but separate, solutions. They found that while the world food supply had improved greatly since 1974, there had been no alleviation of the problem of hunger. The Council commented on this apparent paradox of hunger amidst a plentiful food supply: (*250*)

> The World is feeding nearly 1 billion more people in 1984 than in 1974, and there is ample food produced globally for all the world's people; yet there remains hundreds of millions of hungry and malnourished people.

To specifically address the problem of hunger and not just that of food supply, the Council recommended that future studies address the socioeconomic factors which limit access to available food, primarily lack of income.

Economic and statistical analyses by the 1983 World Bank paper Poverty, Undernutrition, and Hunger further confirm the World Food Council's above recommendation. The paper concludes that "the vast majority of hungry or undernourished people are receiving too few calories because they are poor. (*126*) Using absolute poverty as an indicator of the extent of hunger, in 1980 the World Bank estimated that there were 780 million persons at risk of hunger. Absolute poverty occurs when people are too poor to obtain a calorie-adequate diet; that is, the number of calories needed to lead a reasonably productive and energetic life. Although the proportion of people in absolute poverty in developing countries fell in the 1960's and 1970's, except in sub-Saharan Africa, the number of people in absolute poverty—and at risk of hunger—had increased. (*246*)

The 1983 World Bank staff paper on poverty and hunger, while identifying poverty as the best indicator of hunger, clarifies that income per capita is not sufficient to measure the extent of hunger in every developing nation. The example of Sri Lanka, where "basic needs are so much better fulfilled than real income-per-person would suggest" is cited to support the need to examine money and service resources available per person, rather than simply income per capita. Specifically, the World Bank recommends that the extent of hunger in a particular nation be determined by: (1) the availability of socially provided basic services such as health care; (2) gaps between received and disposable income—disposable for food consumption and not for such payments as interest, rents, et cetera; (3) relative prices and composition of the bundles of needed commodities; and (4) income distribution. (*213*).

Health and Nutrition Indicators

A final group of indicators is used to measure the damaging health and nutrition consequences of hunger in developing nations. An available food supply and income are clearly antecedent to an individual's ability to get enough food. Illness, on the other hand, is both cause and consequence of hunger; death can be the final result.

A limited number of surveys have directly assessed the health and nutrition effects of hunger in developing countries. The World Health Organization and UNICEF keep selected morbidity and mortality statistics worldwide. Country-specific nutrition surveys have been conducted by the Agency for International Development, the World Health Organization, and individual nations for the purpose of planning food distribution and health programs. The most widely accepted indicators of hunger from such data collection are: nutritional deficiency diseases, low birthweight and infant mortality, and childhood illnesses and related child deaths.

Nutritional deficiency diseases. Undernutrition in developing nations is manifested primarily in four major nutritional deficiency diseases: protein-energy malnutrition (PEM), xerophthalimia (vitamin A deficiency), endemic goiter (iodine deficiency), and nutritional anemia (iron deficiency).

Infants and children who are chronically undernourished are most often reported to be growth stunted in height and weight, and have fewer brain cells because of insufficient caloric intake during critical brain growth periods. The children are tiny, with underdeveloped organs and impaired ability to learn. (*328*)

Protein-energy malnutrition is manifested in marasmus, where the body appears to be wasting away, and the limbs are emaciated and weak. Kwashiorkor, another manifestation of protein-energy malnutrition, results in children with swollen bellies, accumulated fluid in the limbs, skin which is tinted reddish-orange, and rashes covering the body.

Xerophthalimia is a result of diets deficient in vitamin A, and results in blindness for 500,000 children each year. (*340*) Endemic goiter is a consequence of diets low in iodine, and can lead to deaf-mutism, deformity, and mental retardation. It affects 200 million persons worldwide. Iron-deficiency anemia, affecting 500 million women, infants, and children in developing countries, leads to serious physical and mental health consequences (described in Hunger in the United States, Extent of Hunger section above). (*246*)

Along with infants and children, women of childbearing age represent a group which is most vulnerable to nutrition deficiency. Comprehensive data on the nutritional status of women in developing countries is severely lacking. A recent review of studies of women's nutrition found large deficiencies in caloric intake for a significant proportion of women in most developing countries. Surprisingly pregnant and lactating women consumed diets similar to other women, even though their nutritional needs are considerably greater. Not only were women found to consistently eat less than men, but, on the average, they consumed a smaller proportion of their recommended daily intake of calories. Iron and vitamin A were commonly deficient in their diets and anemia was highly prevalent among women in all studies. (*339*)

Low birthweight. UNICEF, the World Health Organization (WHO), and the Pan American Health Organization (PAHO), agree that in developing countries a woman's nutritional status before pregnancy and her weight gain during pregnancy are the most important factors in her future infant's birth weight. If a mother is undernourished during pregnancy relative to her own needs plus her fetus' needs, the baby will be deprived nutritionally and have a great risk of being born with a low birthweight. Low birthweight is closely associated with infant illness and death. According to the WHO, the poor nutritional status of women in developing countries is reflected in the low birthweight rate that is 2½ times that in the United States. *(237)*

The effects of undernutrition during pregnancy cause damage long after birth. UNICEF's State of the World's Children reports that low birthweight infants in developing countries suffer a high risk of being malnourished themselves and of dying within 1 year. The deaths of low birthweight infants comprise 4 million out of approximately 12 million infants who die each year. *(237)*

While the World Health Organization estimates of the proportion of low birthweight infants range between 10 and 50 percent in each developing country, *(237)* development and survival outlook for each low birthweight infant is very bleak. It should be noted that the low birthweight infant is a neglected aspect of international child health and survival in the literature reviewed.

Infant mortality. The Infant Mortality Rate (IMR) is the number of deaths under age 1 for every 1,000 live births. Beyond statistics, the IMR is a powerful indicator of the quality of children's lives including health and the absence of hunger. UNICEF reports that the infant mortality rate in developing countries declined from approximately 200/1,000 live births in 1950 to 100/1,000 in 1975—a drop of 50 percent in 25 years. While this improvement is significant, UNICEF's 1980 statistics reveal that the rate of infant mortality in less developed countries remains at over five times the rate in more developed countries. *(237)*

The General Assembly of the United Nations has adopted the target of reducing worldwide infant mortality rates to 50 or less per 1,000 births by the year 2000. UNICEF predicts, however, that "unless there is a sudden acceleration of progress, that target will not be achieved." More than 70 nations are expected to have infant mortality rates above the target, with three out of five of the world's babies born in those 70 nations. Adequate caloric intake during pregnancy is a key factor in preventing low birthweight and would prevent one-third of infant deaths worldwide. *(237)*

Childhood illness and mortality. In addition to women and infants, young children are at particular risk of permanent health damages due to undernutrition. During the critical periods of growth they require higher concentrations of calories, protein, and nutrients in their diets. Consequently, hunger and related diseases have been identified as the most serious child health problem in many developing nations. *(228)*

The World Bank's policy report Malnourished People, for example, states that malnutrition and diarrheal disease frequently simultaneously afflict young poor children in developing nations. The report explains that one problem compounds the damage of the other. Diarrhea is exacerbated by undernutrition and, in turn, the extreme loss of fluids aggravates the poor health status of the already undernourished child. (*328*) UNICEF has reported in The State of the World's Children, 1984 that diarrhea and malnutrition together are the cause of three-fifths of all preventable deaths.

There is also a strong synergistic linkage between hunger and infectious disease. UNICEF found that children with even moderate malnutrition were three times more likely to contract infections. After contracting an infection, undernourished children are found to be 10 times more likely to die from infectious diseases than their well nourished counterparts. With measles infections the relative mortality risk is even greater. The Agency for International Development reports that a child in Guatemala is 268 times more likely to die as a result of inadequate nutrition and no immunization against the disease than a child in a developed nation. (*246*)

World Bank and UNICEF hunger and health studies consistently report that hunger and interrelated episodes of diarrhea and infection are the primary causes of children dying each day in the developing nations. While child survival rates internationally have improved, UNICEF documents that in 44 developing countries children are dying at 20 to 40 times the rate of those in rapidly developing nations such as Costa Rica and Trinidad. UNICEF estimates that 40,000 children under age 5 die each day, with malnutrition estimated to contribute to two-thirds of these deaths. (*237*)

EFFECTIVENESS OF INTERNATIONAL PROGRAMS AND POLICIES

Introduction

World hunger is a problem of immense proportions and subtle complexities. Devising solutions, therefore, depends upon working with those causes which can be affected by efficient and cost-effective change.

Whether a person is hungry is affected by the amount and kinds of food available in the country, in the region, in the market and in the household; whether the individual's household is able to obtain the food that is available; the use of the obtained food by members within the household; and the health status of the individual.

Malnutrition can result from inadequacies in any one or more of these factors. Changes in one factor may be ineffective unless others are changed simultaneously. Efforts to expand the availability of food will have no nutritional effect if the additional food is not made accessible to malnourished people. Although the Green Revolution of the 1960's increased agricultural production in poor countries it did not reduce malnutrition as widely as had been hoped.

In the Philippines, for example, rice production almost doubled in the 1970's as a result of agricultural mechanization. From 1975 to 1981 the value of the GDP (gross domestic product) per worker rose approximately 20 percent. (Data from the Bureau of Agricultural Economics, Ministry of Agriculture and Food, Government of Philippines reported in The Philippines: Recent Trends in Poverty, Employment and Wages, World Bank, January 11, 1985 unpublished report.) This increased productivity was not reflected in the incomes or food available to the farmers who worked the land. In fact, by 1978, the nation's per capita calorie consumption had fallen to the lowest in all Asia (except in war torn Cambodia). (290) According to data from the Government of Philippines, reported by the World Bank, daily wages in agriculture, in real terms, fell sharply. For those workers producing rice, the real wages fell 14 percent from 1970-72 to 1980-82. (World Bank report cited above.)

Efforts to improve the ability of the poor to purchase food may also be unsuccessful if they result in the purchase of nonfood commodities, with no resulting improvement in food consumption among the malnourished members of the household. Before any program to reduce hunger is implemented, the interrelationship of the economic and cultural factors leading to hunger must be carefully considered.

When resources are scarce, programs are often limited to the most vulnerable groups, that is, children less than 3 years old and pregnant and lactating women. But the costs, the intra-household distribution of food, and other difficulties of age-specific programs may make them an inefficient way to address hunger. Alan Berg of the World Bank states: "In planning a program, it is preferable to start, not with a decision to assist a given group, but with the total malnourished population as a target." (328)

Several observations on the effectiveness of anti-hunger efforts can be summarized before examining specific programs and policies. First, programs designed to alleviate hunger must be periodically evaluated to ensure that they are meeting their goals. For example, if a food aid program is causing disincentives to local agricultural production, it may not meet its goals of improving the adequacy of the food supply or access of lower-income people to food. Nutritional intake of individual household members must also be evaluated.

Second, interrelationships of social, political, and economic factors determine the success or failure of strategies in particular situations. Recently, for instance, we have seen how civil unrest can impede the ability of programs to reach people.

Third, assisting people in meeting their basic needs, especially food, health, sanitation, and education, will empower them to move beyond subsistence with its accompanying hunger, disease, and inability to achieve full human potential.

Hunger Intervention Programs

Supplement Programs

Supplemental feeding programs, the largest and often the most popular activities undertaken to alleviate hunger, provide food to nutritionally needy people. In developing nations they are usually designed for pregnant and lactating women and children under age 3.

Two recent reviews summarized data from more than 200 supplementary feeding projects. (*320, 327*) The results from these reviews indicate that nutritional improvement is possible with food supplement programs. Many feeding programs result in significant improvements in growth for infant and child participants, decreases in illness, and improvements in cognitive development. Evaluations of prenatal supplemental feeding programs in Guatemala, India, Colombia, Canada, and the United States found supplementation was associated with increased birthweight, a decreased incidence of low birthweight infants, and/or decreased neonatal mortality. (*341*)

However, evaluation of the effectiveness of these programs does not always show a positive impact on health or nutritional status. The mixed findings from evaluations of these programs is due, in part, to variables in the programs such as adequacy of food quantity distributed, the duration of participation in the program, the timing of supplementation, the nutritional status of persons entering the program, and the degree of targetting of the food programs to those most in need. (*341*)

Programs which are well-designed to reach the neediest populations have documented nutritional improvements. A program in Colombia, by reaching a more chronically malnourished group than children in the community at large, resulted in growth improvements in 45 percent of the children. (*342*) A supplemental feeding program in Mexico City which was reaching only mildly malnourished children, on the other hand, reported no significant impact on the prevalence of malnutrition. (*341*)

School-based supplemental feeding programs are relatively expensive, but have strong political appeal. The support they receive is not readily transferable to other types of nutrition or education interventions. However, if options exist, other strategies should be considered. (*328*)

Food for Work Programs, in which wages are paid totally or in part in food rather than in cash, are a form of food supplement. They were originally developed to provide income generating employment opportunities and improve rural infrastructure. Because of the nature of the work, only the poorest households tend to participate. (*342*)

Data on the nutritional effectiveness of Food for Work Programs is limited. A land-army project in Mysore, India, in which participants were living away from their families increased adult male weight by 8-15 kilograms. (*374*) There is almost no documentation of the effect of food for work projects on individuals within the family. A study currently being conducted in Bangladesh may contribute information about the nutritional impact of Food for Work Programs on families. (*371*)

Food Stamp Programs

Food Stamp Programs are designed to increase the food purchasing power of a household, thus leading to improved food consumption. There are few studies of Food Stamp Programs in developing nations. A preliminary evaluation of the food stamp scheme implemented in 1979 in Sri Lanka indicates positive nutritional effects. In 1981-82 the program increased caloric intake of the poorest fifth of households participating by 11 percent. This occurred although the nominal value of stamps remained constant from the program's inception. It is possible that, if food stamps had been indexed to correlate with inflation, the nutritional benefit may have been greater. (*331*)

To the extent that food stamps increase the purchasing power of a household, an impact on nutritional status can be assumed. However, food stamps vary in their impact on nutrition depending on the effect of prices and income changes on food buying patterns. As noted in the evaluation of the Sri Lanka program, these programs are most cost-efficient if targetted to the poorest households.

Food Subsidies

Governments in many developing countries control food prices, subsidizing either the producer or consumer, or both. Low food prices obviously improve the economic access of poor people to food. However, when food producers cannot obtain an adequate income as a result of artificially low food prices, their nutritional status and the food supply suffers.

If food subsidies are not targetted, program costs are prohibitive. Many countries, therefore, limit subsidies to vulnerable groups, to those foods normally consumed by the low-income population, and/or to specific low-income geographic areas.

Studies in India, Sri Lanka, Bangladesh, Pakistan, and Mexico show improvements in food consumption as a result of food subsidies. (*328*) However, other studies indicate that subsidies have not resulted in a decrease in the prevalence of preschool malnutrition. (*342*)

Food Fortification and Formulated Foods

Alteration of the food supply to make it more nutritious has the potential of reducing specific nutrition deficiency diseases, such as goiter or anemia, in a population. Fortification of sugar with vitamin A and salt with iodine have proven effective in alleviating some forms of malnutrition. (*326*)

Formulated foods were developed to meet the special needs of infants following weaning. Because malnutrition at this stage of a child's development is a serious problem in developing countries, many weaning foods, usually based on a locally available staple food, have been developed and promoted. A number of studies indicate that they can be effective in protecting weanlings from malnutrition, and in stimulating growth. (*326*) Where commercially prepared foods are too expensive for the target population, nutrition education is necessary to promote the development of home-prepared formulated foods.

Primary Health Care

The United Nations Children Fund (UNICEF) has demonstrated the effectiveness of selected primary health care techniques in reducing infant mortality and improving growth among malnourished children. (*237*) Interventions such as vaccinations, oral rehydration for victims of diarrhea, midwifery, maternal education on breastfeeding and weaning, and administration of antibiotics against respiratory disease have been shown to decrease infant and child death rates in Haiti, India, and Thailand. (*329*)

A Worldwatch report notes that such projects have reduced infant mortality by one-half in demonstration projects, for a cost of as little as $2 per person. The report further estimates that extending primary health care to all the world's people would cost an additional $10 billion annually—saving 5 to 10 million lives annually. (*329*) This statistic demonstrates not only that lives of children are saved, but also that millions more have fewer illnesses, better growth, and a greater chance to be economically productive.

Primary health care interventions including Oral Rehydration Therapy (ORT) not only reduce the risk of death from malnutrition and dehydration, they also reduce the short-term negative nutritional impact of the illness. World Health Organization data from the Philippines, Bangladesh, and Turkey show that children treated with ORT showed better weight gain than children to whom ORT was not available. (See Chart No. 1, p 37.) According to UNICEF, with low-cost primary health care interventions, "the downward spiral of malnutrition an infection can be broken and in its place, an upward spiral can be set in motion—less frequent illness, leading to more complete recovery, leading to more normal growth, leading to less frequent illness . . ." The quantitative impact of comprehensive primary health care interventions on children's nutritional status, as measured by the growth curve, is illustrated by UNICEF in Chart No. 2, see p. 38. (*239*)

A secondary achievement of primary health care projects is a reduction in birth rates in densely populated nations. In India, for example, where health care reduced infant and child mortality, the use of contraceptives increased. Family planning was stimulated even in those areas where sterilization campaigns had previously caused intense resentment. (*333*)

The simple and low-cost technique of administering oral salts to children with diarrhea can save millions of children from dying of malnutrition and dehydration. As noted in the section above on Extent of Hunger Internationally, diarrheal disease lowers a child's nutritional level and every episode puts him/her at risk of death from dehydration. In Bangladesh, Costa Rica, Egypt, Haiti, Jamaica, Kenya, Nepal, Papua New Guinea, the Philippines, Sri Lanka, Thailand, and Tonga, oral rehydration salts reduced hospital admissions by more than 50 percent and decreased mortality rates by over 40 percent among those who did have to be hospitalized for diarrheal disease. (See Chart No. 3, p. 39).

The need for maternal education on breast-feeding has been documented by several reviews of the patterns and trends of breastfeeding in developing countries. Compiling national survey data the reviews find that a very large proportion of infants are never breast-fed or breast-fed for less than 3 months in Central and South America, and the Caribbean. In scattered large urban areas in Asia, Africa, and the Near East, similar breast-feeding patterns exist. Elsewhere the extent and duration of breast-feeding is very long, but there are indications that the duration of breast-feeding is declining as formula or infant weaning foods are introduced early in infancy. (*347, 350*)

Integrated Health and Nutrition Interventions

An integrated intervention combines basic health services, such as immunizations and oral rehydration therapy, with nutrition and family planning services. Packaging of the services is more effective and more efficient than individual programs which are not coordinated. (*342*)

Studies clearly indicate the cost-effectiveness of these programs in meeting a number of health and nutrition objectives. In Narangwal, India, the integrated approach was able to decrease mortality and morbidity and improve growth. However, the relative importance of health care versus nutrition supplementation varied for different health outcomes. Prenatal supplementation for underweight women, either alone or in combination with medical care, was the most cost-effective means of reducing prenatal and neonatal mortality. Medical care was the most effective means in reducing infant mortality; and nutrition or health care were equally effective in decreasing mortality in 1-to 3-year-old children. Children receiving nutrition care in combination with medical care services exhibited the highest mean weights. (*343*)

Similar results were reported from an evaluation of a World Bank project in Tamil Nadu, India. Supplementary feeding of high risk children in combination with health care significantly reduced the number of moderately and severely malnourished preschoolers. (*341*) Catholic Relief Service data indicate that clinics supplying food supplements are the ones most regularly attended. (*341*) A chart showing the costs and impacts of various health and nutrition programs follows. (*329*) (See Chart No. 4, p. 40.)

Nutrition Education

Nutrition education promotes the better use of available food resources for meeting nutritional needs. It is especially important for the pregnant woman and mothers of small children so that the special nutritional needs of the fetus and infant are met. Unfortunately, little evidence has been gathered on the effectiveness of nutrition education in improving food practices and nutritional health. The relative merits of different methods of nutrition education in improving nutrition remain largely unknown. Mass media, such as radio announcements, combined with personal counseling, appear to have the greatest effect on changing nutrition behaviors. (*326*)

Agriculture, Development and Food Supply

Agriculture and rural development projects and policies that cause food prices to decrease and to fluctuate less over time offer a high potential for improving the diets of the urban poor. High price levels and severe price fluctuations are much more harmful to the poor than to the better-off urban consumers. (*205*) On the other hand, projects which cause food price levels and/or net farm incomes to increase will benefit low-income food producers.

The type of crop production resulting from specific agricultural policies may influence levels of hunger. Much malnutrition is present in households which consume most of what they produce. For those households, changes in the kinds and amount of food produced, and fluctuations during the year in relation to the harvest, have significant impacts on levels of malnutrition. Agriculture and rural development projects can change both the kind of crops planted and patterns of cropping to improve food availability year round.

In planning agriculture development projects it is necessary to take seasonal variability into account, both in assessing food aid needs and in project implementation. Most poor rural people live in geographic areas of marked variability in wet and dry seasonality. During the wet season, especially before the first harvest, food supply is limited, food prices are high, malnutrition, morbidity and mortality all rise, birth weights drop, and neonatal mortality rises. Further, many remote and poor areas are inaccessible by vehicle during the rains. (*183*)

Appropriate technologies have not been designed for poor farmers in developing nations according to the Office of Technology Assessment (OTA). Agricultural development projects based on large scale models from the United States are not successful. Recommended technologies are low risk, resource conserving, small scale, locally produced, easily repaired, and based on traditional methods. (*380*)

The influence of rural development projects on the control of the intra-household budget, the allocation of the time of women, and the nutritional effect of changes in breast-feeding and child care practices need to be assessed. Research to evaluate these influences has been limited. (*341*) However, studies by AID, the World Bank, and FAO are currently in progress.

Cash Cropping

Agricultural projects can have a negative effect, particularly when cash cropping, that is, producing food for sale, is encouraged among farm households. These households, because they become dependent on income to purchase food, are at risk of fluctuations in food supply and real net income. This financial risk is a result of many factors: the costs of production; the increased vulnerability of their land to pests due to the use of uniformly genetic stock; and farming which is more susceptible to outside market pressures resulting from the international trade environment. (*290*)

In Haiti, where agricultural development has encouraged many farmers to substitute coffee for other foods grown, the farmers produce at a much greater financial risk. They have become more dependent on fertilizer to produce the amount and type of cash crop desired and have become more dependent on middlemen who control the coffee marketing and the price farmers receive for their crops. (*290*) Lower incomes result in less food availability and increased hunger.

Cash cropping projects do not always have negative nutritional impacts. The additional income provided can result in a net gain in the ability of the household to sustain itself, with food and other necessary items. Because the nutritional impact of policies which promote the development of crops for income vary widely, careful study of the effect on subsistence households is necessary. (*328*)

Micro-enterprise Credit

Micro-enterprise credit is the extension of credit in very small amounts to the landless and nearly landless poor, both men and women, in small, interdependent groups, administered by well-trained workers, for the purpose of income generating activities. These activities are based on time-tested survival skills with which the poor are already familiar. The enterprises include such activities as sewing of clothing, rice-husking, pressing mustard seeds for oil, making fishing nets, mats or pottery, trading commodities, and selling cow's milk.

Current evaluations of these direct projects show these to be among those having the greatest positive impact on the landless and nearly landless. The International Fund for Agricultural Development (IFAD) 1982 annual report in its evaluation of rural credit projects found: "the provision of credit is one of the

most powerful means of reaching the poor directly and preferentially and ***
enables them to achieve significant increases in living standards. *(379)*

The Program for Investment in the Small Capital Enterprise Sector
(PISCES), funded by AID, found that the lack of even minimal amounts of
capital is the problem most frequently cited by micro-entrepreneurs *(376)* who
represent 30 to 60 percent of the labor force of Third World countries. *(369)*

The perception of private financial institutions has traditionally been that
lending small amounts to the very poor entails too great a risk with transaction
costs too high. Several recent credit projects have disproven this assumption.
Payback rates of 99 percent are routinely reported, and the cost of delivering
credit assistance has been low. *(379)* The largest of these projects is the Grameen
Bank Project (GBP) in Bangladesh. Preliminary data reveals that the projects are
working positively toward the goal of economic self-sufficiency for poor and
landless people.

Food Supply

Factors which affect whether a country or region has sufficient food to provide for
its population can be divided into two broad categories. Emergency lack of food
results from a sudden occurrence, such as flood, drought, or civil unrest. A
structural lack of sufficient food results when a country cannot produce enough
food locally and when it does not have sufficient foreign exchange to purchase the
food on the international market. Generally, emergency conditions are short-
term, lasting only one growing season. Structural problems take longer to resolve. In some cases, a country can suffer from a food shortage because of both
emergency and structural causes, as in the current crisis in Africa. Appropriate
responses depend upon the particular circumstances involved.

Insufficient food because of an emergency. Because emergency situations vary so
greatly from country to country, there is little consensus on recommendations for
the international community to increase the effectiveness of emergency relief
efforts. In some circumstances, the U.N. Disaster Relief Organization is the
appropriate agency for coordinating emergency efforts; in others the International
Committee of the Red Cross, the World Food Program, or the United National
Development Program may be more appropriate. There is common agreement
that better coordination among UN agencies, donor government relief agencies,
church groups, the Red Cross, and private relief agencies would facilitate relief
efforts.

Chronic insufficiency of the food supply. Chronic food shortages result when a
nation cannot regularly produce enough food for its citizens and cannot purchase
it in international markets. Nations falling in this category are dependent upon
external food aid. The United States is one of the largest providers of food aid,

most of which is channeled through the Public Law 480 program.

Food aid has been the subject of continuing controversy. Certain critics charge that its negative impact on local agricultural production should limit food aid to emergency programs. Some believe that food aid encourages the neglect of agriculture with resulting negative impacts on the majority of the rural population. The most extreme view holds that food aid may "actually increase hunger and repression by reinforcing the power of national and international elites who usurp the resources rightfully belonging to the hungry." *(219)*

Proponents of food aid argue that it can, by increasing food supplies in low-income countries, establish a beginning for development of the rural infrastructure. Two arguments support this view. One is that food aid adds to international transfers, increasing the assets of the recipient country. The second is that food aid can increase the speed of economic growth, facilitating improvements in all sectors of the economy. This view recognizes that economic growth is not necessarily spread across the economic spectrum, and that care must be taken that food aid does benefit the poorest people. Because food aid can lead to lower food prices, poor people thus have increased access to food, which can result in improved nutritional status and improved productivity. *(205)*

A concern is that fluctuation in the level of food aid can cause low agricultural production in years of high food aid flows, and severe economic and nutritional problems in years of low food aid flows. Evidence exists, however, the food aid, when properly used, can help local agriculture, and provide incentives to increased production in rural development programs. *(205)*

Population Growth and Other Development Issues

Population growth creates pressures on food availability. Programs and policies that limit population growth through decreasing family size also have an impact on levels of nutrition.

While the populations of some countries change little in size from year to year, other nations are experiencing the fastest growth ever recorded. For example, the populations of West Germany and Hungary are slowly declining in size, while those of Kenya and Syria will double in two decades. *(246)* Many countries with continued population growth are now moving into a period where a failure to sharply reduce family size is already leading to a decline in per capita consumption of food. *(180)*

Disparities among nations cause stress within the international economic system. Low fertility countries are food aid donors; high fertility countries recipients. *(180)*

Among a number of methods of fertility control discussed in the literature is breast feeding. Women who are breast feeding do not usually ovulate, a precaution taken by nature to avoid the physiological stress associated with lactating and being pregnant at the same time. *(180)*

A broad range of other developmental efforts can affect the extent of hunger. To cite some examples:

Water and sanitation programs can serve to dramatically intercede in the malnutrition-infectious disease cycle. Much disease is linked to inadequate water supply or unsafe sanitation. It is clear that the provision of a safe water supply can decrease the vulnerability of the malnourished to disease.

Reforestation, by reclaiming land that has been lost to food production, or by expanding the potential arable land, has the potential for increasing food availability in poor nations. Land tenure programs designed to make agriculturally productive land available to poor or subsistence farmers have the potential to increase food production among nutritionally vulnerable groups in the population. Marketing, storage, warehousing, and management programs must be coupled with increased production schemes in many countries to assist in assuring food security.

Education can be a significant indicator of hunger. Over 24 separate studies in 15 nations have established that the level of the mother's education is a key determinant of her children's health. In 11 countries studies by the Latin American Demographic Centre, the influence of the mother's education on the child's health was found to be stronger even than the level of household income. Empowering people, and especially women, by education is therefore a key intervention in improving the lives and wellbeing of the world's children. (*237*)

Many private voluntary organizations are implementing educational programs on home gardening, food storage and preservation, and food transport because these are important elements in ensuring that the aggregate food supply is made available with minimal losses to low-income and food-deficit areas.

III

The American Farmer—
Prospects for the Future

Financial Stress on the Farm: How Serious Is It?

Some 214,000 American farms began this year unable to pay last year's bills, according to a study by economists of USDA's Economic Research Service. That's the bad news.

This figure represents around 12 percent of the farms that were covered in a major survey by the Agriculture Department early this year. The brighter side is that the majority of farms—88 percent—had either a positive cash flow or were not overburdened by debt.

The *1984 Farm Costs and Returns Survey* provided detailed financial information applicable to 1.7 million of the nation's 2.3 million farms—in other words, all but the smallest farms. Economists say that this survey, considered to be the most comprehensive to date, can help pinpoint financially stressed farms by type, size, and geographic distribution.

While current financial stress is not limited to any particular class or size of farm or sector of agriculture, says economist Jim Johnson, some groups have been harder hit than others.

"The survey's results enabled economists to get a better grip on the number of farms affected and a clearer understanding of the types and sizes of farms experiencing financial stress," Johnson says. Among the survey's most important findings, he adds, is that "many more commercial-size operations are in financial trouble than most analysts previously thought."

Commercial-size farms—those selling $40,000 or more a year in farm products—form the backbone of American agriculture. Although they represent only a little more than one-third of all farms, they account for 90 percent of all farm sales. "We found that at least one in five commercial operations was experiencing some degree of financial stress," Johnson says. These farms were

---

From *Farmline,* November 1985, pp. 4-6. Reprinted with permission.

carrying high debt loads and were unable to generate sufficient cash to pay their bills. Specifically:

> • Almost 129,000 commercial farms (20 percent of all farms with annual sales of $40,000 or more) were under financial stress because they had both negative cash flow and a debt-to-asset ratio of more than 40 percent.
> • Another 68,000 commercial farms showed the potential for financial stress because their debt-to-asset ratios exceeded 40 percent, even though their cash flow was positive.

Perhaps even more significant, Johnson says, the results of the survey showed that midsize commercial farms (those selling between $40,000 and $99,999 a year) were more financially stressed than farms in any other sales class. Of the 214,000 financially stressed farms, Johnson says, 62,000—or 29 percent—fell into the midsize category. This is particularly telling because the number of farms in this class account for only 18 percent of the 1.7 million farms covered in the survey.

What Portion of American Agriculture Is Financially Stressed?

All farms surveyed (1.7 million)

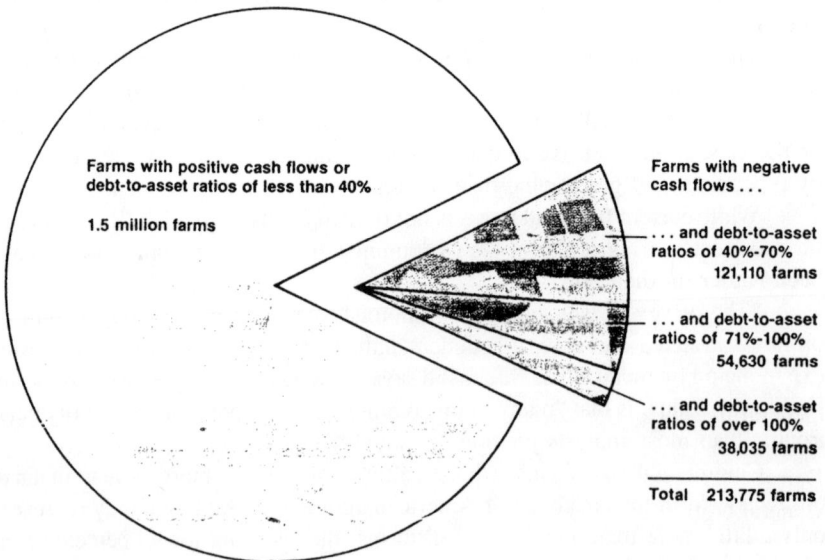

Farms with positive cash flows or debt-to-asset ratios of less than 40%

1.5 million farms

Farms with negative cash flows . . .

. . . and debt-to-asset ratios of 40%-70%
121,110 farms

. . . and debt-to-asset ratios of 71%-100%
54,630 farms

. . . and debt-to-asset ratios of over 100%
38,035 farms

Total   213,775 farms

DEGREES OF STRESS

Just how heavily leveraged an operation is and what kind of cash flow it can generate are two measuring sticks that can be used to determine the financial health of a farm business.

Farms in Trouble by Location, Sales Class, and Commodity[1]

Number of farms by location:

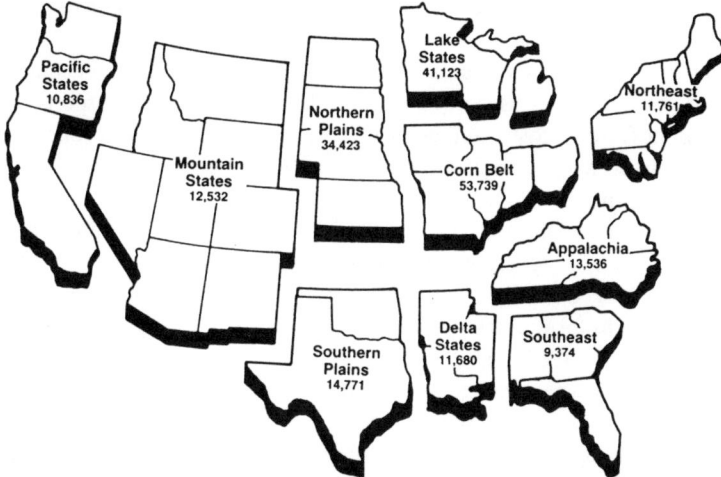

Pacific States 10,836
Mountain States 12,532
Northern Plains 34,423
Lake States 41,123
Corn Belt 53,739
Northeast 11,761
Appalachia 13,536
Southern Plains 14,771
Delta States 11,680
Southeast 9,374

Number of farms by sales class:	
$500,000 and over	5,444
$250,000-$499,999	14,176
$100,000-$249,999	47,216
$ 40,000-$99,999	62,004
$ 20,000-$39,999	32,379
$ 10,000-$19,999	19,776
Less than $10,000	32,780
Number of farms by commodity:	
General livestock	63,705
Cash grain	58,798
Dairy	41,542
General crop	21,493
Field crop	10,925
Poultry	4,578
Fruit and tree nut	4,253
Vegetable and melon	3,612
Other livestock	3,475
Nursery	1,393

First, survey data were used to estimate how much cash from farm and nonfarm income was available to cover production expenses, the interest and principal on outstanding debt, and family living needs. Researchers divided farms into two cash flow positions: negative and positive. A negative cash flow alone is not enough to signal severe financial stress, Johnson says, because a farm that has a strong net worth position would probably be able to weather agriculture's current economic crunch. How? By temporarily leveraging some assets. If assets are too heavily leveraged, however, net worth declines to dangerously low levels, giving the operator little or nothing to fall back on if cash flow is already a problem.

Debt-to-asset ratios—the amount owed to creditors as a percentage of the value of the operator's assets—were calculated from survey responses. Using current prices, input costs, and asset values, researchers defined four categories of debt-to-asset ratios: 0-to-39 percent, 40-to-70 percent, 71-to-100 percent, and over 100 percent.

According to Johnson, farms with ratios of 0-to-39 percent are in strong net worth positions and generally have few financial problems. It's the 40-percent mark that's the critical point, Johnson says. "That's when substantially higher rates of return to farm assets are necessary to maintain a positive cash flow, or farmers begin to have some difficulties."

Farms in the next category of 40-to-70 percent still have fairly strong net worth positions. But, unless they have a large, positive cash flow, they will probably begin having some difficulty meeting the principal repayments on loans, according to Johnson.

When debt-to-asset ratios fall into the 71-to-100 percent category, farms are likely to have trouble meeting their current interest payments as well as their principal payments. For most of these farmers, net worth is declining, Johnson says.

And when debt-to-asset ratios exceed 100 percent, he continues, the farm is considered technically insolvent. "The sale of all the farm's assets would not be sufficient to pay off its debts."

In which categories do most American farms fall?

The majority—88 percent of those covered by the survey—remained financially sound. Their debt-to-asset ratios were in the 0-to-39 percent range or they showed positive cash flow. This is encouraging news, Johnson says, in view of the varied problems facing agriculture in recent years—depressed commodity prices, dwindling farm exports, and plummeting farmland values.

These factors, however, have taken a harsh toll on some operations, he adds, pointing to the flip side of the survey's results. Three percent—or 51,000 of the 1.7 million farms—were technically insolvent.

Most of the farmers who faced some degree of financial problems fell somewhere in between.

FARMERS IN BETWEEN

The survey found about 196,000 farms (11.6 percent of the 1.7 million farms) with debt-to-asset ratios of 40-to-70 percent. Another 72,000 farms (4.2 percent) had debt-to-asset ratios of 71-100 percent.

Again, Johnson points out, a large debt-to-asset ratio alone does not *necessarily* mean that a farm is in financial distress. He explains: "Farms that have less than $40,000 in sales usually earn a large share of total income from nonfarm sources, and often qualify for and repay their loans on the basis of this income. Very large farms with sales of over $500,000 tend to be highly specialized and typically can carry relatively high debt-to-asset ratios because of their positive cash flow positions."

On the other hand, it's a sure sign of trouble when cash flow is low and debt levels are high, Johnson says. These are the farms researchers consider financially stressed, and this was the case for about 214,000 farms. All of these farms had negative cash flow and debt-to-asset ratios of 40 percent or more.

Certain types of farms in certain regions were most affected, Johnson says. Cash grain, general livestock, and dairy farms accounted for more than three-fourths of the 214,000 financially stressed farms. And several geographical regions were also most affected. Sixty percent of the financially stressed farms were concentrated in the Corn Belt, Lake states, and Northern Plains. A contributing factor to this concentration is the steep drop in farmland values in those regions—down more then 20 percent in 1984 alone, compared with a national decline of 12 percent. When a farmer leverages his or her land to borrow operating capital, and the land declines in value, the net worth position also drops, Johnson says.

ANOTHER LOOK FOR BETTER OR WORSE

A lot of farms started 1985 with financial troubles. And this year's developments—still lower crop prices, declining exports, and further drops in farmland values—have not helped matters for many farmers. Exactly how much worse has farming's financial situation gotten during the year?

ERS analysts are going to try and find out with the *1985 Farm Costs and Returns Survey*. But they'll need the help of farmers. Here are some details on the survey:

● If your farm is chosen by USDA's random sampling procedures, you'll be contacted by an interviewer to set up a convenient time to visit your farm. Interviews will take about an hour.

● Participation is voluntary, but remember that each farm represents many other similar operations. For each farm selected, no one else can take its place.

• If you're chosen to participate, you'll receive a notification by mail in early January. Interviews will be conducted between mid-February and early March.

"The response rate to the 1984 survey was tremendous," says ERS economist Jim Johnson. "that's why the results were so revealing." But this year's survey may actually be more important to the nation's farmers and ranchers than last year's survey, according to Johnson, because with the ongoing collection of data, "we'll be able to make a comparison, to see how the problems have changed. We'll know what's getting better and what's getting worse."

The 1985 survey will be almost identical to the one farmers and ranchers answered about last year's income, receipts, expenses, debts, and assets. And, just as they were last year, answers are confidential. After questionnaire data (without names) are fed into a computer, the questionnaires are destroyed so there is no record of any individual's answers. Questionnaires are not sent on to USDA in Washington, nor are they shared with any other government agency.

Again, Johnson stresses the importance of the survey. It's the only way policymakers, farm groups, and the public can be accurately informed of how changing regulations, input costs, returns, and technology affect the agricultural economy, he says.

"The last survey provided the foundation," Johnson adds. "The next one will help us better understand the magnitude of financial problems in the farm sector."

NOTES

Based on the results of USDA's *1984 Farm Costs and Returns Survey.* Analysis was provided by economists Jim Johnson, Ken Baum, and Richard Prescott of the National Economics Division, Economic Research Service.

Super Farms: Giants of Agriculture

If matched against the giants of most other industries, they would barely be noticed. In agriculture, however, they stand out.

Farms with annual sales of $1 million or more belong to a small, but often highly visible, fraternity. They stand out because U.S. agriculture is still overwhelmingly populated by much smaller farms. They also stand out because their role in agriculture is far greater than their numbers might indicate.

The million-dollar-plus operations account for only about 1 out of every 250 U.S. farms, yet they take in more than $1 of every $5 of farm receipts. Together, they control about 47 million acres of land and $52 billion worth of assets.

And their numbers, although small, have been growing.

"Unless farm conditions during the last few years have altered the trend, the million-dollar-and-up farms represent one of the fastest growing sales classes in American agriculture," says USDA economist Paul Velde of the Economic Research Service.

Velde analyzed recently available data from the 1982 Census of Agriculture to construct a profile of these "super farms." Among other things, he found that their numbers increased nearly 50 percent between 1978 and 1982—from 6,290 to 9,190 farms.

Almost half of this growth, he says, was related to inflation and higher prices for farm products. However, many super farms topped the million-dollar mark through increased sales volume, reflecting new investment, expansion, or consolidation.

When combined, both inflation and increased sales volume gave the super farms a larger role in U.S. agriculture. They rang up receipts of $30.3 billion in

From *Farmline*, February 1986, p. 7. Reprinted with permission.

1982, 23 percent of total U.S. farms sales. In 1978, the comparable numbers were $20.3 billion, 21 percent of total U.S. farm sales. Total acreage on super farms reached 47.4 million acres in 1982, up 7 million acres since 1978 and 4.8 percent of all land in farms.

SIZE, TYPE, LOCATION

Velde notes that super farms are not necessarily the biggest farms in terms of acreage. "There are more than a thousand of these million-dollar farms with fewer than 50 acres," he says. "In fact, one-third of all super farms have less than the U.S. average of 440 acres."

The explanation relates mostly to the commodities such farms earn their incomes from. Many super farms specialize in livestock, poultry, or egg production, and others grow high-value crops such as oranges, grapes, and commercial flowers.

Of the various commodity classifications, livestock operations accounted for the most $1-million-or-more farms (2,774). Poultry and egg farms were second (1,245), and dairy operations came in third (1,038). Fruit and tree nut farms were next (812), followed by field crop farms, excluding cash grains (774), and vegetable and melon operations (725).

There were 685 horticultural specialty operations and 610 cash grain farms ringing up $1 million or more in sales.

California had fully a fourth of all farms with sales of $1 million or more (2,398), followed by Florida with 643 such farms and Texas with 618 super farms.

Every state has at least a couple of super farms, according to Velde. Those with the fewest farms of $1 million or more in sales in 1982 were Alaska and Vermont.

IS BIGGER BETTER?

"The 1982 Census numbers of large farms," says Velde, "seems to raise again the old issue: Is bigger better? And if the question cannot be phrased so simply, what impacts are likely with larger farms?"

One concern, he says, centers on the consumer impact as super farms comprise an ever larger proportion of the sales and productive capacity in agriculture. Some observers suggest that concentration is unwise and could lead to higher consumer prices.

"Certainly, the United States has seen and survived the big, highly concentrated nature of other industries," says Velde. "In some other industries, we see only a handful of firms. But in agriculture we are still dealing with thousands of firms producing nearly all commodities—far too many to exert monopoly power on food prices."

For their part, some operators of super farms say that consumer prices might actually go down—largely because of the economies of scale they say are inherent in larger firms.

Velde isn't so sure. "Even if larger farms operated more efficiently, the savings may be absorbed in the marketing process and wouldn't necessarily be passed along to consumers," he says.

On the other hand, he does see some evidence of greater productivity and efficiency with large farms. For example, super farms report greater yields for some crops compared with much smaller farms. His analysis shows that corn growers with farms in the $1 million sales class harvested an average of 122 bushels of corn per acre in 1982, compared with 112 bushels for farms in the $100,000 to $249,999 sales class, and 91 bushels for farms in the $10,000 to $39,999 sales class. Farms in the $500,000-$699,999 sales class had yields per acre roughly equivalent to those of super farms. Farms with annual sales of $10 million or more had the highest average yields per acre, nearly 140 bushels.

Moreover, he says, in contrast to previous years, "farms in the million-dollar sales class appear to be more efficient than their smaller counterparts when measured in terms of returns to investment, for instance."

He cautions, however, that the data he examined from the 1982 Agriculture Census only measures the averages of these groups.

"It doesn't mean that every large farm is more productive or efficient than every small farm," Velde says, "or that all large farms are productive or efficient. And it doesn't take into account the relative status of particular commodities or regions of the country."

Managing Agricultural Pollution

John C. Keene*

INTRODUCTION

Today's agricultural operations, especially those that produce the greatest share of the nation's food and fibre, are often sophisticated industrial activities which produce significant amounts of environmental pollution.[1] Non-point source pollutants such as sediment and associated fertilizers, pesticides, and organic matter are emitted by general land cultivation, pasturing and grazing.[2] At the same time, concentrated activities, such as animal feedlots and mushroom composting operations, emit point source air and water pollution.[3]

Three relatively recent trends have greatly increased the potential for both types of agricultural pollution. First, farming has become increasingly capital intensive and reliant on the products of technology (*e.g.*, pesticides, fertilizers, and heavy equipment). Second, the organizational structure of agriculture has gradually but significantly changed. In 1940 there were 6,350,000 farms in the United States averaging 167 acres each; in 1980 there were only 2,428,000 farms with an average size of 429 acres.[4] The largest of these farms currently produce a disproportionately large share of the nation's total agricultural output.[5] Finally, production from concentrated animal confinement facilities, such as feedlots and poultry barns, has increased markedly and comes from much larger individual facilities, congregated in a few regions of the country.[6]

At the same time that the potential for serious agricultural pollution has increased, so too has the threat to agriculture itself, through the continuing conversion of farmland to other uses.[7] The purpose of this article is to suggest means of managing agricultural pollution without contributing to the often pre-

---

*Professor of City and Regional Planning, University of Pennsylvania; B.A., Yale University, 1953; J.D., Harvard Law School, 1959; M.C.P., University of Pennsylvania, 1966.

From *Ecology Law Quarterly*, 11, 1983, pp. 135-88. Reprinted by permission.

mature removal of land from farm operations. The approach recommended is first to develop and enforce means to minimize the environmentally harmful externalities associated with farming, through government regulation and incentive programs designed to encourage soil conservation and integrated pest management. Second, agricultural areas should be protected from incompatible development by state or local land use control, supplemented by incentives that make it feasible, and in fact desirable, for farmers to keep farming.

After identifying the major sources and types of agricultural pollution, the Article will review four approaches to managing that pollution: (1) judicial resolution of conflicts based on principles of common law nuisance; (2) technology-forcing legislation; (3) legalization of minimally nuisance-creating farming operations through enactment of "right-to-farm" laws; and (4) programs that separate agricultural activities from incompatible non-agricultural activities.[8] The Article concludes by proposing an integrated management strategy that practically and realistically draws from several of these approaches.

PRINCIPAL ACTIVITIES THAT POLLUTE THE ENVIRONMENT

Land Cultivation

Farmers remove the natural cover of the land, then plough, cultivate, irrigate, and apply fertilizers and pesticides. These activities usually tend to increase the amount of soil erosion[9] and run-off, which in turn both increase the risk of flooding and contribute additional sediments, 10 nutrients, organic matter, and toxic substances to hydrological systems. Moreover, agricultural activities increase the rate of topsoil loss above that occurring naturally, thus wasting a critically valuable resource and reducing the long-run productivity of the land.

Application of Fertilizers, Pesticides, and Herbicides

Fertilizers contribute critical nutrients[11] to assure or increase plant growth, but their use often has adverse effects on the natural environment. Annual fertilizer use in the United States has increased from 31.8 million tons in 1965 to 47.6 million tons in 1978, and accounts for some thirty to forty percent of annual crop and fibre production.[12] Yet, crop production utilizes only about fifty percent of the nitrogen, twenty percent of the phosphorus and thirty-five percent of the potassium applied as fertilizer; the remainder is lost through leaching into soils, dissolution in run-off, soil erosion, and through chemical reactions that make it unavailable to plants.[13] In 1975, the National commission on Water Quality estimated that 4.3 million tons of nitrogen and 1.5 million tons of phosphorus dissolved annually into surface waters.[14] The primary damage caused by the introduction of fertilizers into surface waters is an acceleration of the natural rate of eutrophication, the process of nutritional enrichment of natural waters. This acceleration disrupts the natural balance of the aquatic environment, leading to algae blooms and fish kills.[15]

The use of pesticides and herbicides creates well-known hazards to applicators, farm labor, nearby residential areas, and food consumers. Pesticides also run off into surface waters in relatively small amounts.[16] Because farmers have placed more emphasis on integrated pest management during the last few years,[17] the agricultural pesticide use growth rate has slowed.[18]

Operation of Concentrated Production Facilities

In the last two or three decades, American beef, pork, and poultry production has increased significantly.[19] In addition, this production, together with dairy production, has become concentrated in particular regions,[20] and the individual productive unit has become larger and more intense.[21] The concentration of tens of thousands of cattle, hogs, or hens in relatively small areas presents significant potential for air and water pollution.

Irrigation

Irrigation brings arid land into production, protects against drought, facilitates double cropping, and permits more profitable crop production. Its use has tripled since 1940, even though the total amount of land cropped has remained fairly constant.[22] Irrigation may affect water quality in any one of a number of ways. First, irrigation return flow salinity levels may be higher than natural water flows because the irrigation water dissolves salts that exist in relatively dry soils. These salts in turn become further concentrated through evapo-transpiration and may cause a build-up of salinity levels in the root-feeding strata where there is inadequate drainage.[23] Second, irrigation water may either deposit sediment in the receiving soils or cause additional erosion. Third, irrigation may carry nitrogen, phosphorus, and pesticides to the receiving waters. Finally, irrigation may alter the hydrological characteristics[24] of the receiving system.

Irrigation water may infiltrate into the groundwater, or it may flow as "tailwater"[25] to surface waters as either a non-point or a point source (such as a flow from a field drainage system). Irrigational impacts on water quality vary tremendously from one area to another, depending on such factors as initial water quality, soil composition, irrigation technique, agricultural practices and investments, weather, and climate.[26]

Dredging and Filling Activities that Contribute Solid Materials to Rivers, Bays, and Marshes

Sediment is deposited in streambeds, wetlands, and bays as a result of dam and levee construction, terracing, the clearing out of drainage ditches, and to a lesser extent from general cultivation.[27] These areas are ecologically critical—they serve as spawning and nursery areas for commercial and sport fish, act as natural cleansers for airborne and waterborne pollutants, and supply essential nesting and wintering areas for waterfowl[28]—and sediment deposits, especially those containing pesticides, may have adverse impacts on them. As yet, little information is available on the nature and extent of these deposits and their harm.[29]

Other Agricultural Activities

Other agricultural activities may generate pollution, such as the use of noise-producing heavy equipment or devices to scare away birds,[30] burning of stalks, husks and other agricultural debris,[31] and land cultivation that produces dust.[32] For example, the burning of grass straw in the grass seed production area of Oregon and the burning of rice straw in the delta area of California are of sufficient severity so that each state has established expansive permit and monitoring programs, including hour-by-hour meteorological observations to determine safe burning periods.[33] Likewise, dust is more than a minor problem in the High Plains from Montana to the Texas panhandle. Blowing dust from wheat fields in the spring becomes a major traffic problem in certain areas and affects people in a rather wide, though sparsely settled, area.[34]

RESOLUTION OF LAND USE CONFLICTS BASED ON COMMON LAW NUISANCE

General Principles

The term "nuisance" has acquired many meanings over the years, but is used in this context to denote the harm resulting from another's action or from a physical condition caused by another. Nuisance focuses on the effect of the conduct and not on the nature of the conduct itself, and it may not necessarily be remediable in court.[35] Thus, odor from a feedlot and the noise from a "corn cannon" perceived by a neighboring landowner may be nuisances, but whether the neighbor will be able to recover damages or enjoin the conduct because of what he has suffered will depend upon a number of factors.[36]

   The *Restatement of Torts* defines a private nuisance as "a nontrespassory invasion of another's interest in the private use and enjoyment of land."[37] In order to prevail on a nuisance claim, the plaintiff must show (1) some form of property interest in land, (2) impaired enjoyment of that interest, and (3) actions by the defendant that are the proximate cause of the harm.[38] In most cases involving agricultural nuisance, it is easy for a plaintiff to demonstrate these elements.[39]

   An agriculturalist whose activities interfere with the use and enjoyment of another's land will be subject to liability under private nuisance law where the interference is either (1) "intentional and unreasonable," or (2) "unintentional and otherwise actionable under the rules controlling liability for negligent or reckless conduct, or for abnormally dangerous conditions or activities."[40] Adherence to the latter principle produces insensitivity to the particular land use conflicts so often involved in agricultural pursuits and should not be the primary theory of nuisance liability applied to agricultural nuisances. Rather than limiting liability to conduct which is inappropriate in a particular location, reliance on this theory will discourage conduct that can be classified in an abstract sense as wrongful, independent of its location.

The former basis of private nuisance liability requires that the defendant's interference be intentional and unreasonable. According to the *Restatement*, a defendant's interference is intentional if he "(a) acts for the purpose of causing [interference], or (b) knows that it is resulting or is substantially certain to result from his conduct."[41] Most agriculturalists who create nuisances rarely act unintentionally with respect to their neighbors. Feedlot operators, mushroom growers, and farmers who spray crops with pesticides clearly act intentionally in the ordinary course of conducting their businesses. Certainly they are acting intentionally where they continue their activities after the neighbor complains about odors, dust, or spray.

In an agricultural setting, then, the critical inquiry when ascertaining liability under private nuisance will generally be whether the agriculturist's invasion of his neighbor's property interest in unreasonable. To answer this question, the court must determine the reasonableness of the defendant's use by balancing conflicting policies and equities in light of the facts of each case. For this reason, it has been difficult to infer general rules of liability from the cases and to predict the results in particular situations in advance of adjudication.

The *Restatement* defines as "unreasonable" an intentional interference with another's use and enjoyment of land where (1) "the gravity of the harm outweighs the utility of the actor's conduct, or . . . (2) . . . the harm caused by the conduct is serious and the financial burden of compensating for this and similar harm to others would not make the continuation of the conduct not feasible."[42] The latter category encompasses those cases where it may be inappropriate to enjoin the offending activity, but it would be inequitable for the agriculturist not to compensate his neighbors for the harm they suffer because of his continued operations.[43]

In deciding whether the gravity of the harm to the plaintiff outweighs the utility of the defendant's activity, courts consider the degree of the harm, its duration, permanence, and character[44] and whether the nuisance would affect a reasonable person's health, property, or personal comfort.[45] The court also will consider three sets of correlated factors when weighing the relative gravity of the harm and the utility of the conduct: (1) the social value the law places on the type of use that has been invaded and on the primary purpose of the conduct alleged to be actionable; (2) the suitability of the two uses to the character of the locality; and (3) the burden on the plaintiff to avoid the harm and the practicability of the defendant's prevention or avoidance of the invasion.[46]

Over the years, the courts have recognized several defenses to a claim of nuisance.[47] For actions arising out of intentional and unreasonable interferences, one available defense is that the plaintiff "came to the nuisance," meaning that the activity causing a nuisance on the plaintiff's land had been in existence and operating when he bought or improved the land.[48] Coming to the nuisance, however, does not automatically bar recovery. The courts will generally take this factor into account when weighing the social utility of the defendant's conduct, but if the intrusion into the plaintiff's enjoyment of his land is too severe, the defendant's activity still may subject him to liability in nuisance.[49] Moreover, express authorization of a particular nuisance-generating use by a zoning ordinance or applicable police power regulation does not always shield the use against a nuisance complaint.[50]

Remedies

When a landowner demonstrates that his neighbor is liable in nuisance, he often will seek both damages for past injuries and injunctive relief against any continuing invasions. Damages may include compensation for the reduction in rental value of the property for the duration of the nuisance, for physical damage to the property, and for the inhabitants' personal discomfort or sickness.[51]

If the plaintiff can show the inadequacy of his remedy at law, clean hands, no laches, and a threat of irreparable injury, he may secure a temporary or permanent injunction against the nuisance. Courts, however, generally tailor these injunctions to the circumstances of each case in order to minimize the interference with the defendant's activities while protecting the plaintiff's interest. For instance, in some agricultural nuisance cases courts have declined to force defendants to cease operations, but have nonetheless required them to operate their facilities in a manner that does not produce the nuisance on the plaintiff's property.[52]

Occasionally a court will refuse to grant an injunction because of a social policy favoring the particular activity involved. In such cases, the sole remedy available is money damages. For example, in *Boomer v. Atlantic Cement Co., Inc.*,[53] the New York Court of Appeals found that the defendant's operation of a cement plant constituted an actionable nuisance and ordered payment of damages,[54] but declined to enjoin continued operation of the plant. In denying the injunction, the court stressed, first, the cement industry's importance to society generally and, second, the defendant's inability to develop economically feasible and technologically effective pollution control equipment to prevent the nuisance.[55] The Iowa Supreme Court manifested a similar view with respect to a nuisance arising from egg production operations.[56]

One of the leading agricultural nuisance cases, *Spur Industries, Inc. v. Del E. Webb Development Co.*,[57] presents an interesting remedial solution. Webb developed Sun City, a large retirement community 15 miles west of Phoenix,

Arizona.[58] Nearby, Spur Industries operated cattle feedlot having a capacity of 20,000 to 30,000 head.[59] Webb could not market homes near the feedlots because of the odor and flies,[60] and therefore brought a private action based on public nuisance.[61] The trial court found for Webb and permanently enjoined the feedlot operation. The Arizona Supreme Court affirmed, but held that Webb must indemnify Spur for the reasonable cost either of moving the feedlot elsewhere or of shutting it down.[62] The court reasoned that since Webb knowingly had brought the population into a previously agricultural area, thus necessitating the injunction against Spur's lawful business, Webb should bear the costs of the upheaval for which Spur had no adequate relief.[63] The court sought thereby to impose on the developer a more accurate assessment of the costs of his intrusion into a previously agricultural area.

Common Law Nuisance as a Control Over Agricultural Pollution[64]

The utility of judicially-enforced private nuisance law as a means of controlling agricultural pollution varies with the stage of development of the particular geographic area. In an area which is thoroughly rural, nuisance law gives the individual landowner a remedy for harm caused by a neighbor who uses his land in an unreasonable manner. This approach has the distinct advantage of being congruent with landowners' expectations, conserves property values, and preserves the *status quo* against intrusions by inappropriate uses. In an area that is undergoing suburbanization, however, it may be unfair to place sole reliance on the law of private nuisance to allocate the costs and benefits of change. Farmers who have already invested considerable resources in plant and equipment are subject to the continuing risk that their lawful operation will be converted by subsequent development into a private nuisance vulnerable to injunction.

The strengths and weaknesses of private nuisance law as a technique for managing agricultural pollution tend to be opposite sides of the same coin. Thus, one of the main strengths of nuisance law is its case-by-case approach, which permits considerable flexibility and sensitivity both in discerning the right to relief and in fashioning the remedy. Where damages are inadequate to compensate the plaintiff fully, the court can tailor injunctive relief so as to protect the plaintiff's rights without unduly burdening the defendant's use of his land. A legislature, working before the fact and drafting statutes in general terms so as to apply to the myriad of situations likely to arise in the future, will almost never provide such customized solutions. At the same time, the *ad hoc* approach is inimical to the application of any broad plan for development in urban fringe areas. Since judicial action is almost always corrective rather than preventive, the outcome with regard to a particular farm is often unpredictable, especially since changing conditions may legitimate a nuisance-producing activity or turn a proper land use into an actionable nuisance.

Another of the strengths of the law of private nuisance as a land use control is that it is invoked by individuals. The weight, power, and resources of the state will be called into play only with respect to those uses that are sufficiently antagonistic to make an individual willing to expend the time, money, and effort to prosecute an action. Furthermore, a system of control based on litigation gives an individual the right to governmental assistance in gaining resolution of his problem without the need to stir what may be a very stolid and phlegmatic bureaucracy to action. At the same time, a weakness inherent in this aspect of the remedy is that, because it often requires expenditures of large amounts of money and energy, it will not be available to everyone injured by nuisances. Furthermore, by focusing on the rights of a few individuals rather than the interests of the population of an entire region, courts may well fail to give sufficient attention to the broader public interest at stake. Thus, private nuisance law, standing alone, is not an adequate tool for managing agricultural pollution, and to give adequate attention to the needs of the public, legislative intervention is needed. The current extent of such intervention is the subject of the next two parts of this Article.

TECHNOLOGY-FORCING REGULATION

Introduction

As a result of the awakening of interest in environmental protection during the late sixties and early seventies, governmental responsibility for environmental protection shifted to the federal government. Congress assigned primary responsibility for establishing and administering environmental standards to the United States Environmental Protection Agency (EPA), leaving the states the option to assume responsibility if they could show EPA that they possessed both the authority and willingness to protect the environment effectively.[65]

Congress created a complex federal-state-local environmental management scheme, with Congress or EPA usually establishing the standards and EPA or state environmental protection agencies charged with enforcement.[66] While Congress did not entirely preempt state and local regulation, it generally left fairly narrow latitude for state regulatory efforts.[67]

The Principal Federal Environmental Laws Affecting Agriculture

The Clean Water Act

General Structure. The Federal Water Pollution Control Act (FWPCA) Amendments of 1974[68] created the current general framework for managing the nation's efforts to reduce water pollution. The Act has had significant, although difficult to quantify, impacts on agriculture. First, it established stringent water quality standards.[69] Second, it directly affects farming through its new programs for controlling both point source and non-point source agricultural pollution arising from animal wastes, sedimentation, fertilizers, crop residues, agricultural product processing wastes, insecticides, fungicides, and herbicides.[70]

The three elements of the FWPCA Amendments that most directly affect agriculture are: (1) the section 402 National Pollutant Discharge Elimination System (NPDES) permit program, with its effluent guidelines and permit requirements for new and existing feedlots and agricultural products processors;[71] (2) the section 208 areawide waste treatment management program requiring state governments to develop effective means for reducing non-point source pollution;[72] and (3) the section 404 dredge and fill permit program affecting agricultural activities such as wetlands reclamation and the clearing of drainage ditches.[73]

In 1977, Congress conducted a comprehensive review of the FWPCA Amendments and, as part of the "mid-course correction" envisioned in 1972,[74] enacted the Clean Water Act of 1977.[75] Four major elements of the 1977 Act affect agriculture. First, the act authorized funds to support state management of the NPDES, construction grants, section 208, and section 404 programs.[76] Second, it exempted irrigation return flows from NPDES permit requirements and designated them as non-point source discharges to be covered by section 208 areawide waste treatment management plans.[77] Third, it created a new program for providing technical and financial assistance to farmers in order to implement section 208 areawide management programs. Under this program, the Secretary of Agriculture could provide funds for up to fifty percent of the costs of soil conservation and water pollution control practices calculated to reduce agricultural run-off.[78] In 1981, Congress terminated direct funding of section 208 and directed that it be funded from one percent of grants to states for waste water treatment plant construction.[79] Fourth, the Act gave the U.S. Army Corps of Engineers authority to issue general dredge and fill permits for classes of activities with minimal adverse environmental effects.[80] The Act also exempted from the section 404 permit requirement many normal farming and ranching activities, such as farm pond construction and irrigation ditch maintenance.[81]

Despite strong lobbying by agricultural interests, Congress refused to limit the reach of the section 404 dredge and fill permit program to those waters traditionally known as "navigable waters"—"waters that are presently used or susceptible to use in their present condition or with reasonable improvement to transport interstate or foreign commerce."[82] Rather, Congress continued to utilize the very broad definition of "United States waters" as construed in *Natural Resources Defense Council, Inc. v. Callaway.*[83] The 1977 Amendments did provide, however, that if EPA approved, states could administer their own permit program for discharges into navigable waters other than traditional navigable waters.[84]

Point Source Regulation: Feedlots. Feedlot operations produce large amounts of urine, manure, and other organic materials which, in turn, produce biochemical oxygen demand, suspended solids, nitrates, ammonia, phosphorus, and coliform bacteria. To treat these wastes, most operations employ a combination of flushing facilities, lagoons, and secondary water treatment. The highly concentrated nature of the waste requires land application of effluents and solid residues through irrigation or spreading.[85]

NPDES permits must be obtained to discharge pollutants from point sources.[86] EPA's regulations specifically classify "concentrated animal feeding operations" as "point sources subject to the NPDES permit program."[87] A concentrated animal feeding operation is one where (1) animals will be confined and fed for a total of at least forty-five days and (2) vegetation is not sustained over any portions of the facility.[88] An operation is "concentrated" if it meets certain criteria relating to the type and number of animals confined.[89] The regulations divide confinement facilities into three categories. The first consists of those facilities that exceed the criteria set forth in 40 C.F.R. § 122.54, Appendix B, subsection (a).[90] Operation of these facilities requires a permit. The second category consists of facilities which meet the criteria set forth in subsection (b).[91] These operations require a permit only if they discharge directly into navigable waters. The third category of facilities covers those operations for which the EPA regional administrator (or the state director of the state is administering the program[92]) requires permits pursuant to 40 C.F.R. § 122.54(c).[93] The government may initiate criminal prosecution of those who discharge from a point source without a permit.[94]

EPA conditions approval of NPDES permits on compliance with applicable performance standards.[95] The Clean Water Act directed EPA to establish effluent limitations for existing feedlots and other agricultural point sources[96] and new source performance standards for facilities built after September 7, 1973.[97] The amended Act requires dischargers of "conventional pollutants . . . classified as biological oxygen demanding, suspended solids, fecal coliform, [and] pH,"[98] to use the "best practicable control technology currently available" (BPT)[100] no later than July 1, 1984. The Act also requires dischargers of toxic substance to use BPT and the "best available technology economically achievable" (BAT) within three years of promulgation of applicable effluent limitations, but not later than July 1, 1987.[101]

Pursuant to the Act, EPA has promulgated effluent limitations guidelines for feedlots[102] and certain other agricultural processing industries.[103] The feedlot regulations apply to dairy, hog, horse, sheep, poultry, cattle, and duck confinement facilities with animal populations higher than specified sizes.[104] Feedlots[105] constructed prior to September 7, 1973,[106] other than those for ducks, and subject to the BPT requirement, must have storm water management facilities able to prevent both wastewater overflow and the overflow of precipitation from any storm with a return frequency less than a ten year, twenty-four hour rainfall event.[107] Similar feedlots subject to the BAT requirement must be designed to prevent any discharge from storms up to a twenty-five year, twenty-four hour frequency.[108] Parallel guidelines exist for duck feedlots.[109]

Only about 2,000 cattle feedlots—less than two percent of the nation's total[110]—are subject to NPDES review on grounds of size alone. Similarly, well under three percent of dairies, hog feedlots, and egg factories are large enough to be subject to automatic NPDES review.[111] Somewhat higher percentages of broiler houses and turkey farms are covered.[112] In most cases, however, the regulations govern a much higher percentage of the animals marketed.[113] In 1976, the staff of the National Commission on Water Quality estimated the total per animal investment costs of meeting the new guidelines' higher standards for large beef cattle, hogs, and dairy cattle operations (in dry climates) to be approximately $13, $11, and $48, respectively. It concluded that while the requirements might adversely affect a few small operators, "the overall impact on the entire feeding industry will be slight."[114]

Non-point Source Section 28 Planning. Water pollutant discharges that are not from point sources, such as run-off from farmland, irrigation return flows, and discharges from small feedlots not subject to NPDES permits, are classed as non-point sources. The Clean Water Act requires only that areawide waste treatment management planning, required by section 208, attempt to bring these non-point sources under control.[115] The Act requires several interrelated state planning efforts. First, section 209 required long-range regional resource management studies and development of plans for water and related land in every river basin in the country by 1980.[116] Second, section 303(e) establishes a continuing planning process for each river basin as a means of setting major priorities and objectives for pollution control.[117] Third, section 208 of the Act requires each state's governor to designate those areas within his state having significant water quality problems, and create for these areas a twenty-year areawide waste management program that will take an inventory of existing conditions, establish detailed water quality goals, and create the governmental management structure to implement the program.[118] In *Natural Resources Defense Counsel, Inc. v. Castle,*[119] the Court of Appeals for the D.C. Circuit held that state environmental protection agencies must carry out section 208 planning for all parts of their states, including areas not designated as having special pollution problems.[120] Fourth, section 201 of the Act authorizes planning, design, and construction of individual sewage treatment plants,[121] and section 106 establishes criteria for applicants competing for waste-water treatment construction funds.[122] Congress' intention to coordinate water pollution control through these programs is evidenced partially by the fact that activities inconsistent with a section 208 plan are ineligible for waste-water treatment plant construction grants.[123]

Section 208's impact on agriculture has been the subject of considerable comment and evaluation.[124] In 1980, EPA sponsored a study of state agricultural non-point source water pollution programs. The study revealed that: (1) thirty-nine states had begun implementation of their section 208 programs.[125] (2) twenty-seven of those states relied on voluntary programs such as education, technical assistance, and information;[126] and the other twelve utilized some form of land management regulation requiring Best Management Practices;[127] (3) twenty-one states designated state soil and water conservation agencies or departments of agriculture as the managing agencies, sixteen states designated water pollution control agencies, three states designated their departments of natural resources, and nineteen states chose to utilize soil conservation districts either alone or in conjunction with a state agency;[128] (4) thirty states considered agricultural non-point source pollution a "significant" source of non-point pollution;[129] (5) forty states had designated (and thirty-three had ranked) areas where agricultural non-point source pollution was critical;[130] and (6) most states did not have the manpower they considered necessary to administer their section 208 programs and required federal cost-sharing assistance.[131]

Since EPA approved most states' section 208 plans after 1978, and since these plans relied heavily on voluntary implementation methods, there exists to date little evidence that they have had any significant impact on agricultural non-point source pollution. The EPA's guidelines on Best Management Practices stress erosion control as the principal means of controlling non-point source pollution,[132] but also suggest that state programs include integrated pest management, conservation tillage, vegetative cover of bare ground, conservation cropping systems, and animal management systems.[133] Few local governments, however, have instituted strong regulatory programs to control agricultural runoff and erosion.[134] A 1981 analysis of 136 section 208 plans found that many proposed initial voluntary compliance periods, to be followed by stronger regulatory approaches if voluntary efforts failed.[135] In this era of budgetary cutbacks and deregulation, it is impossible to forecast whether state and local governments—working in cooperation with farmers—will marshall both the resources and the will to control agricultural non-point source pollution more effectively.

Section 404 Dredge and Fill Permits. Section 404 of the FWPCA[136] requires that dischargers obtain a permit from the U.S. Army Corps of Engineers before discharging any dredged or fill material into United States "navigable waters."[137] The Conference Report on the Act[138] stated that when Congress defined "navigable waters" as "the waters of the United States, including the territorial seas,"[139] it is intended to assert jurisdiction over all those waters it could regulate under the Interstate Commerce Clause of the Constitution.[140] Despite Congress' expressed intent, however, the Army Corps of Engineers assumed jurisdiction only over water traditionally defined as "navigable,"[141] a more narrow definition than that allowable under the Commerce Clause.

In 1975, a federal district court ordered the Corps to reinterpret its section 404 jurisdiction to encompass the full reach of the commerce Clause.[142] The Corps then proposed interim regulations[143] which raised the spectre of federal regulation of farm ponds, irrigation ditch digging, and plowing.[144] The furor over this perceived intrusion into the domain of private property and local land use control continues today, even though Congress in 1977 created significant exemptions from the section 404 permit requirements.[145]

The 1977 Amendments to the Clean Water Act preserved the broad jurisdiction of the Army Corps of Engineers, but exempted six categories of activities having only minor effects on water quality. The categories include normal farming, silviculture, and ranching activities; farm and stock ponds or irrigation ditch construction or maintenance; farm or forest road construction or maintenance according to prescribed best management practices; and activities regulated by statewide programs approved under section 208(b)(4) for control of minor discharges through best management practices.[146]

Additionally, the 1977 amendments authorized the Corps of Engineers to issue dredge and fill "general permits" to exempt from individual permit requirements several broad classes of activities having only minimally adverse impacts on water quality,[147] even though the Corps had published little information on these programs.[148] Finally, the 1977 Amendments authorized EPA to approve state section 404 programs for waters that do not fall within the traditional definition of navigability.[149]

The Corps of Engineers published its Interim Final Rules for section 404 permits in July 1982.[150] The rules exempt normal farming, silviculture, and ranching activities (plowing, seeding, cultivation, minor drainage, and harvesting) where they are part of an established operation, but not activities that "bring an area into farming or ranching use . . .," including modifications of the hydrological regime necessary to bring back into production land idled for a long period of time.[151] If EPA approves a state's section 404 program, the state may incorporate that program into its section 208 program.[152] This procedure significantly simplifies the approval process.

The Federal Insecticide, Fungicide, and Rodenticide Act

The Federal Insecticide, Fungicide, and Rodenticide Act of 1947 (FIFRA), as amended in 1972,[153] is the centerpiece of current federal efforts to protect applicators, farm labor, and consumers against injury caused by pesticides. FIFRA mandates registration and approval by EPA prior to use of any pesticide,[154] sets labelling and applicators licensing requirements,[155] and makes improper use of pesticides a misdemeanor.[156] The Act further authorizes the Agency to protect farm workers by issuing standards governing when fields may be reentered following pesticide application.[157]

FIFRA authorizes EPA to suspend or cancel the registration of pesticides that it determines have "unreasonable adverse effects on the environment."[158] To date, the Agency has suspended or cancelled the registration of pesticides containing DDT, dieldrin, aldrin, chlordane, heptachlor, mercury, kepone, chlorobenzilate, endrin, DBCP, and 2, 4, and 5-T silvex.[159] EPA estimates show that the economic costs of these cancellations are relatively minor, especially when compared to the estimated half-trillion dollar cost of pollution abatement programs in the United States during the period from 1978 to 1987.[160]

As a result of its registration and licensing requirements, FIFRA and the state regulatory programs it envisages principally affect pesticide manufacturers and commercial applicators. A particular farmer will fall within the Act if he hires an applicator who uses pesticides in violation of the law.[161] The Act also may set or influence the rules of liability to which farmers may be held accountable in private litigation by persons claiming injury from pesticides. Applicators—whether independent commercial contractors or licensed farmers—may be liable on one of several theories, depending on relevant principles of state law:[162] strict liability arising out of an abnormally dangerous activity,[164] or trespass.[165]

The Clean Air Act

Under the regulatory regime created by the Clean Air Act Amendment of 1970,[166] the states retain almost complete responsibility for control of agricultural air pollution. Although EPA sets national ambient air quality standards[167] and provides supervision and technical assistance, the states are primarily responsible for regulating pollution-creating activities so as to meet the Agency's standards.[168] Required State Implementation Plans may incorporate flexible strategies developed through long-range, comprehensive planning processes and may take into account economic and social, as well as environmental, objectives.[169]

One significant source of agricultural air pollution regulated by several states is the open burning of agricultural wastes. California, for instance, has adopted detailed regulations that prohibit open burning unless the owner has obtained a permit.[170] New Jersey also requires a permit for agricultural burning,[171] while Colorado,[172] Texas,[173] Virginia,[174] and Iowa[175] exempt such burnings from their general prohibition against open burning. Nebraska prohibits open fires except those incident to agricultural operations where no nuisance or traffic hazard is created.[176]

Frost protection heaters are another source of agricultural air pollution. California,[177] Florida,[178] and Maryland[179] require that owners of orchards and citrus groves use only state-approved frost protection heaters that do not produce more than one gram per minute of unconsumed carbonaceous material.

Feedlot odors have not escaped regulation. Iowa forbids emissions of odorous substances that are "of such frequency, duration, quality and intensity as to be harmful to human health and welfare,"[180] and has adopted special regulations governing anaerobic lagoons on animal feedlots.[181]

Agricultural activities may also harm air quality by generating large quantities of fugitive dust. Colorado in 1954 enacted the Soil Erosion and Dust Blowing Act[182] which requires landowners to implement cultivation techniques designed to minimize wind erosion. That state's Air Pollution Control Commission further requires feedlot owners to minimize dust from their operations.[183] Arizona simply requires farmers to take reasonable precautions to prevent generation of excessive amounts of airborne particulate matters.[184]

Although less publicized than the burdens of restrictive regulations, the positive impacts of the Clean Air Act's technology-forcing regulatory programs probably are more important to farmers. In his 1981 testimony before Congress, Paul Sacia of the National Farmers Union stated that air pollutants, such as sulfur dioxide and ozone, reduce crop productivity by as much as one to two percent nationwide, according to one estimate.[185] Unfortunately, more precise studies of the agricultural costs and benefits of regulating air pollution have not been made.[186]

The Resource Conservation and Recovery Act

The Resource Conservation and Recovery Act of 1976, as amended,[187] is the major federal statute in the area of solid waste disposal. Although agricultural activities generate large amounts of solid waste,[188] little falls into the category of hazardous wastes.[18] Its disposal is therefore subject to the states' solid waste management plans.[190] Each state's management plan must identify the general strategies it has selected to protect the public against adverse effects of solid waste disposal, indicate how the state will provide adequate sanitary landfill capacity, and show that there are adequate institutional arrangements for implementing the strategies.[191] Some states, such as California,[192] require counties to prepare solid waste management plans that cover, among other materials, wastes resulting from the production and processing of agricultural products, including manure, prunings, and crop residue.[193] Some states exclude agricultural wastes from the requirements of their solid waste acts.[194] As of September 1, 1982, EPA had approved twenty State Solid Waste Management Plans and another twenty had been adopted by states and submitted to the Agency for review.[195]

LEGALIZATION: RIGHT-TO-FARM LAWS

Introduction: The Major Concepts Embodied in Right-to-Farm Laws

In recent years, forty-six state legislatures have adopted statutes intended to protect agricultural activities that would otherwise be subject to abatement through judicial enforcement of common law public or private nuisance principles or by administrative enforcement of local anti-nuisance ordinances.[196] The new statutes, referred to generically as "right-to-farm" laws, seek to accomplish one or both of the following objectives: (1) to strengthen the legal position of established farmers when they are sued in private nuisance by newly-arrived neighbors, and (2) to protect farmers against unreasonably restrictive local land-use controls, building codes, and anti-nuisance ordinances.

States enacted right-to-farm laws in response to a complex set of interrelated developments. First, many agricultural activities have increased both in scale and in degree of concentration so that activities conducted on relatively small acreages may generate levels of environmental pollution markedly higher than in the past.[197] Second, these activities have become subject to a higher degree of government regulation.[198] Third, suburbanization of rural areas has brought large numbers of non-farmer residents to many of the nation's most productive agricultural areas.[199] These newcomers often have found the smell, noise, and other externalities of farming to be unacceptable. Finally farmers have come to fear that they will lose nuisance suits even where they have operated for many years without objections and have complied—often at great expense—with applicable federal and state regulations. These fears are often justified because under the principles of common law private nuisance an activity can be enjoined even though it may be authorized by relevant statutes and ordinances.[200] Moreover, a non-farming newcomer might prevail in a nuisance action despite the fact that he "came to the nuisance."[201]

While the statutes enacted in response to these developments vary, often significantly, from state to state, most fall into one of three major analytical categories. The first and most widely used is the Alabama/North Carolina model, based on a 1915 Alabama statute[202] as modified and adopted by North Carolina in 1979.[203] North Carolina's right-to-farm law protects farming operations that were not nuisances when established against future private nuisance actions which allege that such operations have become nuisances solely because of changed conditions in the locality. Many statutes in this category also protect farmers against restrictive local regulations. The second category of right-to-farm laws is exemplified by New York's 1971 Agricultural Districts Law.[204] This statute forbids local governments from enacting unreasonable regulations affecting structures or practices on farms located in designated agricultural districts. The third type of law, exemplified by Washington's right-to-farm law,[205] provides that where an agricultural activity is conducted in conformity with federal, state, and local laws, it is presumed to be reasonable and therefore not a nuisance. The final category of statutes includes miscellaneous laws that do not fit into any of the first three categories. The discussion that follows will analyze the major provisions of each type of right-to-farm law and examine the legal and public policy issues presented.[206]

A Preliminary Issue: Have Federal Environmental Laws Preempted State Regulations and Common Law?

The implementation of state right-to-farm laws may raise the question of federal preemption in some cases. The United States Supreme Court has enunciated several principles governing federal-state preemption questions. First, the Court has held that "the historic police powers of the states were not to be superseded by [a] Federal Act unless that was the clear intent of Congress."[207] This intent may be stated explicitly in the statute,[208] or it may be inferred from the pervasiveness of the scheme of federal regulation, the dominance of the federal interest in the particular field of regulation, or the purpose of the federal law and the character of obligations imposed.[209] Evidence of an intent to preempt state law must be clearer and more persuasive than that required to show an intent to displace federal common law with federal legislation.[210]

Many of the federal environmental protection laws—the Clean Water Act,[211] the Clean Air Act,[212] the Resource Conservation and Recovery Act,[213] the Safe Drinking Water Act,[214] and the Surface Mining Control and Reclamation Act[215]—expressly do not preclude state and local governments from adopting emission and discharge standards or pollution control requirements that are as strict as or stricter than the applicable federal requirements. Moreover, the Clean Water Act apparently provides for the preservation of state common law actions. The Senate Report accompanying the 1972 amendments to the act specifically noted that "[c]ompliance with requirements under [the] Act would not be a defense to a common law action for pollution damages."[216]

The question of whether federal law preempts state agricultural pollution control laws thus depends on the effects of both the state law and the federal statute concerned, the language of the federal statute, and the intent of Congress. The major federal statutory schemes, such as the Clean Air Act and the Clean Water Act, envision the continuing availability of state remedies that are at least as stringent as federal requirements.[217] Others, such as FIFRA[218] and the Toxic Substances Control Act,[210] provide for a much more preemptive federal posture.

The Categories of Right-to-Farm: An Analysis

The Alabama/North Carolina Model

The Statute. The Alabama/North Carolina model is derived from a 1915 Alabama statute which sought to protect industrial plants that were not nuisances when established from suits based solely on changed conditions in surrounding areas.[220] The Alabama legislature amended the 1915 act in 1978 to protect agricultural operations, facilities, and plants.[221] North Carolina added a paragraph setting forth legislative findings and a declaration of policy, plus a definition of "agricultural operation," thus producing the widely-copied model.[222]

The thirty-two state statutes modeled after the North Carolina law[223] possess two or more of the following provisions: (1) protection of a farming operation after one year's operation; (2) protection against both public and private nuisance actions; (3) protection only from nuisance liability resulting from changed conditions in the locality; (4) preservation of liability resulting from negligent operation; (5) protection only where the facility was not a nuisance at its inception; (6) a definition of protected agricultural activities; (7) preservation of liability for environmental pollution or changes in water flow; (8) insulation against local regulations declaring non-negligent operation a nuisance; (9) failure to protect operations located within an incorporated municipality; (10) preservation of the vitality of pre-existing contracts; (11) continuation of the farming operation's liability resulting from material changes in the nature or size of the operation; (12) preservation of liability for activities conducted in violation of federal, state, or local laws; (13) a definition of the established date of operation; and (14) protection only of farms located within agricultural districts. Table 1 shows which state statutes have which provision; some have additional features of minor importance which have not been included.

Analysis. The following analysis first examines the fundamental question of the degree of protection a farmer actually receives from the Alabama/North Carolina-type statute. It then examines some of the numerous legal issues presented by such statutes.

The Alabama/North Carolina-type right-to-farm law is designed to protect an agricultural activity that, because of changed local conditions, would otherwise be declared a private nuisance. The statute protects, however, only a limited right. First, it does not limit actions based on a trespass theory, such as an action against a farming operation that produces particulate matter which is deposited on a neighbor's land.[224]

Second, the statute does not protect an agricultural activity that becomes a nuisance because of negligent or otherwise improper operation.[225] While the

Table 1
ELEMENTS OF ALABAMA/NORTH CAROLINA TYPE LAWS

Type of Provision[a]

	1	2	3	4	5	6	7	8	9	10	11	12	13	14
North Carolina	x	x	x	x	x	x	x	x	x	x				
Virginia	x	x	x	x		x	x	x		x	x			
South Carolina	x	x	x	x	x	x	x	x	x					
North Dakota	x	x	x	x	x	x	x	x	x	x				
Arkansas	x	x	x		x	x	x	x		x	x			
Colorado	x	x	x	x	x	x		x	x	x	x			
Idaho	x	x	x	x	x	x		x	x					
Minnesota	6		x	x	x	x		x		x	x	x	x	
Kentucky	x	x	x	x	x	x	x	x						
Indiana	x	x	x	x	x	x					x			
New Mexico	x	x	x	x	x	x				x	x			
Utah	3	x	x	x	x	x	x	x			x			
Alabama	x	x	x	x	x		x	x		x				
Missouri	x	x	x	x	x	x	x		x					
Illinois	x	x	x	x	x	x	x							
Louisiana	x	x	x	x	x		x			x				
Maryland	x	x		x		x				x	x	x		
California	3	x	x	x	x	x	x	x						
Hawaii	x	x	x	x	x	x	x				x			x
New Hampshire	x	x	x	x	x	x	x					x		
Pennsylvania	x			x		x	x	x		x	x	x		

Table 1
ELEMENTS OF ALABAMA/NORTH CAROLINA TYPE LAWS

Type of Provision*													
1	2	3	4	5	6	7	8	9	10	11	12	13	14

	1	2	3	4	5	6	7	8	9	10	11	12	13	14
Florida	x	x	x		x	x					x		x	
Iowa				x			x				x		x	x
Delaware	x	x	x	x								x		
Nebraska		x	x			x								
Mississippi	x	x			x	x					x		x	
Georgia	x	x	x											
Rhode Island		x		x		x	x	x				x		
Texas	x	x	x			x			x		x	x	x	
Connecticut	x	x		x							x	x		
Montana	1 day	x	x											
New York	1 day		x											

*The numbers correspond to the number of the provision on the previous page.

concept of "negligence" embodies established legal doctrines, it is not clear what the statute envisions as an "improper" operation. The word has no generally accepted meaning, although dictum in a 1929 Alabama Supreme Court decision construing Alabama's "right to manufacture" law may be enlightening. In *Martin Building Co. v. Imperial Laundry Co.*,[226] the defendant's eight-story-high smokestack emitted large quantities of black smoke that blew into plaintiff's nearby twelve-story office building three or four times daily. The court observed that if the defendant could abate the nuisance at a reasonable cost by using modern operating methods or installing pollution control devices, the failure to do so would constitute "negligent or improper operation" of the laundry, and defeat the laundry's statutory protection.[227]

Third, the Alabama/North Carolina model protects only those activities that fall within the statutory definition of "protected agricultural activities."[228] North Carolina's definition is fairly broad and seems to cover all commercial agricultural activities from raising crops to food processing and packaging.[229] Other definitions are more restrictive,[230] excluding not only non-commercial agricultural activities but also commercial activities falling outside the specific statutory definition.

Fourth, the law provides no protection during the first year of an agricultural activity's operation.[231]

Fifth, the statute does not protect an activity that was a nuisance at the time it began.[232] Presumably, this determination would be governed by legal principles applicable at the time the activity began. In any event, the parties may well have difficulty proving conditions that existed ten, fifteen, or more years prior to trial, especially where the only issue is whether the conduct was unreasonable under all the circumstances.

Sixth, the statute does not afford protection for those activities that were not nuisances at their inception but have become so for some reason other than changed local conditions.[233] Change in local conditions then becomes but one of several factors that are considered in determining whether the activity is a justifiable nuisance. Even ignoring changed conditions, a court may find that the social utility of an agricultural operation is outweighed by interference with a neighboring landowner's use and enjoyment of his property. Thus, a court may hold a defendant farmer liable when it finds that the plaintiff's use of his land has come to be accorded a higher social value or the defendant's use a lower one, than was the case at the inception of his activity. Similarly, if the plaintiff shows that the defendant can prevent the interference more easily now than he could before, because, for example, improved pollution control technology is available, the defendant cannot invoke the statute as a defense. Furthermore, if a change in the defendant's mode of operating his farm, rather than a change in surrounding conditions, produces an unreasonable interference with the neighbor's use of his land, the statute does not apply. Several of the more recently enacted statutes recognize this limitation more explicitly than does North Carolina's.[234]

Finally, the statute does not protect the defendant against nuisance liability where the activity in question causes water pollution or changes in the flow of waters.[235]

Allocation of the burdens of proof—both of persuasion and production[236]—will greatly influence the effectiveness of an Alabama/North Carolina-type statute. If the burdens are allocated in a way that facilitates proof of the plaintiff's case, the statute will afford farmers significantly less protection against nuisance liability. Unfortunately, there is no satisfactory test for assigning the burdens of either persuasion or production.[237] While it has been variously argued that the burden should be allocated to the party who must establish an affirmative proposition, to the party with greater access to knowledge about a disputed fact, or the advocate of a "disfavored contention,"[238] ultimately the choice may be made primarily on the basis of fairness and, where manifest, legislative intent. If the plaintiff is proceeding under theories of trespass or negligence, the defendant can draw no support from the law.[239] In actions based solely on nuisance, the Alabama/North Carolina-type statute provides a defense with some attributes of a statute of limitations. Thus it seems appropriate to require the defendant, in order to invoke statutory protection, to prove as an affirmative defense that his activity falls within the definition of "agricultural operation" and has been in operation for more than one year. Because the legislature intended to protect farmers who met these two prerequisites, the plaintiff should then be required to show either that the defendant's operation created a nuisance when it began or that it created a nuisance because of changed methods of operation, failure to use newly available pollution control technology, changing social valuations of conflicting land uses, or some other reason other than "changed conditions in or about the locality."[240] Although this may place a heavy burden on newcomers to prove facts more probably within the ken of the long-time farmer, it seems proper in light of the legislative intent. Furthermore, the fact that in most cases neighbors will not have complained earlier of the farm's water or air pollution will suggest that conditions were not clearly nuisance-producing before the suit in question.

Constitutional Issues. Neighbors whose nuisance actions are barred by an Alabama/North Carolina statute may seek to challenge the statute on grounds it violates the Fifth and Fourteenth Amendments' strictures against the taking of property without just compensation.[241] To succeed, a challenger would need to prove (a) that a legally cognizable property interest was adversely affected by the statute's operation and, (b) that the statute affected this interest in such a manner as to constitute a taking.[242] A thorough analysis of the constitutional issues raised by such a challenge is beyond the scope of this article.[243] The following preliminary analysis, however, suggests that the challenge would be unlikely to succeed.

The first hurdle encountered by plaintiff challenging an Alabama/North Carolina statute is to define the precise property interest allegedly taken. A challenger who bought property after the enactment of the statute would be hard pressed to show that it caused him any loss. Presumably he bargained for and bought his property with knowledge of the law and of local conditions. Thus, his purchase price should have reflected the value of the property given the remedies for nuisance afforded or denied by the statute. Under these circumstances, the statute would not operate so as to effect a taking.

No challenger owning land before the enactment of the statute would be likely to succeed in an action against a farm established after the statute was enacted. An Alabama/North Carolina statute does not protect farms from suit until they have been in operation for one year.[244] Before the year has elapsed, plaintiffs may bring nuisance suits on a changed conditions theory. Hence, with respect to nuisance-producing farms established after the statute becomes effective, the statute functions merely as a statute of limitations.

Thus, only a challenger who bought his property before the enactment of an Alabama/North Carolina statute and who is suing a farm established before the effective date of the statute could potentially show that the statute operated so as to effect a taking of a property interest. As discussed above, however, these statutes protect only those farming operations that (1) fall within the statutory definition of an agricultural operation, (2) do not produce water pollution, (3) are not being conducted negligently or improperly, (4) did not create a nuisance at their inception and have not changed so as to presently constitute one, and (5) have become nuisances solely because of changed conditions in the locality surrounding the defendant's farm rather than on the farm itself.[245] If any one of these five conditions is absent, the statutes do not provide a defense, so no property interest is affected.

Even if the defendant farmer's operation falls within the scope of right-to-farm protection, the plaintiff-neighbor continues to use and enjoy his property as before, subject only to externalities from the defendant's farm that would not constitute a nuisance but for changes on surrounding properties. The only interest that the statute takes away, therefore, is the ability to recover nuisance damages from the farmer because changes on third parties' land have changed the character of the locale such that the farm would not be deemed a nuisance. Such an interest may well be too insubstantial to be characterized as a property interest entitled to constitutional protection.

Moreover, even if a plaintiff is able to show that he has a constitutional protected property interest, it seems clear that an Alabama/North Carolina right-to-farm law does not cause a taking of that interest. The question of whether or not a legislature can insulate a property owner from private nuisance liability to its neighbors arose with some frequency in the nineteenth century, when both Congress and state legislatures sought to protect railroad companies as they constructed facilities across the nation.[246] The railroads' neighbors argued that these laws affected a taking of their property by authorizing railroads to deprive them of the enjoyment of their property and by subjecting them to serious physical discomfort and annoyance without just compensation.[247] In *Richards v. Washington Terminal Co.*,[248] a case involving a congressionally authorized railroad facility in Washington, D.C, the Supreme Court held that Congress could (1) legalize the operation of a railroad so that it could not be deemed a public nuisance,[249] and (2) insulate it against nuisance liability for ordinary damages to neighboring property caused by the normal, necessary and non-negligent operations of the railroad.[250] In the case before the Court, however, the railroad subjected plaintiff to special damages by installing fans which blew gases and soot from a nearby tunnel onto plaintiff's house. The Court held that Congress could not empower the railroad to impose a "direct and substantial and peculiar"[251] burden on an adjoining landowner's property (as opposed to incidental inconveniences unavoidably attendant to the operation of a railroad).[252] The Court indicated that this result was required in order to avoid a taking, noting by way of dicta that:

> We deem the true rule, under the Fifth Amendment, as under state constitutions containing a similar prohibition, to be that while the legislature may legalize what otherwise would be a public nuisance, it may not confer immunity from an action for a private nuisance of such a character as to amount in effect to a taking of private property for public use.[253]

Thus, *Richards* stands for the principle that neither Congress nor state legislatures may exempt railroads from private citizens' damage claims for special inconvenience and discomfort not experienced by the public at large.[254]

The precise wording and operation of the Alabama/North Carolina law distinguishes it from the railroad authorization act considered in *Richards*. The law does not authorize a farmer to engage in new or more destructive interferences with neighbors' use and enjoyment of their property, and thus avoids imposing "direct and substantial and peculiar" burdens.[255]

Recent case law has recognized that common law remedies (and the underlying property rights they protect) are not immutable. In *Duke Power v. Carolina Environmental Study Group*,[256], for example, the Supreme Court addressed the issue of whether the Price-Anderson Act,[257] which limits liability for nuclear accidents, violates due process by eliminating common-law tort remedies. "Initially," the Court observed, "it is not at all clear that the Due Process Clause in fact requires that a legislatively enacted compensation scheme either duplicate the recovery at common law or provide a reasonable substitute remedy."[258] The Court did not have to decide whether due process requires a substitute remedy because it found that Congress had in fact provided a reasonable substitute.[259] Nevertheless, the Court took pains to note that:

> Our cases have clearly established that "[a] person has no property, no vested interest, in any rule of the common law." [citation] The "Constitution does not forbid the creation of new rights, or the abolition of old ones recognized by the common law, to attain a permissible legislative object," [citation] despite the fact that "otherwise settled expectations" may be upset thereby. [citation] Indeed, statutes limiting liability are relatively commonplace and have consistently been enforced by the courts.[260]

Therefore, even if a neighbor were able to demonstrate that a property interest previously enjoyed (the private nuisance remedy) was diminished by the legislation, he may nonetheless be denied relief because he lacks a vested right in the permanency of that remedy.

New York's Agricultural District Law

In 1971 New York adopted the Agricultural District Law,[261] which provides incentives to encourage farmers to create agricultural districts. The statute then gives farmers of land within a district limited protection against local regulations, such as zoning ordinances restricting agricultural uses.[262] Virtually identical provisions are found in the agricultural district laws of Illinois,[263] Oregon,[264] Pennsylvania,[265] Virginia,[266] and for the Twin Cities Metropolitan Area of Minnesota.[267]

Although more than seventy percent of the land in agricultural production in New York is in agricultural districts,[268] the law has yet to be interpreted by that state's courts. On its face, the statute does not provide much protection for farmers. It permits regulations that do not "unreasonably" restrict or regulate farm structures or practices or that further the purposes of the Agricultural

District Law.[269] The act permits even those laws that are unreasonable or that contravene its purposes so long as they bear a direct relationship to public health and safety.[270]

Statutes That Create a Presumption That Agricultural Operations That Comply With Federal, State, and Local Regulations Are Not Nuisances

The third type of right-to-farm statute creates a presumption that farming conducted in conformity with federal, state, and local law is "reasonable" and not a nuisance. The three major variants of this type of statute are based, respectively, on Washington's 1979 right-to-farm law,[271] Michigan's 1981 law,[272] and feedlot statutes such as that enacted by Kansas in 1963.[273]

The Washington Model. Washington adopted its right-to-farm law in 1979.[274] Oklahoma,[275] Arizona,[276] Kansas,[277] and Vermont[278] soon thereafter enacted virtually identical statutes. These laws provide agricultural activities conducted in conformity with federal, state, and local laws and regulations with a complete defense against nuisance suits brought by owners of adjacent lands, where the plaintiffs undertook nonagricultural activities subsequent to the initiation of farming activity.

To determine whether an agricultural activity is protected by the Washington statute, one initially must determine whether the activity conforms with applicable regulations. If so, the statute presumes that the activity is a good agricultural practice.[279] The statute then establishes that any agricultural operation consistent with good agricultural practices (and established prior to surrounding non-agricultural activities) is "presumed" to be reasonable, and hence not a nuisance.[280] This construction leaves open the possibility, however, that an operation not in compliance with regulations could still be found to be a good agricultural practice and thus protected by the statute. It is unclear, however, precisely what would constitute proof of good agricultural practice. Presumably, "best management practices" promulgated by EPA, the U.S. Department of Agriculture, or the state department of agriculture would qualify. Alternatively, the phrase could be construed to refer to practices actually followed by careful farmers in the area.

The Washington statute's protection is limited in several ways. First, the statute explicitly excludes activities having a substantial adverse effect on public health and safety.[281] This provision might be construed to mean that only activities that are public nuisances are not protected. Another interpretation would protect minor interferences with neighboring landowners' uses, but withdraw protection from activiites that cause substantial harm to a neighbor's health and safety. Second as was the case with the Alabama/North Carolina type of right-to-farm law, the Washington statute does not protect farmers against liability based on trespass or negligence, or arising out of non-commercial agriculture.[282] Third, the law provides no protection against nuisance suits brought by neighbors who are conducting agricultural activities even where these activities began after those of the farm operator against whom relief is sought.[283] This is an important omission since a large share of nuisance suits against agricultural operations have been brought by farmer neighbors.[284] Finally, the Washington statute is silent as to the consequences of a substantial change in the nature of the agricultural activities after the establishment of a nearby non-agricultural use. Such new farm activities would appear to fall outside the protection of the statute and have priority only over those subsequently commenced non-agricultural activities.

Like the Alabama/North Carolina right-to-farm laws, the Washington statute raises several burden of proof issues. As outlined above, the statute embodies two presumptions—first, that activities conforming to applicable regulations are presumed to be good agricultural practices; and second, that good agricultural practices are presumed to be reasonable. Even though each presumption is rebuttable, they do impose the burden of producing evidence on the plaintiff. Because the statute carves an exception to the general rules of nuisance, however, the farmer should have the burdens of production and persuasion with respect to the propositions that trigger the affirmative defense, specifically, that: (1) his activity fits the definition of agricultural activity and is on farmland as defined, (2) it was established prior to the plaintiff's surrounding non-agricultural activity, and (3) it complies with applicable federal, state, and local laws.

The Washington model does not present a serious "taking" problem because it does not affect neighbors whose nonagricultural uses predate the agricultural activity. Those neighboring landowners whose non-agricultural activities began subsequent to the farming operations but before enactment of the statute may have to prove somewhat different elements to make out a case from what they might have had to prove before the enactment, but if they can show that the farmer's operations are not consistent with good agricultural practices or have a substantial adverse effect on the public health and safety, they may still secure relief through a nuisance suit. Those who begin operations after the enactment of the statute are in the same position and, in addition, are less entitled to argue that their investment-backed expectations have been frustrated.

The Michigan Model. The Michigan right-to-farm law,[285] which has been copied in various forms by Maine,[286] Tennessee,[287] and New Jersey,[289] provides that a farmer has an absolute defense against a public or private nuisance action if he can show either (1) that his operation conforms to generally accepted agricultural and management practices as determined by the director of the Department of Agriculture or (2) that his operation existed before a change in use or occupancy of land within one mile and was not a nuisance before such change. The second defense is virtually identical to the essence of the protection afforded by the Alabama/North Carolina model, so much of the analysis developed there is applicable here.

Tennessee's right-to-farm law[289] creates only a rebuttable presumption and not an absolute defense. Thus, neighbors may secure relief against a substantial interference with the use and enjoyment of their property by showing that the conduct causing the harm is unreasonable according to general principles of nuisance law. In fact, this statute appears not to change common law rules of nuisance liability significantly, since evidence that the defendant conducted the damage-producing activities in accordance with generally accepted practices always has been a factor to be considered in assessing the reasonableness of his conduct.[290]

Laws Pertaining to Animal Confinement Facilities. The final type of right-to-farm law covers only animal confinement facilities. One version, found in Kansas,[291] and Oklahoma,[292] protects animal confinement facilities for cattle, swine, sheep, and horses (and for poultry in Oklahoma) over a specified size. The statute provides that the operation of a feedlot in compliance with regulations promulgated by the responsible state official will be *prima facie* evidence that a nuisance does not exist. The presumption thereby created can be rebutted by a neighbor's showing of substantial interference with his use and enjoyment of his property. There have been no judicial decisions interpreting this statute.

A second variant of the statute, found in Iowa,[293] Tennessee,[294] and Wyoming,[295] applies to cattle, swine, sheep, poultry, and other animal confinement facilities. It provides that when a nuisance plaintiff has obtained title to or established residential or commercial use of his property after the date of establishment of the feedlot operation, proof that the defendant feedlot has complied with the regulations of the responsible state agency provides an absolute defense, provided that the activities causing the alleged nuisance are subject to such regulation.

These statutes also provide limited exemptions from state environmental regulations and local zoning and farm nuisance regulations. To qualify for these exemptions, feedlots must comply, first, with regulations and standards applicable under a NPDES permit,[296] second, with regulations of the responsible state agency and local governments that were in effect at the date of adoption of the state feedlot law, and third, with any such regulations that take effect before the agricultural activity is established. The farming activities are thus exempt from regulations adopted both after the effective date of the law and after the date they began operations. The statute also exempts the protected agricultural activities from post-1979 zoning and anti-nuisance regulations that become applicable to them because a city has annexed the land on which they are conducted.

Other Statutes

Four states have enacted right-to-farm laws that do not fit easily into one of the categories discussed above. West Virginia's statute[297] gives limited protection to agricultural operations against subsequently begun nonagricultural uses. The statute enacted by Ohio[298] provides similar protection to agricultural activities that are located within an agricultural district and are not operated in violation of any federal, state, or local law. Massachusetts' law[299] provides simply that the odor from the normal maintenance of livestock or the spreading of manure upon agricultural or horticultural lands shall not be deemed a nuisance.

Wisconsin's law[300] has some interesting features. It establishes guidelines for use by judges in resolving conflicts between agricultural and other uses. First, it distinguishes between agricultural uses that are not in an exclusive agricultural use zone pursuant to Wisconsin's farmland protection program[301] and those that are. For those that are not, closure is not to be ordered unless the use is a threat to public health or safety, plaintiffs coming to the nuisance may be granted only nominal damages, but the court may direct the farmer to adopt agricultural practices that will reduce the adverse impacts of the activity found to be causing a nuisance. For agricultural uses that are in exclusive agricultural use zones, the relief granted cannot restrict or regulate the use unless necessary to protect public health or safety. Further, if the farmer-defendant prevails, he is entitled to collect both costs and reasonable attorney's fees.

Summary

The widespread adoption of the vast majority of right-to-farm laws in the short period from 1971 to 1982 presents an intriguing instance of parallel action by almost all state legislatures. It is intriguing for several reasons. First, the scope of the various right-to-farm laws is limited in so many ways by narrow definitions, exclusions, exceptions and rebuttable presumptions that most farmers will not be able to avail themselves of their protection. Second, as the technology forcing provisions of most federal environmental protection acts take hold, operators of the large concentrated animal confinement facilities that are the object of most agricultural nuisance suits will install better equipment and thereby reduce the amount of pollutants their operations generate. The need for right-to-farm protection will thus be reduced. Despite these considerations, right-to-farm laws, especially those that protect agricultural operations that are located in agricultural districts and being managed in conformity with federal, state and local laws against private nuisance liability, are sensible as one provision of a comprehensive farmland protection program.[302]

SEPARATION: PROGRAMS DESIGNED TO PROTECT AGRICULTURAL AREAS AGAINST INTRUDING CONFLICTING USES

The final approach to managing agricultural pollution is to separate agricultural uses from other uses which are adversely affected by agricultural pollution. The principle of separation of mutually incompatible uses, the core of standard Euclidean zoning, has recently been resurrected as the functional means of achieving various environmental protectionist objectives.[303] These new programs are designed primarily to protect critical environmental areas, such as Massachusetts' wetland program[304] and the Wisconsin Shoreland Protection Program.[305] But others are more broadly conceived and advance comprehensive land use objectives, such as Hawaii's Land Use Law of 1961,[306] which established statewide zoning, Oregon's Land Use Act of 1973,[307] which established the Land Conservation and Development Commission as lead agency in a state/local land use planning and management process,[308] and New Jersey's Pineland Protection Act[309] and its State Development Guide Plan.[310] The objective in each case is to build legal barriers around statutorily demarcated land areas and prevent the intrusion of incompatible uses.

The promulgation in 1976 of the American Law Institute's Model Land Development Code[311] advanced the notion that land areas with special characteristics could be protected through separation. Article 7 of the Code is especially significant because it proposes state designation and regulation of "areas of critical state concern."[312] Even before final adoption, the Code served as a model for several state laws, including the Florida Environmental Land and Water Management Act of 1972,[313] and Minnesota's Critical Areas Act of 1973.[314]

Not surprisingly, several commentators have advocated the creation of agricultural districts incorporating many of the mechanisms and approaches embodied in the model code.[315] While recognizing the obvious differences between agricultural land and critical environmental areas, they argue that the principle of separation applies with the same force to the protection of farmland as it does to the protection of the natural environment.

At least fourteen state, two regional, and numerous local agricultural programs, of varying degrees of complexity and sophistication, but all based in part on spatial separation, have been enacted. Many of these laws seek to accomplish objectives other than reducing the impact of agricultural pollution, most notably control of urban growth and reduction of the rate of conversion of agricultural land to non-agricultural uses. Eight states[316] have enacted agricultural district laws that (1) rely on voluntary participation by farmers, (2) provide various types of tax relief and other incentives to induce such participation, and (3) impose few if any sanctions for withdrawal of land from the district. Six other states[317] and two metropolitan areas[318] have enacted stronger and more comprehensive agricultural land protection programs, some of which are voluntary, but all of which provide (1) varying types of incentives and (2) significant sanctions to deter conversion of land to non-agricultural use. Several have a strong planning component. The key elements of seventeen programs containing a wide variety of approaches to the twin problems of agricultural pollution and premature conversion of farmland are set out in Table 2. In several other states, most notably Illinois, Iowa, Pennsylvania, Maryland, and Washington, local governments have enacted similar agricultural zoning ordinances.[319]

In Canada, the provinces of British Columbia, Saskatchewan, and Prince

Table 2

Program Element

Program Element	Agricultural District Laws										Comprehensive Programs						
	Kentucky	Illinois	Virginia	New York	Iowa	Pennsylvania	Ohio	New Jersey	Maryland	Calif. Wmson	Twin Cities	Lexington	Wisconsin	California Coastal Comm.	Vermont	Hawaii	Oregon
1. Differential Assessment or tax credit	*	*	×	×	*	*	*	×	*	×	×	*	×	×		×	×
2. Right-to-Farm Protection	*	*	*	*	*	*	×	×	*	*	*	*	*	*	*	*	*
3. Protection from restrictive local ordinances		×	×	×	×	×	×	×	×		×						×
4. Limitations on special assessments		×	×	×	×	×	×				×		×				×
5. State agency policies must support farming	×	×	×	×	×						×			×			×
6. Limits on public investments for non-farm development			×	×		×	×	×		×	×		×	×	×		×
7. Limits on use of eminent domain			×	×		×	×	×		×	×			×			×
8. Limitations on annexation within districts	×								×		×		×	×			
9. Sound conservation practices required								×	×		×		×				
10. Limits on rate of tax increases											×						
11. Compensation to local governments for tax losses			×	×						×	×						
12. Zone adjacent lands to reduce conflict																	

160 The Agriculture Crisis

	Agricultural District Laws								Comprehensive Programs								
	Kentucky	Illinois	Virginia	New York	Iowa	Pennsylvania	Ohio	New Jersey	Maryland	Calif. Wmson	Twin Cities	Lexington	Wisconsin	California Coastal Comm.	Vermont	Hawaii	Oregon
13. Eligible for purchase of development rights	x					x		x	x								
14. Limits on development of district land by zoning or other techniques									x	x	x	x	x	x	x	x	x
15. Mediation for right to farm conflicts								x									
16. Strong sanctions on withdrawal									x	x	x	x	x	x	x	x	x
17. Mandatory consistency with state or regional plans										x	x	x	x	x		x	x
18. Control over public facilities such as sewers									x		x	x					x
19. Growth boundary divides rural and urban areas											x	x		x			x
20. State funding of local planning activities													x				
21. State or regional permit needed for development												x		x	x	x	x

* Available to all eligible farmers in state

Edward Island have created farm and protection programs based on agricultural preserves.[320] In France, for over 20 years, the *Societes d' Amenagement Foncier et d' Etablissement Rural* (SAFERs) have implemented an agricultural reserves program.[321] The local SAFER requests the prefect of te *departement* within which it operates to designate areas that should remain in agricultural use. After the designation is approved, the SAFER may either buy farmland in the market or assert a right of first refusal in the event that land in the reserve is offered for sale. Between 1969 and 1975, SAFERs bought about twelve percent of the agricultural land sold in France each year, and resold most of it to prospective farmers.[322]

The various programs discussed are much too complex to describe in detail and evaluate fully here. It is important, however, to recognize that these programs represent a spectrum of responses to the problems caused by the intrusion of non-agricultural activities into farm areas. Such programs are also major building blocks of effective programs for protecting farmland and reducing the damage caused by agricultural pollution, by keeping distant uses and populations that the pollution may adversely affect.

To evaluate spatial separation one must weigh the attractiveness of incentives to participate, the comprehensiveness of the controls imposed, the severity of penalties for withdrawal, and the rigor of enforcement. If the program is voluntary, like the eight agricultural district programs and the more comprehensive approaches of Maryland and California's Williamson Act, it will be effective only to the extent that individual farmers voluntarily keep their land in the program. If the incentives for initial participation are strong, but the penalties for withdrawal weak, little actual deterrence exists when the pressure to sell and convert is high. New York's agricultural district program falls into this category. Although 70% of the state's farmland is enrolled,[323] there is little evidence that farmers have availed themselves of the protections of the act or that it has reduced farmland conversion significantly.[324] If the incentives are modest and the penalties for withdrawal strong, few farmers who are entertaining intentions of developing their land in the near future will voluntarily enroll in the program. California's Williamson Act best typifies this situation. Basically a strong act, in that it prevents conversion of farmland for at least ten years after enrollment, it has been used principally by farmers in remote rural areas where development pressures are weak.[325]

Thus, voluntary programs are caught in a paradox: if they are strong enough to protect agricultural areas from the intrusion of incompatible uses, they will not attract farmers in the very areas where the pressure to sell is the greatest. If their controls are so weak that farmers will not be deterred from enrolling, they will not be effective. Nevertheless, basic voluntary agricultural district programs do have some important benefits. The protections and incentives that they provide negate some of the causes of the intrusion of non-agricultural uses into agricultural areas. Moreover, they create new entities or organizations that are committed to the objective of maintaining agriculture. The mere existence of such entities may prevent some conversions that might otherwise take place.

The attractiveness of incentives and the stringency of controls are also critical when considering the political feasibility of mandatory programs like those in Oregon, Hawaii, the Twin Cities Region, Vermont, Lexington-Fayette Urban County (Kentucky), Wisconsin, and California's Coastal Zone. The greater the incentives and the weaker the controls on conversion, the easier they are to enact, and vise versa.

Perhaps the most important spatial separation technique is the "urban growth boundary." Used in its purest form in Oregon, Lexington-Fayette Urban County, and the California Coastal Zone, the urban growth boundary delineates an area within which five, ten or more years' worth of development is allowed to take place. In rural areas outside the boundary, development is barred, while present agricultural or undeveloped uses are permitted.[326] The boundary serves to shape landowners' and developers' expectations and, thereby, to deflect land-value-inflating development pressures away from prime agricultural land.

While it is beyond the scope of this article to propose an agricultural reserve program in full, such a program should have most of the following elements, allowing for variations in values and conditions among the states.

1. A state land planning agency with authority:
(a) to establish a comprehensive plan for the development and protection of the state's resources, including agricultural land, and
(b) to create urban growth boundaries around all major cities and towns located in or near agricultural reserves, within which fifteen to twenty years' anticipated growth can be accommodated.
2. A state agricultural land agency with authority:
(a) to regulate land use in agricultural reserves,
(b) to delegate the authority to regulate land use in agricultural reserves to local governments that enact regulations meeting state criteria, and
(c) to exercise a right of first refusal with respect to farmland that comes on the market and to buy it at publicly appraised fair market value and then resell it to farmers at below market value.
3. Appropriate combinations of tax reduction and other economic compensation to owners of land which has a reduced market value because placed in an agricultural reserve.

CONCLUSION

This article has reviewed several major approaches to managing agricultural pollution, including: (1) judicial resolution of land use conflicts based on principles of common law nuisance; (2) recent legislative attempts to limit the application of those principles by the enactment of right-to-farm laws; (3) technology-forcing regulation; and (4) spatial separation of agricultural activities from land uses with which they conflict, by the creation of agricultural districts or comprehensive farmland protection programs.

The essence of the law of private nuisance is that it involves the application of a set of general principles to a particular set of circumstances. The court must decide whether there is a substantial interference, whether the social value of one activity outweighs that of another, which of two uses is more appropriate for a particular neighborhood, and whether the harm can be either avoided or prevented at relatively little cost. The strengths of this process are first, that a landowner can do what he wants with his property so long as he does not interfere unreasonably with the rights of his neighbor, and second, that landowners can take advantage of developments in technology.

Judicial enforcement of nuisance law does have some serious weaknesses, however. *Ad hoc* resolutions often fail to produce the kind of broad information needed to solve land use problems wisely. Judges are not sufficiently responsible to the electorate to authorize them to perform what is often a political function in balancing competing social values. Moreover, judges are not equipped with the technical and financial expertise needed to decide whether or not existing techniques for reducing the injurious impact of a particular land use are adequate or financially practicable.

Legislative approaches to the management of agricultural pollution have rested on the principles of forcing technological change, inducing spatial separation, and encouraging voluntary reduction of pollution by means of subsidies. The major federal environmental laws have led to the identification of the most serious forms of agricultural pollution and the establishment of standards that farmers are required to meet. In most cases, compliance with these standards has not been particularly onerous and has redounded to the benefit of neighboring farmers more than it has to non-farmers. The costs, benefits and practical problems associated with the management of non-point source pollution under section 208 of the Clean Water Act are in the early stages of exploration. The program is operating under a clause of uncertainty because of budgetary cutbacks and recurring financial adversity in the agricultural sector.

The various agricultural district and farmland programs represent a rich array of techniques for enticing, rewarding, and forcing actions that support the continuation of farming in the most appropriate and fertile locations. Here, again, many programs are in such an early stage of development that their long-term effectiveness cannot be evaluated with confidence.

If there is one lesson to be learned from this review of approaches to managing agricultural pollution, it is that while some of the elements of an effective program must be nationwide in scope (such as those governing major point source pollution and the use of pesticides), the best combination of strategies must be determined on a state-by-state or region-by-region basis, so as to take into account varying conditions and values. At the core of such programs should be significant technology-forcing requirements such as those now in effect for large feedlots and pesticide production and application, perhaps supplemented by greater emphasis on conservation tilling, integrated pest management, and subsidies for soil conservation measures. These strategies should be integrated with more or less comprehensive farmland protection programs that are premised on sound analysis of soil data, farm ownership patterns, and economic trends.[327] Protection against private nuisance suits and excessive local regulation should be conditioned on participation in a farmland protection program. Landowners should be allowed to assert rights under principles of common law nuisance, but such suits should be primarily interstitial; they would apply only to the neighboring activities that either were not complying with applicable federal and state pollution control standards, or were not subject to such standards and not protected by responsible participation in a state or local farmland protection program. As these programs became effective, farming and non-farming activities would be separated so there would be fewer and fewer conflicts between agricultural and non-agricultural land uses and therefore less need for private nuisance remedies. Thus, strategies aimed at the twin goals of protecting prime agricultural land from inappropriate conversion to non-agricultural uses and managing agricultural pollution can be woven together in ways that best serve the interests of both the agricultural industry and society at large.

NOTES

1. *See, e.g.,* Bower v. Hog Builders, Inc. 461 S.W.2d 784 (Mo. 1970); Rust v. Guinn, 429 N.E.2d 299 (Ind. App. 1981); Lacy Feed Co. v. Parrish, 517 S.W.2d 845 (Tex. Civ. App. 1974).

2. *See Schloesser,* Agricultural Non-Point Source Water Pollution Control Under Sections 208 and 303 of the Clean Water Act: Has Forty Years of Experience Taught Us Anything?, 54 N.D.L. REV. 589 (1978).

3. The Clean Water Act defines a point source as "any discernible, confined and discrete conveyance including but not limited to any pipe, ditch, channel, tunnel, conduit, well, discrete fissure, container, rolling stock, concentrated animal feeding operation, or vessel or other floating craft, from which pollutants are or may be discharged. . . ." 33 U.S.C. § 1362(14) (Supp. V 1981).

4. 1981 STATISTICAL ABSTRACT OF THE UNITED STATES 660 (table 1165).

5. *See* ECONOMIC RESEARCH SERVICE, U.S. DEPT. OF AGRICULTURE, AGRICULTURAL OUTLOOK 11 (Table) (Oct. 1982).

6. *See infra*notes 19-21 and accompanying text.

7. The Council on Environmental Quality reported that more than eight million acres of prime farmland were converted to urban development, reservoirs, highways, recreation, surface mining and other uses from 1967 to 1975. U.S. COUNCIL ON ENVIRONMENTAL QUALITY, EIGHTH ANNUAL REPORT 90 (1977). The Council's tenth report estimated that agricultural land of all types (not only prime) is currently being converted at a rate of three million areas a year. U.S. COUNCIL ON ENVIRONMENTAL QUALITY, TENTH ANNUAL REPORT 396 (1979). *See also* NATIONAL AGRICULTURAL LANDS STUADY, FINAL REPORT (1981)

8. A fifth approach, the provision of financial assistance, tax incentives and technical services, for decades a primary activity of the federal and state departments of agriculture especially in the area of soil conservation and erosion control, is beyond the scope of the article. *See generally* R. HELD & M. CLAWSON, SOIL CONSERVATION IN PERSPECTIVE (1965); SOIL, CONSERVATION SOCIETY OF AMERICA SOIL CONSERVATION POLICIES: AN

ASESSMENT (1979); THE FUTURE OF AMERICAN AGRICULTURE AS A STRATEGIC RESCOURCE (S. Batie & R. Healy eds., 1980) [hereinafter cited as Batie & Healy]; R. DALLAVALLE & L. MAYER, SOIL CONSERVATION IN THE UNITED STATES: THE FEDERAL ROLE (1980); N. SAMPSON, FARMLAND OR WASTELAND: A TIME TO CHOOSE (1981); SOIL CONSERVATION POLICIES, INSTITUTIONS, AND INCENTIVES (H. Halcrow, E. Heady & M. Cotner eds. 1982) Schloesser, *supra* note 2; Uchtmann & Seitz, *Options for Controlling Non-Point Source Water Pollution: A Legal Perspective*, 19 NAT. RESOURCES J. 587 (1979); Garner, *Innovative Strategies for Conserving Soil and Water*, 1982 AGRIC. L.J. 543 (1982).

9. Recent studies indicate that as much as one-third of the topsoil from U.S. cropland has been lost through erosion, NATIONAL AGRICULTURAL LANDS STUDY, SOIL DEGRADATION: EFFECTS ON AGRICULTURAL ACTIVITY (INTERIM REPORT NO. 4) (1980) [hereinafter cited as SOIL DEGRADATION], and that cropland soil loss continues at the rate of over 2.5 billion tons per year. CONSERVATION FOUNDATION, STATE OF THE ENVIRONMENT 1982, at 234-35 (1982) [hereinafter cited as CF ENVIRONMENT 1982]. Whereas the average annual rates of sheet and rill erosion for forestland and pastureland are 1.2 and 2.6 tons per acre per year, respectively, the rate for cropland is 4.7 tons per acre. SOIL DEGRADTION, *supra*, at 12, 20.

10. Sediment is itself a pollutant because it clouds the water, settles to the stream bed and interferes with the natural cycles of stream and lake wildlife, and acts as a carrier for pesticides and fertilizers, CF ENVIRONMENT 1982, *supra* note 9, at 225-26.

11. Mainly nitrogen, phosphorus and potassium, CF ENVIRONMENT 1982, *supra* note 0 at 230.

12. Batie & Healy, *supra* note 8, at 100.

13. *Id.* at 82.

14. REPORT OF THE STAFF TO THE NATIONAL COMMISSION ON WATER QUALITY 11-183 (1976) [hereinafter cited as NCWQ STAFF REPORT].

15. *See* Beeton, *Eutrophication of the St. Lawrence Great Lakes*, 10 LIMNOLOGY & OCEANOGRAPHY 240 (1965), *reprinted in* T. DETWYLER, MAN'S IMPACT ON ENVIRONMENT 225, 238 (1971) (discussing the effects of domestic and agricultural run-off on the Great Lakes).

16. *See* N. SAMPSON, *supra* note 8, at 167. The *amount* of pesticide run-off is often a secondary consideration, however, since some pesticides are so toxic or persistent that any quantity in surface waters presents a serious problem. *Id.*

17. *See* D. BOTTRELL, INTEGRATED PEST MANAGEMENT (1979); U.S. COUNCIL ON ENVIRONMENTAL QUALITY, ELEVENTH ANNUAL REPORT 321-22 (1980).

18. ECONOMIC ANALYSIS BRANCH, BENEFITS AND FIELD STUDIES DIVISION, OFFICE OF PESTICIDE PROGR/ MS, U.S. ENVIRONMENTAL PROTECTION AGENCY, REGULATORY IMPACT ANALYSIS: DATA REQUIREMENTS FOR REGISTERING PESTICIDES UNDER THE FEDERAL I9N-SECTICIDE, FUNGICIDE, AND RODENTICIDE ACT 24-25 (1982) [hereinafter cited as REGULATORY IMPACT ANALYSIS]

19. *See generally* Martin, *Beef*, in L. SCHERTZ, ANOTHER REVOLUTION I: U.S. FARMING? 90 (1979); STATISTICAL REPORTING SERVICE, U.S. DEPT. OF AGRICULTURE, LIVESTOCK AND MEAT: OUTLOOK AND SITUATION 17 (Aug. 1982); Rogers, *Poultry and Eggs*, in L. SCHERTZ, *supra*, at 153-56; ECONOMIC RESEARCH SERVICE, U.S. DEPT. OF AGRICULTURE, POULTRY AND EGGS: OUTLOOK AND SITUATION 13 (Aug. 1982).

20. Martin, *supra* note 19, at 94, 104; Forest & Frick, *Dairy*, in L. SCHERTZ, *supra* note 19, at 121-27; ECONOMIC RESEARCH SERVICE, U.S. DEPT. OF AGRICULTURE, LIVESTOCK AND MEAT: OUTLOOK AND SITUATION (LMS 244) at 23 (Feb. 1982); ECONOMIC AND STATISTICS SERVICE, U.S. DEPT. OF AGRICULTURE, POULTRY AND EGG OUTLOOK AND SITUATION 19 (May 1982).

21. Martin, *supra* note 19, at 101; STATISTICAL REPORTING SERVICE, U.S. DEPT. OF AGRICULTURE, LIVESTOCK AND MEAT STATISTICS (STAT. BUL. 522) SUPPLEMENT FOR 1980, at 55 (table) (1981); Forest & Frick, *supra* note 20, at 145; ECONOMIC AND STATISTICS SERVICE, U.S. DEPT. OF AGRICULTURE, POULTRY AND EGG OUTLOOK AND SITUATION 19 (May 1982).

22. Frederick, *Irrigation and the Future of American Agriculture,* in Batie & Healy, *supra* note 8, at 157. Most of that increase has come from groundwater withdrawals, which increased 300 percent during the same period. *Id.* at 175. In many parts of the country, these groundwater withdrawals are extracting water at a much greater rate than the rate of natural replenishment. This not only increases the cost of withdrawal but also threatens the long term continuation of agriculture in those areas.

23. NCWQ STAFF REPORT, *supra* note 14, at II-169.

24. The timing and rate of flow and the allocation between ground and surface water.

25. "Railwater" is the water that flows back into the natural hydrological system after having passed through the network of irrigation facilities.

26. NCWQ STAFF REPORT, *supra* note 14, at II-169.

27. Blumm, *Wetlands Protection and Coastal Planning: Avoiding the Perils of Positive Consistency,* 5 COLUM. J. ENVT'L. L. 69 (1978)

28. *Id.* at 69-70.

29. Blumm, *The Clean Water Act's Section 404 Permit Program Enters Its Adolescence: An Institutional and Programmatic Perspective,* 8 ECOLOGY L.Q. 410, 431-32 (1980)

30. *See, e.g.,* Maykut v. Plasko, 170 Conn. 310, 365 A.2d 114 (1976).

31. *See, e.g.,* CAL. HEALTH & SAFETY CODE: §§ 41850-64 (West 1980).

32. *See, e.g.,* Has v. Levin, 625 F.2d 1384 (10th Cir. 1980).

33. OR. ADMIN. RULES 340-26-010 to -025 (1982), *reprinted in* ENV'T REP. (BNA) 486.0575-.0583; CAL. ADMIN. CODE tit. 17, § 80150(d) (1983), *reprinted in* EVT'T REP. (BNA) 321.0510.

34. Letter from Prof. Donald T. Epp, Pennsylvania State University, to author (Mar. 3, 1983).

35. *See* RESTATEMENT (SECOND) of torts § 821A comment b (1979).

36. *See infra* text accompanying notes 4346.

37. RESTATEMENT (SECOND) OF TORTS § 821D (1979).

38. *Id.* §§ 821E, 822.

39. If a plaintiff has a fee simple of leasehold interest, he will have the requisite property interest. Proximate cause is easy to demonstrate because agricultural activities are generally open and discrete. *See, e.g.,* Schloesser, *supra* note 2 and cases cited therein.

40. RESTATEMENT (SECOND) OFTORTS § 822 (1979).

41. *Id.* § 825 (1979).

42. *Id.* § 826.

43. *See, e.g.,* Boomer v. Atlantic Cement Co., 26 N.Y.2d 219, 257 N.E.2d 870, 309 N.Y.S.2d 312 (1970).

44. RESTATEMENT (SECOND) OF TORTS § 827 comment c (1979).

45. *Id.* 827 comment d; *see also* Arbor Theatre Corp. v. Campbell Soup Co., 11 Ill. App. 3d 89, 296 N.E.2d 11 (1973); Kriener v. Turkey Valley Community School Dist., 212 N.W.2d 526, 536 (Iowa 1973).

46. RESTATEMENT (SECOND) OF TORTS §§ 827-28 (1979).

47. *See, e.g., id.* §§ 840B-C (contributory negligence and assumption of risk).

48. *Id.* § 840D. *See* Dill v. Excel Packing Co., 183 Kan. 513, 331 P.2d 539 (1958), Arbor Theatre Corp. v. Campbell Soup Co., 11 Ill. App. 3d 89, 296 N.E.2d 11 (1973);

Spur Industries, Inc. v. Del E. Webb Development Co., 108 Ariz. 178, 494 P.2d 700 (1972).

49. Most of the right-to-farm laws, *see infra* text accompanying notes 197-302, limit the time within which later purchaser may bring nuisance suits, thus strengthening the position of the farmer who was there first.

50. RESTATEMENT (SECOND) OF TORTS § 821B (1979).

51. *See* RESTATEMENT (SECOND) OFTORTS §§ 905 comment b, 929, 929 comment d (1979); Yeager and Sullivan, Inc. v. O'Neill, 163 Ind. App. 466, 324 N.E.2d 846 (1975).

52. *See, e.g,.* Fortin v. Vitali, 28 Mich. App. 565, 184 N.W.2d 609 (1970); Schiller v. Raley, 405 S.W.2d 446 (Tex. Civ. App. 1966); Gerrish v. Wishbone Farm of New Hampshire, Inc., 108 N.H.2d 237, 231 A.2d 622 (1967).

52. 26 N.Y.2d 219, 257 N.E.2d 870, 309 N.Y.S.2d 312 (1970).

54. *Id.* at 228, 257 N.E.2d at 875, 309 N.Y.S.2d at 319.

55. *Id.* at 225-26, 257 N.E.2d at 873, 309 N.Y.S.2d at 316-17.

56. Patz v. Farmegg Products, Inc., 196 N.W.2d 557 (Iowa 1972).

57. 108 Ariz. 178, 494 P.2d 700 (1972).

58. *Id.* at 180, 494 P.2d at 702.

59. *Id.* at 183, 494 P.2d at 705.

60. *Id.*

61. Public nuisance is "an unreasonable interference with a right common to the general public." RESTATEMEMT (SECOND) OF TORTS § 821B (1979). *Spur Industries* was brought as a private action based on public nuisance because Webb was able to show that it had suffered particular harm over and above that experienced by the general public. 108 Ariz. at 183, 494 P.2d at 705. Even though the case was really a public nuisance action rather than a private nuisance action, the remedy developed by the court can be easily applied to private nuisance cases.

62. *Id.* at 179, 494 P.2d at 701.

63. *Id.* at 185, 494 P.2d at 707.

64. A careful search of reported appellate decisions from1966-81 produced 37 private and six public nuisance actions involving the externalities from various agricultural operations. While these cases do not constitute a statistically valid sample of all the nuisance actions brought during the period, they indicate that most of the serious complaints about farming concern concentrated animal feeding operations.

65. *See, e.g.,* Clean Water Act of 1977, 33 U.S.C. §§ 1251-1376 (Supp. V 1981); Clean Air Act, 42 U.S.C. §§ 7401-7642 (1976 & Supp. V 1981); Resources Conservation and Recovery Act of 1976, 42 U.S.C. §§ 6901-86 (1976 & Supp. V 1981); National Environmental Policy Act of 1969, 42 U.S.C. §§ 4321-47 (1976); Safe Drinking Water Act, 42 U.S.C. §§ 300f to 300j-10 (1976 & Supp. V 1981); Coastal Zone Management Act of 1972, 16 U.S.C. §§ 1451-464 (1976 & Supp. V 1981); Federal Environmental Pesticide Control Act of 1972, 7 U.S.C. §§ 136-136y (1982); Toxic Substances Control Act, 15 U.S.C. §§ 2601-2629 (Supp. V 1981).

66. *See supra* note 65.

67. *See infra* text accompanying notes 206-219. Congress did leave the states power to establish more stringent standards. *Id.*

68. 33 U.S.C. §§ 1251-1376 (1976 & Supp. V 1981).

69. *Id.* § 1313 (1976 & Supp. V 1981).

70. *Id.* 1288, 1342. For a more detailed analysis of the Act, its antecedents, and its applicability to agricultural pollution, see Beck, *Agricultural Water Pollution Control Law,* in 2 R. DAVIDSON, AGRICULTURAL LAW 141 (1981 & Supp. 1982); Montgomery, *Control of Agricultural Water Pollution: A Continuing Regulatory Dilemma,* 1976 U. ILL. L.F. 533.

71. 33 U.S.C. § 1342 (1976 & Supp. V 1981).

72. *Id.* § 1288.
73. *Id.* § 1344.
74. *See* S. Rep. Mo 95-370, 95th Cong., 1st Sess. 1-2 (1977); 123 Cong. Rec. S 39,170 (1977) (comments of Sen. Muskie).
75. Pub. L. No. 95-217, 91 Stat. 1566 (1978) (codified as amended at 33 U.S.C. §§ 1251-1376 (Supp. V 1981)).
76. 33 U.S.C. §§ 1251(b), 1285(g) (Supp. V 1981).
77. *Id.* § 1342(*l*), 1362(14). This portion of the amendments statutorily reversed the ruling in Natural Resources Defense Council, Inc. v. Train, 396 F. Supp. 1393 (D.D.C. 1975), *aff'd,* 568 F.2d 1369 (D.C. Cir. 1977).
78. Although never funded, this program served as a precursor to the Rural Clean Water Program created by the 1980 Agricultural Appropriations Act. Pub. L. No. 96-108, 93 Stat. 821, 835 (1980) (codified as amended at 33 U.S.C. § 1288(j)(1) (Supp. V 1981)).
79. 33 U.S.C. § 1285(j) (Supp. V 1981).
80. *Id.* § 1344(e).
81. *Id.* § 1344(f).
82. H.R. Conf. Rep. No. 95-830, 95th Cong., 1st Sess. 97, *reprinted in* [1977] U.S. Code Cong. & Ad. News 4424, 4472.
83. 392 F. Supp. 685 (D.D.C. 1975). This definition is coextensive with the reach of federal government powers. *Id.* at 686
84. 33 U.S.C. § 1344(g) (Supp. V 1981).
85. 1 Pollution Control Guide (CCH) 990. Much of this collection and treatment would occur anyway for health and sanitation reasons. *Id.* at 991.
86. 33 U.S.C. § 1342 (1976 & Supp. V 1981).
87. 40 C.F.R. § 122.54(a) (1982). These regulations are part of the consolidated permit requirements which also include regulations for the Hazardous Waste Management Program of the Resources Conservation and Recovery Act of 1976, 42 U.S.C. §§ 6901-86 (1976 & Supp. 1981); the Section 404 Dredge and Fill Program of the Clean Water Act, 33 U.S.C. § 1344 (1976 & Supp. V 1981); and the Prevention of Significant Deterioration Program of the Clean Air Act, 42 U.S.C. §§ 7470-91 (Supp. V 1981). 40 C.F.R. pt. 122, especially subpt. 19D.81 (1982).
88. 40 C.F.R. § 122.54(b)(1) (1982).
89. *Id.* § 122.54 (b)(3).
90. An animal feeding operation is a concentrated feeding operation for purposes of § 122.54 if . . . the following criteria are met:
(a) More than the numbers of animals specified in any of the following categories are confined:
(1) 1,000 slaughter and feeder cattle,
(2) 700 mature and dairy cattle, (whether milked or dry cows),
(3) 2,500 swine each weighing over 25 kilograms (approximately 55 pounds),
(4) 500 horses,
(5) 10,000 sheep or lambs,
(6) 55,000 turkeys,
(7) 100,000 laying hens or broilers (if the facility has continuous overflow watering),
(8) 30,000 laying hens or broilers (if the facility has a liquid manure handling system),
(9) 5,000 ducks, or
(10) 1,000 animal units. . . .
91. An animal feeding operation is a concentrated animal feeding operation for purposes of § 122.54 if . . .
(b) More than the following number and types of animals are confined:

(1) 300 slaughter or feeder cattle,

(2) 200 mature dairy cattle (whether milked or dry cows),

(3) 750 swine each weighing over 25 kilograms (approximately 55 pounds),

(4) 150 horses,

(5) 3,000 sheep or lambs,

(6) 16,500 turkeys,

(7) 30,000 laying hens or broilers (if the facility has continuous overflow watering),

(8) 9,000 laying hens or broilers (if the facility has a liquid manure handling system),

(9) 1,500 ducks,

(10) 300 animal units;

and either one of the following conditions are met: pollutants are discharged into navigable waters through a manmade ditch, flushing system or other similar manmade device; or pollutants are discharged directly into waters of the United States which originate outside of and pass over, across, or through the facility or otherwise come into direct contact with the animals confined in the operation.

Provided, however, that no animal feeding operation is a concentrated animal feeding operation as defined above if such animal feeding operation discharges only in the event of a 25 year, 24-hour storm event.

The term "animal unit" means a unit of measurement for any animal feeding operation calculated by adding the following numbers: the number of slaughter and feeder cattle multiplied by 1.0, plus the number of mature dairy cattle multiplied by 1.4, plus the number of swine weighing over 25 kilograms (approximately 55 pounds) multiplied by 0.4, plus the number of sheep multiplied by 0.1, plus the number of horses multiplied by 2.0.

The term "manmade" means constructed by man and used for the purpose of transporting wastes.

92. Between 35 and 40 states have assumed primary responsibility for administering the NPDES program. BUDGET FOR THE UNITED STATES, FISCAL YEAR 1983, app. I-54 (1982). Their statutes and regulations set standards at least as high as those of the EPA guidelines and often cover smaller operations. *See, e.g.,* IOWA DEPT. OF ENVIRONMENTAL QUALITY, RULES, tit. II (Water Quality), ch. 20 (Animal Feeding Operations) (1976), *reprinted in* ENV'T REP. (BNA) 776:0601; NEBRASKA DEPT. OF ENVIRONMENTAL CONTROL, RULES AND REGULATIONS PERTAINING TO LIVESTOCK WASTE CONTROL (1979), *reprinted in* ENV'T REP. (BNA) 836:0581.

93. 40 C.F.R. § 122.54(c) (1982) provides:

(1) the Director may designate any animal feeding operation as a concentrated animal feeding operation upon determining that it is a significant contributor of pollution to the waters of the United States. In making this designation the Director shall consider the following factors:

(i) The size of the animal feeding operation and the amount of wastes reaching waters of the United States;

(ii) The location of the animal feeding operation relative to waters of the United States;

(iii) The means of conveyance of animal wastes and process waste waters into waters of the United States;

(iv) The slope, vegetation, rainfall, and other factors affecting the likelihood or frequency of discharge of animal wastes and process waste waters into waters of the United States; and

(v) Other relevant factors.

(2) No animal feeding operation with less than the numbers of animals set forth in Appendix B shall be designated as a concentrated animal feeding operation unless:

(i) Pollutants are discharged into waters of the United States through a manmade ditch, flushing system, or other similar manmade device; or

(ii) Pollutants are discharged directly into waters of the United States which originate outside of the facility and pass over, across, or through the facility or otherwise come into direct contact with the animals confined in the operation.

(3) A permit application shall not be required from a concentrated animal feeding operation designated under this paragraph until the Director has conducted an on-site inspection of the operation and determined that the operation should and could be regulated under the permit program.

94. *See, e.g.,* United Staes v. Frezzo Brothers, Inc., 602 F.2d 1123 (3rd Cir. 1979), *cert. denied,* 444 U.S. 1074 (1980), *reopened under* 28 U.S.C. § 2255 (1976), 642 F.2d 59 (3rd Cir. 1981).

95. 33 U.S.C. § 1342 (1976 & Supp. V 1981).

96. *Id.* § 1311(b)(2).

97. *Id.* §§ 1314(b), 1316(b)(1)(A).

98. *Id.* § 1314(a)(4) (Supp. V 1981).

99. *Id.* § 1311 (b)(1)(A).

100. *Id.* § 1311(b)(2)(E).

101. *Id.* §§ 1311(b)(2)(A), (c)-(D).

102. 40 C.F.R. pt. 412 (1982).

103. Dairy Products, 40 C.F.R. pt. 405 (1982); Grain Mills, 40 C.F.R. pt. 406 (1982); Canned and Preserved Fruits and Fruits and Vegetables, 40 C.F.R. pt. 407 (1982); Canned and Preserved Seafood, 40 C.F.R. pt. 408 (1982); Sugar Processing, 40 C.F.R. pt. 409 (1982); Meat Products, 40 C.F.R. pt. 432 (1982).

104. 40 C.F.R. § 412.10 (1982) defines applicability as follows:

The provisions of this subpart are applicable to discharges of pollutants resulting from feedlots in the following subcategories: Beef cattle—open lots; beef cattel—housed lots; dairy cattle—stall barn (with milk room); dairy—free stall barn (with milking center); dairy—cowyards (with milking center); swine—open dirt or pasture lots; swine—housed, slotted floor; swine—solid concrete floor, open or housed lot; sheep—open lots; sheep—housed lots; horses—stables (race tracks); chickens—broilers, housed; chickens—layers (egg production), housed; chickens—layer, breeding or replacement stock, housed; turkeys—open lots; turkeys—housed; and for those feedlot operations within these subcategories as large or larger than the capacities given below: 1,000 slaughter steers and heifers; 700 mature dairy cattle (whether milkers or dry cows); 2,500 swine weighing over 55 pounds; 10,000 sheep; 55,000 turkeys; 100,000 laying hens or broilers when facility has unlimited continuous flow watering systems; 30,000 laying hens or broilers when facility has liquid manure handling system; 500 horses; and 1,000 animal units from a combination of slaughter steers and heifers, mature dairy cattle, swine over 55 pounds and sheep.

105. As defined in 40 C.F.R. § 412.11(b) (1982).

106. Feedlots constructed after September 7, 1973, are subject to new source performance standards which are identical to the BAT effluent guidelines. 40 C.F.R. § 412.17.25 (1982).

107. 40 C.F.R. § 412.12 (1982). *See also* 1 POLLUTION CONTROL Guide (CCH) 989-96. A 10 year, 24 hour rainfall is a storm that produces, in 24 hours, precipitation in an amount that would be expected to fall once every 10 years in a 24 hour period on the average. 40 C.F.R. § 412.11(c) (1982).

108. 40 C.F.R. § 412.17 (1982).

109. 40 C.F.R. § 412.20-.26 (1982).

110. These 1,880 feedlots, however, produce nearly 70% of fed cattle. *See* Martin, *supra* note 19, at 101; STATISTICAL REPORTING SERVICE, U.S. DEPT. OF AGRICULTURE, LIVESTOCK AND MEAT STATISTICS (STAT. BUL 522), SUPPLEMENT FOR 1980, at 55 (table).

111. Forest & Frick, supra note 20, at 122; Rogers, *supra* note 19, at 152; U.S. DEPT. OF AGRICULTURE, ECONOMIC RESEARCH SERVICE, LIVESTOCK AND MEAT; OUTLOOK AND SITUATION 23 (Aug. 1982).

112. Rogers, *supra,* note 19, at 152.

113. *See supra* note 110 and sources cited therein.

114. NCWQ STAFF REPORT, *supra* note 14, at 11-165.

115. I J. JUERGENSMEYER & J. WADLEY, AGRICULTURAL LAW 576 (1982); 33 U.S.C. § 1288(b)(2)(F) (Supp. V 1981).

116. 33 U.S.C. § 1289 (1976), referring to the so-called "level B" plans of the Water Resources Planning Act. 42 U.S.C. §§ 1962 to 1962d-18 (1976 & Supp. V 1981).

117. 33 U.S.C. § 1313(e) (1976).

118. *Id.* § 1288.

119. 546 F.2d 573 (D.C. Cir. 1977).

120. *Id.* at 578.

121. 33 U.S.C. § 1281 (1976 & Supp. V 1981).

122. *Id.* § 1256(f)(1) (1976).

123. *Id.* § 1281(g) (1976 & Supp. V 1981).

124. Beck, *supra* note 70, at 215-35; Schloesser, *supra* note 2; Uchtmann & Seitz, *supra* note 8; Note, *A Procedural Framework for Implementing Non-point Source Water Pollution Control in Iowa*, 63 IOWA L. REV, 184 (1977); Pimentel & Pimentel, *Ecological Aspects of Agricultural Policy*, 20 NAT. RESOURCES J. 55 (1980); Hines, *Farmers, Feedlots and Federism: The Impact of the 1972 Federal Water Pollution Control Act Amendments on Agriculture*, 19 S.D.L. REV. 540 (1974).

125. OFFICE OF WATER AND WASTE MANAGEMENT, U.S. ENVIRONMENTAL PROTECTION AGENCY, IMPLEMENTATION STATUS OF STATE 208 AGRICULTURAL PROGRAMS (draft) 2 (Sept. 1980).

126. *Id.*

127. The twelve states were Maine, Massachusetts, Pennsylvania, Illinois, Michigan, Ohio, Iowa, Montana, South Dakota, Hawaii, New York (with no enforcement provision), and California (water rights regulation). *Id.* at chart I.

128. *Id.* at 2.

129. *Id.*

130. *Id.* at 3.

131. *Id.*

132. U.S. ENVIRONMENTAL PROTECTION AGENCY, GUIDELINES FOR STATE AND AREAWIDE WATER QUALITY MANAGEMENT PROGRAM DEVELOPEMNT app. 4 (1976); 40 C.F.R. § 35.1521-4(c)(1) (1982)

133. U.S. ENVIRONMENTAL PROTECTION AGENCY, *supra* note 132, at app. 4-5; Beck, *supra* note 70, at 228-29.

134. *See* R. Coughlin, Regulatory Approaches by State and Local Governments for Reducing Erosion from Agricultural Lands: A report to the American Farmland Trust (193) (unpublished manuscript)

135. Beck; *supra* note 70, at 225, 227.

136. 33 U.S.C. § 1344 (Supp. V 1981).

137. *Id.* § 1344(a).

138. S. REP. NO. 1236, 92d Cong., 2d Sess. 144 (1972).

139. 33 U.S.C. § 1362(7) (1976).

140. U.S. CONST. art. I, § 8, cl. 3.

141. *I.e.*, those waters below the ordinary high water mark in fresh water and below the mean high water in tidal waters. Blumm, *supra* note 29, at 416.

142. Natural Resources Defense Council, Inc. v. Calloway, 392 F. Supp. 685 (D.D.C. 1975).

143. 40 Fed. Reg. 31,320 (1975). Final regulations were adopted in 1977. 33 C.F.R. 323.3(a)(4) (1982).

144. *Hearings on the Federal Water Pollution Control Act Amendment of 1977 Before the Senate Committee on Environment and Public Works*, 95th Cong., 1st Sess. 517-20 (1977).

145. *See infra* note 146-149 and accompanying text.

146. 33 U.S.C. § 1344(f)(1) (Supp. V1981).

147. *Id.* § 1344(e)(1).

148. Blumm, *supra* note 29, at 431-32.

149. 33 U.S.C. § 1344(g)-(h) (Supp. V 1981). Presumably the states had valid regulatory power over activities that were exempt from Section 404 prior to 1977. Blumm, *supra* note 29 at 455.

150. 47 Fed. Reg. 31, 794-834 (1982) (to be codified at 33 C.F.R. pts. 320-30).

151. 40 C.F.R. § 123.92 (1982). See 45 Fed. Reg. 33,290 33,397-400 (1980) for an evaluation of the farming provisions of these regulations.

152. 33 U.S.C. § 1288(b)(4)(B) (Supp. V 1981).

153. 7 U.S.C. §§ 136-136y (1982).

154. *Id.* § 136a.

155. *Id.* § 136a, 136b.

156. *Id.* § 136j, 136l.

157. Organized Migrants in Community Action, Inc. v. Brennan, 520 F.2d 1161 (D.C. Cir. 1975).

158. 7 U.S.C. § 136a(c)(6) (1982). *See* Spector, *Regulation of Pesticides by the Environmental Protection Agency*, 5 ECOLOGY L.Q. 233 (1975); 2 J. JUERGENSMEYER & J. WADLEY, *supra* note 115, at 50-54; 40 C.F.R. § 1502.22 (1982).

159. OFFICE OF PESTICIDE PROGRAMS, U.S. ENVIRONMENTAL PROTECTION AGENCY, EPA PESTICIDE CANCELLATIONS/SUSPENSIONS: A SURVEY OF ECONOMIC IMPACTS (1980).

160. REGULATORY IMPACT ANALYSIS, *supra* note 18, at 2.

161. *See* United States v. Corbin Far Service, 444 F. Supp. 510 (E.D. Cal), *aff'd.* 578 F.2d 279 (9th Cir. 1978).

162. *See* 2 J. JUERGENSMEYER & J. WADLEY *supra* note 115, at 60-70; Annot., 37 A.L.R.3d 833 (1971).

163. *See, e.g.,* Langan v. Valicopters, Inc., 88 Wash. 2d 855, 567 P.2d 218 (1977).

164. *See, e.g.,* Binder v Perkins, 213 Kan. 365, 516 P.2d 1012 (1973).

165. *See, e.g.,* Shronk v Gilliam, 380 S.W.2d 743 (Tex. Civ. App. 1964).

166. 42 U.S.C. §§ 7401-7642 (Supp. V 1981).

167. *Id.* § 7409.

168. *Id.* § 7410.

169. 123 CONG. REG.. S 26,851 (1977) (statement of Sen. Stafford); *id*, at S 26,852 (statement of Sen. Randolph).

170. CAL. HEALTH & SAFETY CODE: §§ 41850-64 (West 1977 & Supp. 1983), *reprinted in* ENV'T REP. (BNA) 321:0124; CAL. ADMIN. CODE tit. 17, §§ 80100-300 (1983) (Agricultural Burning Guidelines), *reprinted in* ENV'T REP. (BNA) 321.0508.

171. N.J. ADMIN. CODE tit. 7, §§ 7.27-2.1 to .13 (1981), *reprinted in* ENV'T REP. (BNA) 451:0502.

172. COLO. REV. STAT. § 25-7-109 (1973); CODE COLO. REG. pt. 1, Reg. No. 1, § II.C.1.d (1983), *reprinted in* ENVT REP. (BNA) 326:0513.

173. TEX. ADMIN. CODE tit. 31, § 111.2(6) (1982), *reprinted in* ENV'T REP. (BNA) 521:0541.

174. Va. State Air Pollution Control Bd. Regs. app. D (Forest Management and Agricultural Practices) (1983), *reprinted in* Env't Rep. (BNA) 536:0570.

175. Iowa Dept. Rules, div. 400 (Environmental Quality Dept.), tit. 1, ch. 3, § 4.2(3) (1982), *reprinted in* Env't Rep. (BNA) 376:0511.

176. Neb Dept. of Envir. Control, Air Pollution Control Rules and Regs., R 11, §§ 1, 2(d) (1982), *reprinted in* Env't Rep. (BNA) 436:0551.

177. Cal. Health & Safety Code § 41860 (West 1982), *reprinted in* Env't Rep. (BNA) 321:0125.

178. Fla. Dept. of Envir. Reg. Rules § 17-5.06 (1975), *reprinted in* Env't Rep. (BNA) 346:0641.

179. Md. Admin. Code tit. 10, § 10.18.20.04 (1982), *reprinted in* Env't Rep. (BNA) 401:0533.

180. Iowa Dept. Rules, div. 400 (Environmental Quality Dept.), tit. I, ch. 3, § 4.5(1) (1982), *reprinted in* Env't Rep. (BNA) 376:0516.

181. *Id.* § 4.5(3).

182. Colo. Rev. Stat. §§ 35-72-101 to -107 (1973 & Supp. 1982).

183. Code Colo. Regs. pt. 1, Reg. No. 1, § III.D.2.k (1983), *reprinted in* Ev't Rep. (BNA) 326.0518.

184. Ariz. Admin. Comp. R. tit. 9, ch. 3, § $ 9-3-409 (1982), *reprinted in* Env't Rep. (BNA) 311:0523.

185. *Prevention of Significant Deterioration and Nonattainment [Clean Air Act]: Hearings Before the Subcomm. on Health and the Environment of the House Committee on Energy & Commerce*, 97th Cong., 1st Sess. 784 (1981) (statement of Paul Sacia, Legislative Assistant, National Farmers Union).

186. Several studies have examined the macroeconomic efforts on agriculture of federal environmental regulations. *See, e.g.*, Chase Econometric Associates, Inc., The Macroeconomic Impacts of Federal Pollution Control (1975); Hollenback, *The Employment and Earnings Impacts of the Regulation of Stationary Source Air Pollution*, 6 J. Envtl. Econ.& Mgmt. 208 (1979). These studies are inconclusive but had they taken non-market benefits into account, they may well have found that the impact of federal environmental laws on agriculture has been positive. *See* Portney, *The Macroeconomic Impacts of Federal Environmental Regulation*, 21 Nat. Resources J. 459 (1981).

187. 42 U.S.C. §§ 6901-87 (1976 and Supp. V. 1981).

188. In 1976, EPA estimated that between 1970 and 1974 agriculture produced 687 million tons (dry weight) of solid waste. Staff of Subcommittee on Transportation and Commerce of the House Committee on Interstate and Foreign Commerce, 94th Cong., 2d. Sess., Materials Relating to the Resource Conservation and Recovery Act of 1976, at 3 (Comm. Print 1976).

189. *See* 40 C.F.R. §§ 261.4(b)(2), 262.51 (1982).

190. These plans are prepared according to the EPA's Guidelines promulgated pursuant to 42 U.S.C. § 6942 (1976 and Supp. V 1981). *See* 40 C.F.R. § 256.02 (1982).

192. Cal. Govt. Code §§ 66700-96 (West Supp. 1982).

193. Cal. Admint. Code tit. 14, §§ 17129, 17131(a), 17225.3 (1978), *reprinted in* Env't Rep. (BNA) 1121.0504, .0508. The State's Agricultural Solid Waste Management Standards set general levels of performance that are to be met by agricultural operations with respect to disposal of manure, prevention of excessive odor, dust, feathers ad excessive numbers of rodents, flies and other insects. The appropriate state, regional or county enforcement agency is empowered to inspect areas where agricultural wastes are stored and determine whether these levels have been exceeded. *Id.* §§ 17801-24.

194. *See, e.g.*, Colo. Rev. Stat. § 30-20-101(b) (1973); 401 Ky. Admin. Regs. § 2:050 (1981), *reprinted in* Env't Rep. (BNA) 1186.0505 (exempting agricultural wastes returned to the soil as fertilizers or soil conditioners).

195. Letter from James F.Michael, State Programs Branch, Office of Solid Waste, U.S Environmental Protection Agency, to the author (Sept. 16, 1982).

196. See infra notes 223, 261-267, 274-278, 285-288, 291-296, and 297-300.

197. *See supra* notes 10-32 and accompanying text.

198. *See supra* notes 65-195 and accompanying text.

199. *See supra* note 2.

200. RESTATEMENT (SECOND) OF TORTS § 821B (1979).

201. *See supra* notes 48-50 and accompanying text.

202. 1915 Ala. Acts 691 (codified as amended at ALA. CODE § 6-5-127 (Supp. 1982)).

203. N.C. GEN. STAT. §§ 106-700 to -701 (Supp. 1981).

204. N.Y. AGRIC. & MKTS. LAW 1§ 300-309 (McKinney 197 & Supp. 1982).

205. WASH. REV. STAT. ANN. §§ 7.48.300-.310 (Supp. 1983).

206. *See also* Grossman & Fischer, *Protecting the Right to Farm: Statutory Limits on Nuisance Actions Against Farmers*, 1983 WIS. L. REV. 95.

207. Ray v. Atlantic Richfield Co., 435 U.S. 151, 157 (1978).

208. *See, e.g.,* the Federal Pesticide Act of 1978, 7 U.S.C. § 136v (1982); the Noise Control Act of 1972, 42 U.S.C. § 4905(e)(1)(A) (1976); and the Toxic Substances Control Act, 15 U.S.C. § 2617 (1976 & Supp. V 1981), which explicitly prohibit any state or local government from setting standards for new products covered by the federal acts that are not identical to those established by the EPA.

209. Rich v. Santa Fe Elevator Corp., 331 U.S. 218, 230 (1947).

210. City of Milwaukee v. Illinois, 451 U.S. 304, 316-17 (1981). In this case, the Supreme Court held that Congress had occupied the field of water pollution control through establishment of a comprehensive regulatory program, administered by EPA, and thereby had supplanted federal common law principles of nuisance. *Id.* at 317-19. *See also* Middlesex Co. Sewerage Auth. v. National Sea Clammers Ass'n, 450 U.S. 1.22 (1981), where the Court reached the same conclusion with respect to the Marine Protection, Research and Sanctuaries Act of 1972, U.S.C. §§ 1404-44 (1976 & Supp. V 1981).

211. 33 U.S.C. § 1370 (1976). *See* Scott v. City of Hammond, 519 F. Supp. 292, 298 (N.D. Ill. 1981).

212. 42 U.S.C. § 7416 (1976).

213. 42 U.S.C. § 6929 (Supp. V 1981).

214. 42 U.S.C. § 300g-3(e) (1976).

215. 30 U.S.C. §§ 1253, 1255 (Supp. V 1981).

216. S. REP No. 414, 92d Cong. 2d Sess. 81 (1971) *reprinted in* [1972] U.S. CODE CONG. & AD. NEWS 3668, 3746-47

217. *See supra* notes 211-12.

218. 7 U.S.C. § 136v (1982).

219. 15 U.S.C. § 2617 (1976).

220. 1915 Ala. Acts 691 (codified as amended at ALA. CODE § 6-5-127 (Supp. 1982)). The Alabama "right to manufacture" law was passed in response to the Alabama Supreme Court's decision in Shelby Iron Co. v. Greenlea, 184 Ala. 496, 630 So. 470 (1913). The court held that a landowner has no right to build and operate a factory which would be a nuisance to the adjoining land and thus measurably control the uses to which the plaintiff's land might be put in the future. It could not, by the use of its own land, deprive the adjoining owner of the lawful use of this property. It was no defense that the defendant conducted his business with care and skill and with the best equipment available.

221. 1978 Ala. Acts 1967 (codified at ALA. CODE § 6-5-127 (Supp. 1982)).

222. N.C. GEN. STAT. §§ 106-700 to -701 (Supp. 1981). The statute provides as follows:

Nuisance Liability of Agricultural Operations

§ 106-700. Legislative determination and declaration of policy. It is the declared policy of the State to conserve and protect and encourage the development and improvement of its agricultural land for the production of food and other agricultural products. When nonagricultural land uses extend into agricultural areas, agricultural operations often become the subject of nuisance suits. As a result, agricultural operations are sometimes forced to cease operations. Many others are discouraged from making investments in farm improvements. It is the purpose of this Article to reduce the loss to the State of its agricultural resources by limiting the circumstances under which agricultural operations may be deemed to be a nuisance.

§ 106.701. When agricultural operations, etc., not constituted nuisance by changed conditions in locality.

(a) No agricultural operation or any of its appurtenances shall be or become a nuisance, private or public, by any changed conditions in or about the locality thereof after the same has been in operation for more than one year, when such operation was not a nuisance at the time the operation began, provided, that the provisions of this subsection shall not apply whenever a nuisance results from the negligent or improper operation of any such agricultural operation or its appurtenances.

(b) For the purposes of this Article, "agricultural operation" includes, without limitation, any facility for the production for commercial purposes of crops, livestock, poultry, livestock products, or poultry products.

(c) The provisions of subsection (a) shall not affect or defeat the right of any person, firm, or corporation to recover damages for any injuries or damages sustained by them on account of any pollution of, or change in conditions of, the waters of any stream or on the account of any overflow of lands of any such person, firm, or corporation.

(d) Any and all ordinances of any unit of local government now in effect or hereafter adopted that would make the operation of any such agricultural operation or its appurtenances a nuisance or providing for abatement hereof as a nuisance in the circumstance set forth in this section are and shall be null and void; provided, however, that the provisions of this subsection shall not apply whenever a nuisance results from the negligent or improper operation of any such agricultural operation or any of its appurtenances. Provided further, that the provisions of this subsection shall not apply whenever a nuisance results from an agricultural operation located within the corporate limits of any city at the time of enactment hereof.

(e) This section shall not be construed to invalidate any contracts heretofore made but insofar as contracts are concerned, it is only applicable to contracts and agreements to be made in the future.

223. ALA. CODE § 6-5-127 (Supp. 1982); ARK. STAT ANN. §§ 34-120 to -126 (Supp. 1983); CAL. CIV. CODE § 3482.5 (West 1982); COLO. REV. STAT. §§ 35-3.5-101 to -103 (Cumm. Supp. 1982); CON. GEN. STAT. ANN. § 19a-341 (1983); DEL. CODE ANN. tit. 3 § 1410 (Supp. 1982); FLA. STAT. ANN. § 823.14 (West supp. 1983); GA. CODE ANN. § 72-107 (Supp. 1982); HAWAII REV. STAT.§§ 165.1-.4 (Supp. 1982) IDAHO CODE §§ 22-4501 to -4504 (Supp. 1983); ILL. ANN. STAT. ch. 5, § 1101-03 (Smith-Hurd Supp. 1982); IND. CODE § 34-1-52-4 (1983); IOWA CODE ANN. ch. 93A, § 3.12 (West Supp. 1982); KY. REV. STAT. § 413.072 (Supp. 1982); LA. REV. STAT. ANN. tit. 51, § 1202 (Supp. 1982); MD. CTS. & JUD. PROC. CODE ANN. § 5-308 (Supp. 1982); MINN. STAT. ANN. § 561.19 (West Supp. 1982); MISS. CODE ANN. 95-3-29 (Supp. 1982); 1982 Mo Laws 665; 1981 Mont. Laws ch. 123, 170; NEB. REV. STAT. 2-4401 to -4404 (Cumm. Supp. 1982); N.H. REV. STAT. ANN. ch. 430-C (Supp. 1982); N.M. STAT. ANN. §§ 49-9-1 to -4 (1982 Repl. Pampl.); N.Y. PUB. HEALTH LAW § 1300-C (McKinney Supp. 1981); N.C. GEN. STAT. §§ 106-700 TO -701 (Supp. 1981); N.D. CENT. CODE §§ 42-04-01 to -05 (Supp. 1981); PA. STAT. ANN. tit. 3, §§ 951-57 (Purdon Supp. 1983); R.I. GEN. LAWS §§ 2-23-1 to -7 (Supp. 1983); S.C. CODE §§ 46-45-10 to -50 (Supp. 1982); TEX. AGRIC. CODE ANN. §§ 251.001-.004 (Vernon 1981); UTAH CODE ANN. § 78-38-7 to -8 (Supp. 1981); VA. CODE §§ 3.1-22.28 to -22.29 (1983).

224. *See, e.g.,* Born v. Exxon Corp., 388 So. 2d 933 (Ala. 1980) (construing Alabama's "right to manufacture" predecessor to the North Carolina law). *See also* RESTATEMENT (SECOND) OF TORTS §§ 157-66 (1965); Schronk v. Gilliam, 380 S.W.2d 743 (Tex.

Civ. App. 1964) (aerial sprayer held liable in trespass for flying over land and spraying it with a toxic substance).

225. *See, e.g.*, Stone Container Corp. v. Stapler, 263 Ala. 524, 83 So. 2d 283 (1955).

226. 220 Ala. 90, 124 So. 82 (1929).

227. *Id.* at 94, 124 So. at 85.

228. *See* Herrin v. Opatut, 248 Ga. 148, 281 S.E.2d 575 (1981).

229. N.C. GEN. STAT. § 106.701(b) (Supp. 1981).

230. *See, e.g.*, R.I. GEN. LAWS § 2-23-4 (Supp. 1982), which limits the definition to horticulture, viticulture, viniculture, floriculture, forestry, dairy farming, or aquaculture, or the raising of livestock, furbearing animals, poultry or bees."

231. N.C. GEN. STAT. § 106-701(a) (Supp. 1981).

232. *Id. See also* Beam v. Birmingham Slag Co., 243 Ala. 313, 10 So. 2d 162 (1942). The decision points out that even though Alabama's one year statute of limitations for nuisance actions may limit the plaintiff to one year's damages, an activity that was a nuisance at its inception is still subject to being declared a nuisance and is not protected by Alabama's right to manufacture law.

233. *See* Herrin v. Opatut, 248 Ga. 140, 281 S.E.2d 575 (1981).

234. *See, e.g.*, VA. CODE §§ 3.1-22.28 to -22.29 (1983); UTAH CODE ANN. § 78-38-7 (Supp. 1981).

235. N.C. GEN. STAT. § 106.701(c) (Supp. 1981).

236. *See* F. JAMES & G. HAZARD, CIVIL PROCEDURE 240-61 (2d Ed. 1977).

237. *Id.* at 249.

238. *Id.* at 249-53.

239. *See* St. Louis-San Francisco Ry. Co. v. Wade, 607 F.2d 126, 131-32 (5th Cir. 1979), where the court held, in a case involving Alabama's right to manufacture law, that the jury need not consider a plaintiff's second cause of action based on negligence unless it were to conclude that the defendant fell within the statutory exemption and therefore was not liable under non-negligent nuisance theories.

240. N.C. GEN. STAT. § 106.701(a) (Supp. 1981).

241. U.S. CONST. amend. V; amend. XIV, § 1.

242. *See* Penn Central Transportation Co. v. City of New York, 438 U.S. 104 (1978).

243. For a more thorough discussion of the issue see Grossman & Fischer, *supra* note 206, at 136-42.

244. N.C. GEN. STAT. § 106.701(a) (Supp. 1981).

245. *See supra* notes 223-240 and accompanying text.

246. *See, e.g.*, Richards v. Washington Terminal Co., 233 U.S. 546 (1914).

247. *See, e.g., id.* at 548-50.

248. 233 U.S. 546 (1914)

249. *Id.* at 551.

250. *Id.* at 554.

251. *Id.* at 557.

252. *Id.* at 555.

253. *Id.* at 553.

254. *Id.* at 556-47.

255. Justice Holmes noted long ago that: "It is settled that within constitutional limits not exactly determined the legislature may change the common law as to nuisances, and may move the line either way, so as to make things nuisances which were not so, or to make things lawful which were nuisances, although by doing so, it affects the use or value of property." Commonwealth v. Parks, 155 Mass. 531, 532, 30 N.E. 174 (1892).

256. 438 U.S. 59 (1978).

257. 42 U.S.C. § 2210 (1976).

258. 438 U.S. at 88. *But see* In re Air Crash in Bali, Indonesia on April 22, 1974, 684 F.2d 1301, 1312 n. 10 (9th Cir. 1982).

259. 438 U.S. at 88.

260. *Id.* n. 32 (citations omitted).

261. 1971 N.Y. Laws 479 (codified as amended at N.Y. AGRIC. & MKTS. LAW §§ 300-309 (McKinney 1972 & Supp. 1982)).

262. N.Y. AGRIC. & MKTS. LAW § 305(2) (McKinney Supp. 1982) provides:

> No local government shall exercise any of its powers to enact local laws or ordinances within an agricultural district in a manner which would unreasonably restrict or regulate farm structures or farming practices in contravention of the purposes of the act unless such restrictions or regulations bear a direct relationship to the public health or safety.

263. ILL. STAT. ANN. ch. 5 § 1018 (Smith-Hurd Supp. 1982).

264. OR. REV. STAT. § 215.253 (Repl. 1981).

265. PA. STAT. ANN. tit. 3 § 912 (Purdon Supp. 1983).

266. VA. CODE § 15.1-1512B (Repl. 1982).

267. MINN. STAT. ANN. § 473H.12 (Supp. 1982). New York, Illinois, Minnesota, Pennsylvania, and Virginia have also passed right-to-farm laws that follow the Alabama/North Carolina model but are not limited to farming operations located in agricultural districts. *See supra* note 223.

268. Letter from Eileen S. Stommes, Special Assistant for Legislative Affairs, N.Y. Dep't of Agriculture and Markets, to the author (Mar. 3, 1982).

269. N.Y. AGRIC. & MKTS. LAW § 305(2) (McKinney Supp. 1982).

270. *Id.* Since these laws do not restrict private property rights, they do not present any constitutional questions involving the taking or due process clauses. They may, however, impermissibly restrict the powers of home rule municipalities in violation of stat constitutional provisions. *See* Myers, *The Legal Aspects of Agricultural Districting,* 55 IND. L.J. 1, 35 (1979).

271. WASH. REV. CODE ANN. §§ 7.48.300-.310 (Supp. 1983).

272. MICH. COMP. LAWS ANN. §§ 286.471-.474 (1981).

273. KAN. STAT. ANN § 47.1505 (1981).

274. 1979 Wash. Laws, ch. 122, §§ 1-3 (codified at WASH. REV. CODE § 7.48.300-310 (Supp. 1982)). The Act provides:

> [Section 1]. The legislature finds that agricultural activities conducted on farmland in urbanizing areas are often subjected to nuisance lawsuits, and that such suits encourage and even force the premature removal of the lands from agricultural uses. It is therefore the purpose of RCW 7.48.300 through 7.48.310 to provide that agricultural activities conducted on farmland be protected from nuisance lawsuits.
> [Section 2]. Notwithstanding any other provision of this chapter, agricultural activities conducted on farmland, if consistent with good agricultural practices and established prior to surrounding nonagricultural activities, are presumed to be reasonable and do not constitute a nuisance unless the activity has a substantial adverse effect on the public health and safety.
> If that agricultural activity is undertaken in conformity with federal, state, and local laws and regulations, it is presumed to be good agricultural practice and not adversely affecting the public health and safety.
> [Section 3]. As used in Section 2 of this act:
> (1) "Agricultural activity" includes, but is not limited to, the growing or raising of horticultural and viticultural crops, berries, poultry, livestock, grain, mint, hay, and dairy products.
> (2) "Farmland" means land devoted primarily to the production, for commercial purposes, of livestock or agricultural commodities.

275. OKLA. STAT. ANN. tit. 50, §§ 1 to 1.1 (Supp. 1982).

276. ARIZ. REV. STAT. ANN. §§ 3-1051, 3-1061 (Supp. 1982). *See* Comment, *The Arizona Agricultural Nuisance Protection At,* 1982 ARIZ. ST. L.J. 689.

277. KAN. STAT. ANN. § 2.3201-03 (1982).

278. VT. STAT. ANN. tit. 12 §§ 5751-53 (Supp. 1982).

279. WASH. REV. CODE § 7.48.305 (Supp. 1983).

280. *Id.*

281. *Id.*

282. *Id.* § 7.48.310

283. *Id.* § 7.48.305.

284. *See supra* note 64.

285. MICH. COMP. LAWS ANN. §§ 286.471-.473 (Supp. 1982). The Act provides:

Section 1. This act shall be known and may be cited as the "Michigan right to farm act."

Section 2. (1) As used in this act, "farm" means the land, buildings, and machinery used in the commercial production of farm products.

(2) As used in this act, "farm operation" means a condition or activity which occurs on a farm in connection with the commercial production of farm products, and includes, but is not limited to: marketed produce at roadside stands or farm markets; noise; odors; dust; fumes; operation of machinery and irrigation pumps; ground and aerial seeding and spraying; the application of chemical fertilizers, conditioners, insecticides, pesticides, and herbicides; and the employment and use of labor.

(3)As used in this act, "farm product" means those plants and animals useful to man and includes but is not limited to: forages and sod crops, grains and feed crops, dairy and dairy products, poultry and poultry products, livestock, including breeding and grazing, fruits, vegetables, flowers, seeds, grasses, trees, fish, apiaries, equine and other similar products; or any other product which incorporates the use of food, feed, fiber or fur.

Section 3. (1) A farm or farm operation shall not be found to be a public or private nuisance if the farm or farm operation alleged to be a nuisance conforms to generally accepted agricultural and management practices according to policy as determined by the director of the department of agriculture.

(2) A farm or farm operation shall not be found to be a public or private nuisance if the farm or farm operation existed before a change in the land use or occupancy of land within 1 mile of the boundaries of the farm land, and before such change in the land use or occupancy of land, the farm or farm operation would not have been a nuisance.

286. ME. REV. STAT. ANN. tit. 17, § 2805 (1982).

287. TENN. CODE ANN. §§ 43-26-101 to -104 (Supp.1983). It is interesting to note that House Bill No. 1556, the original version, followed Michigan's law virtually verbatim and did not cast the protection in the form of rebuttable presumptions, as did the legislation finally enacted.

288. Right-to-Farm Act, 1983 N.J. Sess. Law Serv. ch. 31 (West) (to be codified at N.J. STAT. ANN. §§ 4:1C-1 to -10).

289. TENN. CODE ANN. § 42-26-101 to 104 (Supp. 1982).

290. *See supra* text accompanying notes 35-50.

291. KAN. STAT. ANN. § 47-1501, -1505 (Supp. 1981).

292. OKLA. STAT. ANN. tit. 2, § 9-202, -210 (West 1941).

293. IOWA CODE ANN. §§ 172D.1-.4 (West Supp. 1982). *See* McCarty & Matthews. *Foreclosing Common Law Nuisance for Livestock Feedlots: The Iowa Statute,* 1980-81 AGRIC. L.J. 186.

294. TENN. CODE ANN. §§ 44-18-101 to -104 (Supp. 1928).

295. WYO. STAT. §§ 11-39-101 to -104 (1979).

296. *See supra* notes 85-114 and accompanying text.

297. W. VA. CODE ANN. §§ 19-19-1 to -5 (Supp. 1983).

298. OHIO REV. CODE ANN. § 929.0 (Supp. 1983).

4399. MASS. GEN. LAWS ANN. ch. 111, § 125A (West Supp. 1982).

300. WIS. STAT. ANN. §§ 814.04(9), 823.08 (West Supp. 1983).

301. *Id.* §§ 91.01-.79. *See infra* text accompanying note 317.

302. For a thoughtful proposal for a "second generation" right-to-farm law, see Thompson, *Defining and Protecting the Right to Farm*, 5 ZONING & PLAN, L. REP. 57, 65 (1982).

303. *See* F. BOSSELMAN & D. CALLIES, THE QUIET REVOLUTION IN LAND USE CONTROL (1973); R. HEALY & J. ROSENBERG, LAND USE AND THE STATES (2d ed. 1979); N. ROSENBAUM, LAND USE AND THE STATE LEGISLATURES (1976); R. COUGHLIN, J. KEENE, J. ESSEKS, W. TONER & L. ROSENBERGER, THE PROTECTION OF FARMLAND: A REFERENCE GUIDEBOOK FOR STATE AND LOCAL GOVERNMENTS (1981) [hereinafter cited as R. COUGHLIN & J. KEENE *et. al.*].

304. MASS. GEN. LAWS ANN. ch. 130, § 105 (West 1981); MASS. GEN. LAWS ANN. ch. 131, § 40, 40A (West 1981).

305. WIS. STAT. ANN. §§ 59.971, 144.26 (West Supp. 1982).

306. HAWAII REV. STAT. ch. 205 (1976 & Supp. 1982). *See* R. COUGHLIN & J. KEENE *et. al., supra* note 303, at 236-38.

307. OR. REV. STAT. ch. 197 (1981 Repl.).

308. *See* R. COUGHLIN & J. KEENE *et. al., supra* note 303, at 239-49; Gustafson, Daniels & Shirock, *The Oregon Land Use Act: Implications for Farmland and Open Space Preservation*, 48 J. AM. PLAN. A. 365 (1982)

309. N.J. STAT. ANN. § 13:18A-1 (Supp. 1983).

310. Adopted pursuant to *id.* § 13:1B15.52. The Guide Plan was given significant effect by the New Jersey Supreme Court when it used the Plan as the centerpiece of its order implementing anti-exclusionary zoning doctrines. Southern Burlington County NAACP v. Mt. Laurel Township, 92 N.J. 158, 456 A.2d 390 (1983).

311. MODEL LAND DEV. CODE (1976).

312. *Id.* art. 7, *See* Mandelkier, *Critical Areas Controls: A New dimension in American Land Use Regulation*, 41 J. AM. INST. PLANNERS 21 (1975).

313. FLA. STAT. ANN. §§ 380.012-.12 (1977 & Supp. 1983). *See* R. HEALY, LAND USE AND THE STATES 103-35 (1976).

314. MINN. STAT. ANN. §§ 16G.01-.14 (1977 & Supp. 1983). *See also* N. ROSENBAUM LAND USE AND THE LEGISLATURES: THE POLITICS OF STATE INNOVATION 73-75 (1976).

315. *See, e.g.,* Geier, *Agricultural Districts and Zoning: A State-Local Approach to a National Problem*, 8 ECOLOGY L.Q. 665 (1980); Gustafson, *Farmland Protection Policy: The Critical Areas Approach*, 36 J. SOIL & WATER CONSERV. 194 (1981); Little, *Farmland Conservancies: A Middleground Approach to Agricultural Land Preservation*, 35 J. SOIL & WATER CONSERV. 204 (1980).

316. ILL. STAT. ANN. ch. 5, §§ 1001-20 (Smith-Hurd Supp. 1982); IOWA CODE ANN. ch. 93, § 1.13 (West Supp. 1982); KY. REV. STAT. ANN. § 262.850 (Baldwin Supp. 1982); Agricultural Retention and Development Act, 1983 N.J. Sess. Law Serv. cha. 32 (West) (to be codified at N.J. STAT. ANN. §§ 4:1C-11 to 37); N.Y. AGRIC. & MKTS. LAW §§ 301-07 (McKinney Supp. 1982); OHIO REV. CODE ANN. § 929 (Page 1983 Leg. Bull.); PA. CONS. STAT. ANN. tit. 3, § 901-15 (Purdon Supp. 1981); VA. CODE §§ 15.1-1506 to - 1513.8 (1950 & Supp. 1982).

317. CAL. GOV'T CODE §§ 51200-295 (West 1983) (Williamson Act); CAL. PUB. RES. CODE §§30000-30900 (West 1977 & Supp. 1982) (California Coastal Act of 1976); HAWAII REV. STAT. § 226 (Supp. 1982); MD. AGRIC. CODE ANN. §§ 2-501 to -515 (Supp. 1982); MINN. STAT. ANN. §§ 473.851-.872 (West 1977 & Supp. 1983); OR. REV. STAT. §§ 197, 215.203-.273 (1981); VT. STAT. ANN. tit. 10, §§ 6000-6092 (1973 & Supp. 1982); WIS. STAT. ANN. § 91 (West Supp. 1982).

318. MINN. STAT. ANN. § 473H (West 1977 & Supp. 1983); Lexington-Fayette County, Ky., Zoning Ordinance 160-80 (Oct. 30, 1980).

319. For an extended discussion of the characteristics, strengths, and weaknesses of agricultural districts, agricultural zoning, and comprehensive agricultural land programs, see R. COUGHLIN, J. KEENE *et. al., supra* note 303, at 76-97, 104-47, 188-253.

320. B.C. REV. STAT. ch. 110 (1970); P.E.I. REV. STAT. ch. L-2 (1974); SASK. REV. STAT. ch. L-2 (1978). *See* W. FLETCHJER & C. LITTLE, THE AMERICAN CROPLAND CRISIS 146-50 (1982); Little, *Farmland Conservancies: A Middleground Approach to Agricultural Land Preservation,* 35 J. SOIL & WATER CONSERV. 204, 206-08 (1980).

321. This program is authorized by Law No. 60-808, 1960 Journal Official de la Republique Francaise (Aug. 7), 1960 Bulletin Legislatif Dalloz 616; Decree 61-610, 1961 J.O. (June 15), 1961 B.L.D. 407; Law No. 62-933, 1962 J.O. (Aug. 10), CODE RURAL art. 188; Ordinance No. 67-824, 1967 J.O. (Sept. 28), 1967 B.L.D. 642.

322. *See* W. FLETCHER & C. LITTLE, *supra* note 320, at 150-53; A. STRONG, PREEMPTION AND FARMLAND PRESERVATION: THE FRENCH EXPERIENCE (1976); A. STRONG, LAND BANKING 171-84 (1979).

323. Letter from Eileen Stommes, Special Assistant for Legislative Affairs, N.Y. Dept. of Agriculture and Markets, to the author (Mar. 3, 1982).

324. R. COUGHLIN, J. KEENE, *et. al. supra* note 303, at 76-93.

325. *Id.* at 206-10.

326. *Id.* at 239-53. *See also* Gustafson, Daniels & Shirock, *supra* note 308, at 365.

327. *See* F. STEINER, ECOLOGICAL PLANNING FOR FARMLANDS PRESERVATION (1981).

Agricultural Research

Policy Issues

B.Y. Morrison Memorial Lecture[1]
Vernon W. Ruttan[2]

Over the last 50 years, U.S. agriculture has been transformed from a resource-based industry to a science-based industry. It has been transformed from a traditional to a high-technology sector. There are relatively few sectors in the U.S. economy that have been able to maintain their technological leadership. Agriculture is one of those sectors. The future growth of the U.S. economy will depend very heavily on those sectors that are able to maintain their technological leadership—that can continue to generate the dividends resulting from productivity growth. We are part of a world in which scientific and technological leadership in agriculture can no longer be ours by default. Some countries seem more willing than the United States

---

[1]The B.Y. Morrison Memorial Lectureship, created in 1968 to recognize outstanding accomplishments in the environmental sciences, is sponsored by the Agricultural Research Service of the U.S. Dept. of Agriculture. The Lectureship commemorates the life and work of the first director of the U.S. National Arboretum. Presented at the 80th Annual Meeting of the American Society for Horticultural Science, McAllen, Texas, on Oct. 18, 1983. The paper draws on material presented at hearings on Industrial Policy by the Subcommittee on Economic Stabilization of the House Committee on Banking, Finance and Urban Affairs, Aug. 4, 1983; Hearings on Agricultural Research, Subcommittee on Departmental Operations, Research and Foreign Agriculture of the Committee on Agriculture, U.S. House of Representatives, June 28, 1983; the Annual Meeting of the American Association for the Advancement of Science, Detroit, May 27, 1983; and the National Industry-State Agricultural Research Council (NISARC) Conference on Recent Federal and State Policy Initiatives Affective Agricultural Research, Arlington, Va., Oct. 12-13, 1982. The author is indebted to Glenn Fine for assistance in preparing the tables and figures.

[2]Ruttan (BA, Yale Univ.; MA, PhD, Univ. of Chicago) has held academic appointments at Purdue Univ. and Univ. of Minnesota. He has served as President of the Agricultural Development Council (1973-1978) and President of the American Agricultural Economics Association (1971-1972). His research has been on the economics of ethical change and agricultural development.

From *HortScience*, December 1983, pp. 809-817. Reprinted with permission.

to recognize and to build on complementarity between the public and private sectors. If we are to realize the gains from this complementarity it will place a special burden on each of the 3 major performers of agricultural research—federal, state, and private—to recognize their responsibility for supporting policies that will maintain the strength of the other two.

Since the mid-1960s, the U.S. federal-state agricultural research system has undergone a series of internal and external reviews. It has been criticized and defended from a variety of scientific, populist, and ideological perspectives. A basic thrust of much of this effort has been to achieve more effective planning and coordination among the several components of the federal-state system. Attempts have also been made to exercise greater federal control over resource allocation in the state system. There have been pressures from the populist front to give greater weight in the research agenda to rural development and to environmental and consumer concerns relative to commodity production; and, there have been pressures from the federal science bureaucracies to substitute competitive grant-funding mechanisms for institutional support in both the federal and the state agricultural research systems.

I do not attempt, in this paper, to review the proposals and counterproposals that have been put forth for reform of the U.S. agricultural research system in detail. The earlier literature has been reviewed in recent books by Anderson (2), Busch and Lacy (4), Hadwiger (9), and Ruttan (21). The more diligent reader is referred to the massive analysis carried out by the U.S. Office of Technology Assessment (16). Many of the issues have been addressed in the recent Winrock Workshop on Critical Issues in American Agricultural Research (25).

I would like to emphasize several of the agricultural research policy issues that have concerned me as I look to the need to strengthen the U.S. agricultural research system.

I am concerned about the tendency to embrace overly simplistic decision rules for the allocation of responsibility for research between the public and private sectors.

One of these dangerous simplifications is the frequently encountered perception that the public sector should have primary responsibility for basic research and the private sector primary responsibility for applied research.

The perception on which this decision rule is based is the "spillover principle." The spillover principle occupies a highly respected niche in the history of economic thought. The implications that flow from application of the spillover principle to the research enterprise are fairly clear. When the benefits from a research activity are sufficiently pervasive or elusive that they cannot be captured in sufficient amount to enable the organization performing the research to realize a reasonable return on its investment, it is in society's interest to bear the cost of the research (15). The only way that society can realize the benefits is to bear the cost.

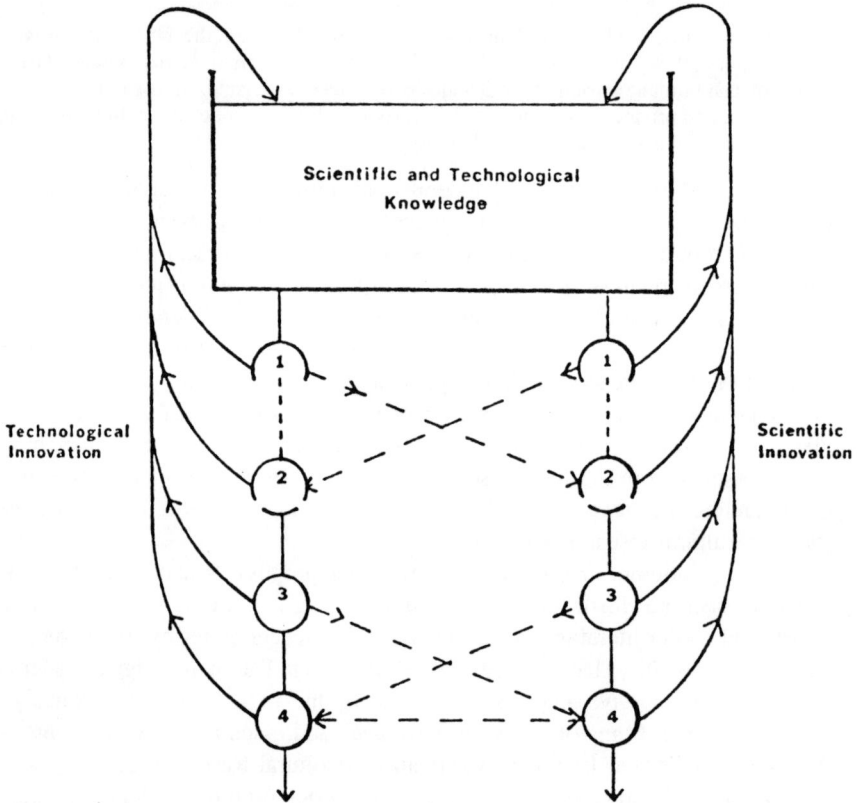

Fig. 1.   The interaction between advances in scientific and technical knowledge.

The spillover principle is so obviously relevant to much of the activity that is conventionally labeled basic research that it elicits very little dissent from even the most libertarian of political philosophers. It helps explain why those private-sector firms that have broad enough product lines to capture the random fallout from basic research—the Du Ponts, General Electrics, IBMs—have been consistently large performers of basic research.

The danger posed by the spillover principle is that its application is so obvious in the case of basic research. Indeed, it is so obvious that there is a temptation to classify any research activity that meets the spillover principle as "basic." But the temptation should serve to remind us that there are broad areas of applied research that meet the test of the spillover principle. For example, much of the agronomic research leading to the design of new production practices, minimum tillage, and other conservation practices will not be done at all unless it is performed by the public sector. We have not yet invented an effective way to package and market the results in a manner that would pay for the cost of the research.

Much of agricultural and industrial research fits an intermediate category. Sufficient gains can be captured to induce a modest level of research expenditure but not enough to induce anywhere near a socially optimum level of research activity. Research in genetics and plant breeding is a useful example. The best available estimates indicate that only about half of the social returns from industrial research and development are captured by the innovating firm (14, 23). I see no reason why these estimates should not apply to industrial research on mechanical technology for agriculture. My guess is that in the area of chemical technology the share of the benefits captured by the innovative firm is somewhat lower than this and in the area of biological technology it may be substantially lower. The result is a substantial underinvestment in agriculturally related research in the private sector. We have not yet designed incentives that induce an efficient level of private research investment.

I am concerned about the need to maintain and to strengthen the articulation between advances in knowledge and technology development and between technology development and improvements in practice.

The productivity of modern agriculture is the result of a remarkable fusion of technology and science. This fusion did not come easily. The advances in cropping practices and tillage equipment in western Europe, from the Middle Ages until well into the 19th century, evolved entirely from husbandry practices and mechanical insights. Lynn White has observed: "Science was traditionally aristocratic, speculative, intellectual in intent; technology was lower class, empirical and action oriented" (24). This cultural distinction persisted in the folklore regarding the priority of basic science over applied science and professional practice (in medicine, engineering, agronomy) long after the interdependence of science, technology, and practice had eliminated the functional and operational value of the distinction.

It is now clear that the basic-applied dichotomy is nowhere near as clear-cut as it appeared to Vannevar Bush and the other architects of post-World War II science policy (5). The orthodox view implies a simple linear relationship between advances in science and technology: "basic science developed theory and understanding; technology took that knowledge and provided blueprints for a change in technology."

As historians of science and technology have begun to examine the processes by which advances in knowledge and technology have actually come about, it has become clear that patterns of interaction tend to be much more complex (Fig. 1). Instead of a single path running from scientific discovery through applied research to development, it is more representative to think of science-oriented and technology-oriented research as two parallel but interacting paths that both lead from, and feed back into, advances in scientific and technical knowledge (12, 13). There are also many direct linkages or interactions that occur at the leading edges of advances in both science and technology.

In some cases a single individual or research team may occupy a leading role in advancing both knowledge and technology. An important historical example is the case of William Shockley and his associates in the solid state research group at Bell Laboratories, which both advanced the theory of semiconductors and made the initial advances in transistor technology. This pattern was clearly evident in the interaction among George H. Schull (Carnegie Institution), Edward M. East and Donald F. Jones (Connecticut Agricultural Experiment Station), and Paul C. Mangelsdorf (Harvard Univ.) in the development and extension of the theory of hybrid vigor and the invention of the double cross method of hybrid seed production (3). It also appears to represent a valid interpretation of some of the interrelationships between scientific and technological advances in biotechnology—in molecular genetics and genetic engineering—that are underway at the present time (21, p. 56-58).

As we reform the institutions that fund and perform agricultural research, it is important that we strengthen the articulation between advances in knowledge, [missing copy] technology, development. The classic explanation for the lag in technology in the United Kingdom during the interwar and early postwar period was that the U.K. had not solved the problem of linking advances in knowledge with advances in technology—that the U.K. had failed to institutionalize the linkages between discovery and development. The recommendations in the 1971 Rothschild report for the establishment of a customer-contract relationship to direct the activities of the national [missing copy] concern (20).

We are now hearing the same explanation that used to be advanced for lagging productivity growth in the U.K., advanced to explain the dramatic decline in productivity growth in U.S. industry since the late 1960s (19). Although the evidence is not yet conclusive, it is hard for me to escape to the conclusion that the institutional changes introduced to implement national science policy

Table 1.   Estimated impacts of research and extension investments in U.S. agriculture (8).

Period and subject	Annual rate of return (%)	Percentage of productivity change realized in the state undertaking the research
1868–1926: All agricultural research	65	not estimated
1929–1950: Technology-oriented agricultural research	95	55
Science-oriented agricultural research	110	33
1948–1971: Technology-oriented agricultural research		
South	130	67
North	93	43
West	95	67
Science-oriented agricultural research	45	32
Farm management and agricultural extension	110	100

after World War II have contributed to the disarticulation rather than to the strengthening of the linkages between advances in knowledge and technology development (22). There is a critical need for the architects of national science policy to give attention to the problem of how to institutionalize more effective articulation between advances in knowledge and advances in technology. And we must be particularly careful, in those areas where articulation is effectively institutionalized, that the reforms that are introduced do not lead to further disarticulation.

I am concerned about the ability of the agricultural sector to sustain a rate of productivity growth that approaches the rate that prevailed during the first 3 decades after World War II.

There are several sources of this concern. One is *the growth of maintenance research relative to productivity enhancing research.* Maintenance research is the research needed to offset the forces that would otherwise result in productivity losses, such as the evolution of pests and pathogens or declines in soil fertility and structure. There is a substantial basis for hypothesizing that the research effort needed to maintain existing productivity levels is a positive function of the level of productivity—that maintenance research must be larger when maize yields are at 8 MT/ha than when they were 2 MT/ha. This implies that if research budgets remain relatively static, a larger share of the total budget will be devoted to maintenance research relative to research designed to advance productivity (21, p. 60).

A second reason for concern is *lagging productivity growth in the agricultural input industries.* These are the industries that embody new scientific and technical knowledge in inputs used in agricultural production—new mechanical, chemical, and biological technologies. This concern about the agricultural input industries goes beyond the weakening of productivity growth in manufacturing. There is also substantial evidence of a decline in productivity in industrial research itself. In the pesticide and animal drug industries, the share of the research budget allocated to defensive research has arisen. And the identification of new chemical entities that eventually are embodied in new products per scientist year is declining (6).

When these considerations are added to a 3rd source for concern, *the lag in public sector research support since the mid-1960s and the more recent slowing of productivity growth indicators* (7), it leads me to anticipate a slower rate of productivity growth in 1980-2000 than in 1950-1980. Even a significant reversal of the lag in research funding can be expected to have little impact on agricultural productivity growth until at least the mid-1990s.

I am concerned about the limited understanding of the implications of the Hatch "formula funding" for state incentives to support agricultural research.

It is becoming increasingly clear from the research productivity studies that a substantial share of the benefits from technology development at the state level

Table 2.   The international agricultural research institutes.'

Center	Location	Research	Coverage	Date of initiation	Core budget for 1980 ($000)^y
IRRI (International Rice Research Institute)	Los Banos, Philippines	Rice under irrigation, multiple cropping systems; upland rice	Worldwide, special emphasis on Asia	1959	16,119
CIMMYT (International Center for the Improvement of Maize and Wheat)	El Batan, Mexico	Wheat (also triticale, barley); maize (also high-altitude sorghum)	Worldwide	1963	17,035
IITA (International Institute of Tropical Agriculture)	Ibadan, Nigeria	Farming systems: cereals (rice and maize as regional relay stations for IRRI and CIMMYT); grain legume (cowpeas, soybeans, lima beans); root and tuber crops (cassava, sweet potatoes, yams)	Worldwide in lowland tropics, special emphasis on Africa	1967	15,106
CIAT (International Centre for Tropical Agriculture)	Palmira, Colombia	Beef; cassava; field beans; swine (minor); maize and rice (regional relay stations to CIMMYT and IRRI)	Worldwide in lowland tropics, special emphasis on Latin America	1968	14,998
WARDA (West African Rice Development Association)	Monrovia, Liberia	Regional cooperative effort in adaptive rice research among 13 nations with IITA and IRRI support	West Africa	1971	2,768
CIP (International Potato Centre)	Lima, Peru	Potatoes (for both tropical and temperate regions)	Worldwide, including linkages with developed countries	1972	8,048
ICRISAT (International Crops Research Institute for the Semi-Arid Tropics)	Hyderabad, India	Sorghum; pearl millet; pigeon peas; chickpeas; farming systems; groundnuts	Worldwide, special emphasis on dry semiarid tropics, nonirrigated farming; special relay stations in Africa under negotiation	1972	12,326

IBPGR (International Board for Plant Genetic Resources)	FAO, Rome	Conservation of plant genetic material with special reference to crops of economic importance	Worldwide	1973	3,124
ILRAD (International Laboratory for Research on Animal Diseases)	Nairobi, Africa	Trypanosoiasis; theileriasis	Mainly Africa	1974	10,443
ILCA (International Livestock Center for Africa)	Addis Ababa, Ethiopia	Livestock production system	Major ecological regions in tropical zones of Africa	1974	8,986
ICARDA (International Centre for Agricultural Research in Dry Areas)	Lebanon and Syria	Crop and mixed farming systems research, with focus on sheep, barley, wheat, broad beans, and lentils	West Asia & north Africa, emphasis on the semiarid winter precipitation zone	1976	11,825
IFPRI (International Food Policy Research Institute)	Washington, D.C.	Food policy	Worldwide	1975	2,400
ISNAR (International Service for National Agricultural Research)	The Hague, Netherlands	Strengthening the capacity of national agricultural research programs	Worldwide	1979	1,199

Source: Crawford, J.G. 1977. Development of the International Agricultural Research System. p. 282–283. In: T.M. Arndt, D.G. Dalrymple, and V.W. Rutan (eds.). *Resource allocation and productivity in national and international agricultural research.* Univ. of Minnesota Press, Minneapolis.
²Budget data for 1980 obtained from the Secretariat for the Consultative Group on International Agricultural Research, World Bank, Washington, D.C.

spill over into other states (or parts of states) with similar agro-ecological (or geoclimatic environments). And a substantial share of the benefit from research designed to produce new knowledge spills over into other agro-ecological regions. In the United States, in the neighborhood of 50% of the benefits from agricultural research in the typical state are captured by other states (Table 1; also 8, 17). It is hard to escape the conclusion that state legislators take this geographic spillover into account, if only implicitly, in decisions about the level of agricultural research fundings.

Federal funds allocated to the states for support of the state agricultural experiment stations are—except for funds reserved for competitive grants— allocated by a formula based on the number of farms and the size of the rural population in each state. Most state legislators provide support for the state experiment stations substantially in excess of the federal matching requirements. It is not unreasonable to view the formula funds as a partial compensation to the individual states for their contribution to economic growth in neighboring states. It also seems clear that the incentive effect would be greater if the formula required the federal government to match state expenditures rather than that the state governments match the federal transfer.

In stressing the importance of institutional support to sustain long-term research efforts, I am not questioning the contribution that an effective competitive grants program can make to the strengthening of agricultural research. Indeed, I consider it important to move the competitive grant funding levels to the

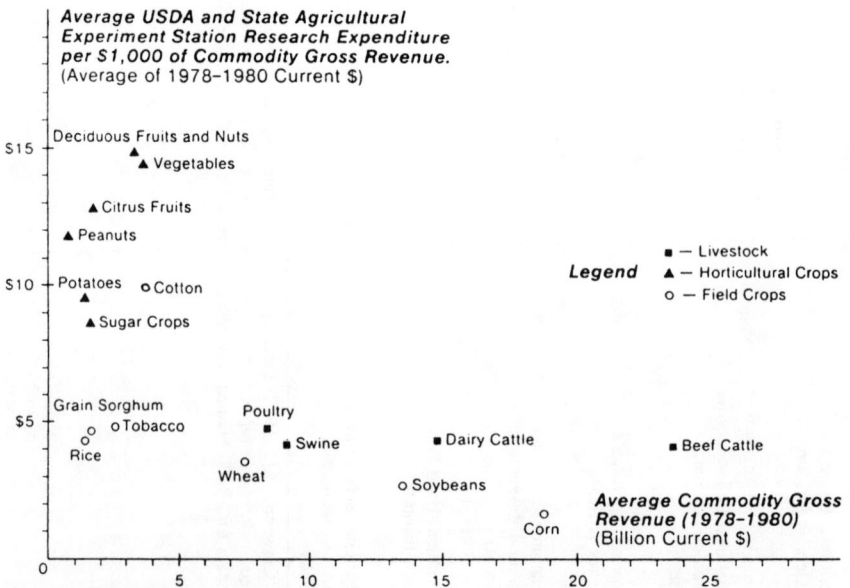

Fig. 2   Average USDA and state agricultural experiment station research expenditures per $1000 of commodity gross revenue.

Table 3. Commodity specific agricultural research expenditure, 1978–1980.[a]

Commodity	1978			1979			1980			Avg research expenditure (million current $)		
	USDA	SAES	TOTAL	USDA	SAES	TOTAL	USDA	SAES	TOTAL	USDA	SAES	TOTAL
Vegetables	14.7	36.4	51.1	15.8	39.6	55.4	15.4	46.7	62.1	15.3	40.9	56.2
Deciduous fruit	13.7	31.6	45.3	14.7	33.7	48.4	13.9	38.9	52.8	14.1	34.7	48.8
Citrus fruit	9.7	11.8	21.5	9.2	12.7	21.9	9.8	13.6	23.4	9.6	12.7	22.3
Potatoes	4.2	8.0	12.2	4.2	8.8	13.0	4.2	9.9	14.1	4.2	8.9	13.1
Sugar crops	6.2	5.1	11.3	7.8	5.0	12.8	7.9	5.4	13.3	7.3	5.2	12.5
Tobacco	5.9	6.2	12.1	4.7	7.0	11.7	4.8	7.9	12.7	5.1	7.0	12.2
Peanuts	3.8	4.3	8.1	3.6	4.5	8.1	3.9	4.9	8.9	3.8	4.6	8.4
Cotton	24.1	11.9	36.0	23.1	12.8	35.9	22.7	15.3	38.0	23.3	13.3	36.6
Rice	2.3	3.5	5.8	2.0	4.0	6.0	2.3	4.6	6.9	2.2	4.0	6.2
Sorghum	2.1	4.7	6.8	2.3	4.9	7.2	2.4	6.7	9.1	2.3	5.4	7.7
Wheat	10.7	12.7	23.4	10.8	14.0	24.8	10.9	17.5	28.4	10.8	14.7	25.5
Soybeans	12.7	20.3	33.0	13.5	22.5	36.0	14.6	28.4	43.0	13.6	23.7	37.3
Corn	11.4	18.3	29.7	12.8	20.6	33.4	12.3	24.7	37.0	12.2	21.2	33.4
Sheep and wool	8.6	8.9	17.5	8.9	9.2	18.1	8.9	11.1	20.0	8.8	9.7	18.5
Poultry	12.8	25.5	38.3	12.6	28.3	40.9	12.3	31.7	43.0	12.6	28.5	40.7
Swine	13.3	21.1	34.4	14.7	24.6	39.3	15.2	29.4	44.6	14.4	25.0	39.4
Dairy cattle	16.3	39.3	55.6	21.7	44.8	66.5	20.0	51.7	71.7	19.3	45.3	64.6
Beef cattle	29.8	56.9	86.7	28.6	64.6	93.2	29.5	75.4	104.9	29.3	65.6	94.9
Subtotal (commodities above)	202.3	326.5	528.8	211.0	361.6	572.6	211.0	423.8	634.8	208.1	370.6	578.7
Other commodities	33.2	67.3	100.5	35.0	74.5	109.4	36.8	87.1	123.9	35.0	76.3	111.3
Not commodity-specific	272.1	255.1	527.3	267.9	282.0	549.9	301.3	342.3	643.5	280.4	293.1	573.6
Total	507.7	648.9	1156.6	513.9	718.1	1231.9	549.1	853.1	1402.3	523.6	740.0	1263.6
Commodity-specific research as a proportion of total (%)	46.4	60.7	54.4	47.9	60.7	55.4	45.1	59.9	54.1	46.5	60.4	54.6

Note: Research expenditure columns for 1978, 1979, 1980 are in million current $.

[a]Sources: 1) *Inventory of Agricultural Research FY 1978*, Vol. 2, USDA, Science and Education Administration, Apr. 1981. 2) Inventory Agricultural Research FY 1979, FY1980, USDA, Cooperative State Research Service, Oct. 1982.

$30 million range as soon as possible. A competitive grant system can be an effective instrument to open up innovative areas of research. Arguments about the merits of institutional and project research support should be cast in terms of the relative mix of the two types of support rather than the absolute merits of either system. But the productivity of the traditional institutional support system has been high. This places a heavy burden on those who would argue for the substitution of a centralized competitive grant system for the traditional institutional support system to demonstrate that such a shift would substantially enhance the productivity of the research effort or draw substantial new resources into agricultural research (21, p. 231).

I am concerned about what appears to be a decline in the attractiveness of graduate education in the agricultural sciences and in the sciences related to agriculture on the part of American students.

Graduate enrollment in the agricultural sciences, and in the sciences generally, on the part of American students declined in the last half of the 1970s and has continued into the 1980s. The decline has been greater in the science-oriented fields than in the more applied or professional fields. Part of the decline in enrollment by American students has been offset by increases in enrollment by non-U.S. citizens. In many departments, non-U.S. citizens now account for more than half of all graduate students (10).

Table 4.   Commodity gross revenue, 1978–1980.[1]

Commodity	Gross revenue (million current $)			Avg gross revenue[2] (million current $)
	1978	1979	1980	
Vegetables	3,661	3,950	4,047	3,886
Deciduous fruit	3,034	3,405	3,489	3,309
Citrus fruit	1,594	1,773	1,905	1,757
Potatoes	1,224	1,172	1,979	1,458
Sugar crops	1,133	1,406	2,084	1,541
Tobacco	2,680	2,154	2,720	2,518
Peanuts	834	819	578	744
Cotton	3,045	4,391	3,987	3,808
Rice	1,087	1,384	1,873	1,448
Sorghum	1,464	1,880	1,696	1,680
Wheat	5,281	8,070	9,278	7,543
Soybeans	12,450	14,250	13,560	13,420
Corn	16,281	19,904	20,571	18,919
Sheep and wool	459	501	494	485
Poultry	7,753	8,606	8,850	8,403
Swine	9,066	9,416	8,847	9,110
Dairy cattle	12,957	14,949	16,890	14,932
Beef cattle	19,554	25,994	25,365	23,638
Total	103,557	124,024	128,213	118,598

[1]*Agricultural Statistics, 1982*, USDA, Washington, D.C., 1982.
[2]Calculated as a simple average of 1978, 1979, and 1980 in current dollars.

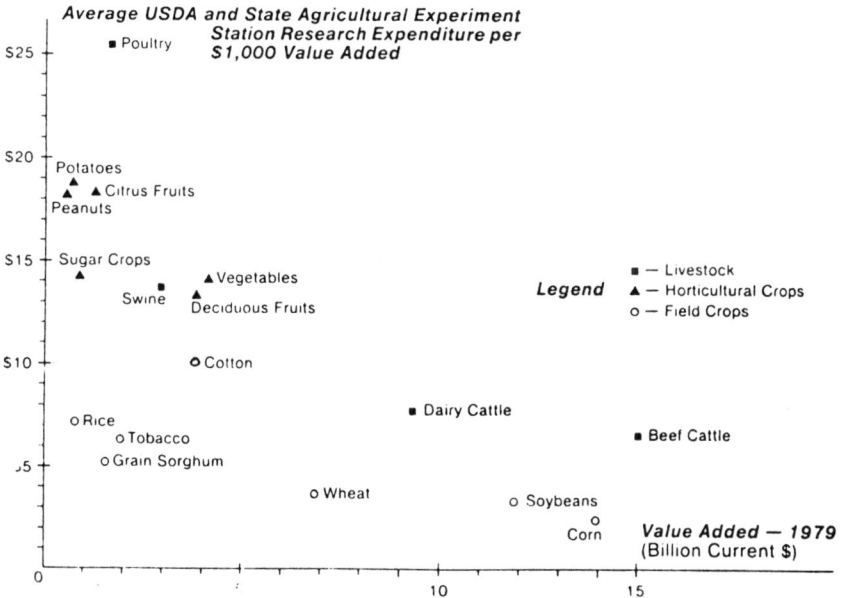

Average USDA and State Agricultural Experiment Station Research Expenditure per $1,000 Value Added

Fig. 3   Average USDA and state agricultural experiment station research expenditures per $1000 of

One implication of these trends is that in another decade students who entered graduate training as non-U.S. citizens will represent a much larger share of graduate research faculty in universities and of research scientists in both public- and private-sector research institutions. In the past, foreign-born and foreign-trained scientists have made major contributions to the advancement of knowledge and the development of technology in the United States. One only has to recall the migration of scientists to the United States from Europe in the 1930s and 1940s. We should welcome growth in the proportion of foreign-born scientists in our laboratories and experiment stations if it is based on the ability of American agricultural research institutions to attract the best graduates in the agricultural and agriculturally related biological and physical sciences. But I would be very worried if the proportion of foreign-born scientists should increase because agricultural research careers become unattractive to the brightest students in our undergraduate programs.

It is doubtful that one can address these issues of the attractiveness of agricultural science effectively without reference to the erosion of the salary structure in the public sector. The erosion has been most severe at the federal level. The lag in federal salaries has resulted not only in the erosion of scientific capacity but also of executive and professional capacity throughout the federal government. I must admit to being surprised that the authors of the Winrock Workshop report on "Critical Issues in American Agricultural Research" (25) were able to address the question of strengthening the federal agricultural research system without addressing the issue of salary level and structure. At present, the primary factor that holds a first-rate federal scientist within the system beyond the midcareer is his or her stake in the federal retirement system. And the federal system is clearly not in a position to bid effectively against either the state system or the private sector for first-rate agricultural scientists or research managers.

I am concerned about the erosion of scientific leadership in federal agricultural research.

My concern includes both scientific leadership and leadership in technology development and programming. This concern does not reflect a lack of confidence in the scientific excellence of the universities or the commitment to technology development and introduction by the private sector. But, neither the universities nor the private sector are capable of providing national program leadership. Fragmentation along institutional and disciplinary lines at the university levels and the pressures arising out of marketing considerations in the private sector preclude such leadership.

Nor is the federal agricultural research system in a position to exercise such leadership. It neither has the scientific capacity nor the bureaucratic structure that it would take to exercise such leadership. But it is the only organization that has

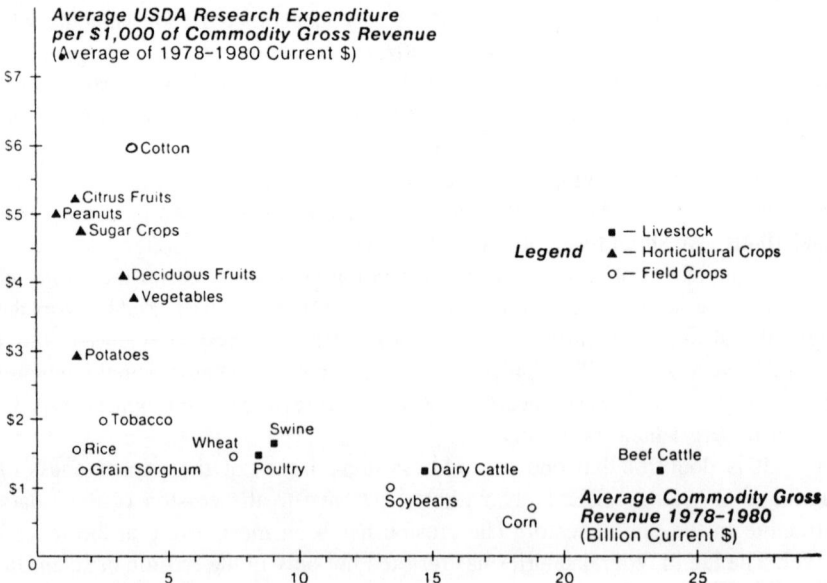

Fig. 4.   Average USDA research expenditures per $1000 of commodity gross revenue.

Table 5. Congruence ratios and average research expenditures per $1000 commodity gross revenue.[a]

| | Congruence ratios[b] | | | | | | | | | Avg (1978–1980) | | | | | |
| | 1978 | | | 1979 | | | 1980 | | | Congruence ratio | | | Research expenditures per $1000 gross revenue | | |
Commodity	USDA	SAES[c]	TOTAL	USDA	SAES	TOTAL	USDA	SAES	TOTAL	USDA	SAES	TOTAL	USDA	SAES	TOTAL
Vegetables	2.05	3.15	2.73	2.35	3.44	3.04	2.30	3.49	3.10	2.23	3.36	2.96	3.95	10.52	14.47
Deciduous fruit	2.31	3.30	2.98	2.54	3.39	3.08	2.42	3.37	3.06	2.42	3.35	3.04	4.28	10.49	14.87
Citrus fruit	3.11	2.35	2.69	3.05	2.46	2.68	3.13	2.16	2.48	3.10	2.32	2.62	5.49	7.26	12.81
Potatoes	.76	2.07	1.99	2.11	2.57	2.40	1.29	1.51	1.44	1.72	2.05	1.94	3.04	6.42	9.49
Sugar crops[d]	2.80	1.43	1.99	3.26	1.22	1.97	2.30	0.78	1.29	2.79	1.14	1.75	4.94	3.57	8.56
Tobacco	1.13	0.73	0.90	1.28	1.11	1.18	1.07	0.88	0.94	1.16	0.91	1.01	2.05	2.85	4.94
Peanuts	2.33	1.66	1.94	2.58	1.88	2.14	4.10	2.57	3.11	3.00	2.04	2.40	5.31	6.39	11.74
Cotton	4.05	1.24	2.36	3.09	1.00	1.77	3.46	1.16	1.93	3.53	1.13	2.02	6.23	3.54	9.89
Rice	1.08	1.02	1.06	0.85	0.99	0.94	0.75	0.74	0.75	0.89	0.92	0.92	1.58	2.89	4.50
Sorghum	0.73	1.02	0.93	0.72	0.89	0.83	0.86	1.20	1.08	0.77	1.04	0.95	1.36	3.26	4.65
Wheat	1.04	0.76	0.88	0.79	0.59	0.67	0.71	0.57	0.62	0.85	0.64	0.72	1.50	2.00	3.52
Soybeans	0.52	0.52	0.53	0.56	0.54	0.55	0.64	0.63	0.64	0.57	0.56	0.57	1.01	1.75	2.79
Corn	0.36	0.36	0.36	0.38	0.35	0.36	0.36	0.36	0.36	0.37	0.36	0.36	0.65	1.13	1.76
Sheep and wool	9.59	6.15	7.60	10.44	6.30	7.82	10.95	6.80	8.18	10.34	6.42	7.87	18.30	20.09	38.58
Poultry[e]	0.84	1.04	0.98	0.86	1.13	1.03	0.84	1.08	0.98	0.85	1.08	1.00	1.50	3.38	4.89
Swine	0.75	0.74	0.75	0.92	0.87	0.90	1.04	1.01	1.02	0.90	0.87	0.89	1.59	2.72	4.35
Dairy cattle	0.64	0.96	0.86	0.85	1.03	0.96	0.72	0.93	0.86	0.74	0.97	0.89	1.31	3.04	4.35
Beef cattle	0.78	0.92	0.88	0.65	0.85	0.78	0.71	0.90	0.84	0.71	0.89	0.83	1.27	2.79	4.06
	1.00	1.00	1.00	1.00	1.00	1.00	1.00	1.00	1.00	1.00	1.00	1.00			
Research expenditure per $1000 gross revenue	1.95	3.15	5.11	1.70	2.92	4.62	1.65	3.31	4.95	1.77	3.13	4.89			

[a]Sources: 1) *Inventory of Agricultural Research FY 1978*, Vol. 2, USDA, Science and Education Administration, Apr. 1981. 2) *Inventory of Agricultural Research FY 1979, FY 1980*, USDA, Cooperative State Research Service, Oct. 1982. 3) *Agricultural Statistics 1982*, USDA, Washington, D.C., 1982.

[b]Computed as dollars of research expenditure per $100 of total revenue for each commodity divided by the average research expenditure per $100 of total revenue. That is:

$$CR_i = \frac{RE_i}{TR_i} \bigg/ \left[\frac{\sum RE_i}{\sum TR_i} \right].$$

where CR_i is the congruence ratio for commodity i in year t, RE is research expenditure, and TR is total revenue.

[c]State Agricultural Experiment Stations.

[d]Includes beets and cane.

[e]Includes eggs, turkeys, and chickens.

the potential capacity for national leadership. I wonder whether today, for example, if it would be possible to mobilize the scientific effort, the technology development, and the field organization that it took to put the screw worm eradication effort into place (18, p. 97-126).

In the past, each of the three major performers of agricultural research—federal research, state research, and private research—could assume the effectiveness of the other two. In such an environment, the rivalry between the state experiment stations and the federal system over budgets and between the public and private sectors over their appropriate roles was not too unhealthy. But we are now in a different world. Any opportunity to strengthen one element in the system must be eagerly embraced and supported by the other agricultural research performers if we are to avoid erosion of the strength of the total system. If the federal system continues to weaken it will weaken the total system.

I am concerned about inadequate articulation among the agricultural research systems in the developed countries.

During the last decade and a half, we have seen the emergence of a new system of international agricultural research institutes in the tropics. This system consists of ten research institutes and three programs (Table 2). It is funded by the Consultative Group for International Agricultural Research (CGIAR) with a general secretariat located at the World Bank and a Technical Advisory Committee (TAC) secretariat located at the Food and Agriculture Organization (FAO) in Rome. Each institute is incorporated separately and has an independent governing board (21, p. 116-146).

The new international system has evolved a highly effective set of institutional linkages with national research systems. It performs an important role in facilitating communication of scientific information, technical knowledge, and genetic material among the national research systems in developing countries. The effectiveness of researchers at remote stations in countries with weak agricultural research systems is greatly enhanced by the international system. For example, the research team at the Mopti rice station in Mali has access, through the West African Rice Development Association (WARDA), to the world collection of rice germ plasm at the International Rice Research Institute in the Philippines and to a communication network that makes the methods and results of rice research throughout the world available to them.

The linkage between the international research system and the national research system in the developed countries is primarily through the bilateral development assistance agencies (the U.S. Agency for International Development and the Canadian International Development and Research Centre, for example) rather than directly to the national research agencies in the developed countries. And there is no comparable institution or set of institutions that provide similar linkages among the national research institutions, or even the research institutions of neighboring provinces or states (between Ontario and Ohio or Michigan, for example) of the developed countries.

Table 6. Value added in U.S. agriculture and research expenditure per $1000 value added for selected commodities, 1979.[z]

Commodity	Value added (million current $)	Value added as % of total revenue[y]	Research expenditure per $1000 value added (1979)		
			USDA	SAES	Total
Vegetable[x]	3,957	89.1	3.99	10.01	14.00
Deciduous fruit[w]	3,586	75.6	4.10	9.40	13.50
Citrus fruit[v]	1,225	66.5	7.51	10.37	17.88
Potatoes	703	58.4	6.04	12.47	18.51
Sugar crops[u]	908	74.9	8.60	5.55	14.15
Tobacco	1,859	85.4	2.51	3.75	6.26
Peanuts	444	54.1	8.18	10.09	18.27
Cotton	3,514	68.9	6.57	3.63	10.20
Rice	849	61.3	2.38	4.67	7.05
Sorghum[t]	1,418	71.3	1.63	3.45	5.08
Wheat	6,408	78.8	1.69	2.19	3.88
Soybeans	11,237	80.0	1.20	2.00	3.20
Corn	13,204	64.4	0.97	1.56	2.53
Sheep and wool[s]	315	75.2	28.39	29.06	57.45
Poultry[r]	1,628	18.6	7.74	17.36	25.10
Swine	2,834	30.0	5.20	8.67	13.87
Dairy cattle[q]	8,686	58.1	2.49	5.15	7.64
Beef cattle[p]	14,358	54.7	1.99	4.50	6.49

[z]Sources: 1) Kunz, J.J. and J.C. Purcell. 1982. Value added (created) in United States agriculture. Interregional Cooperation Publication of the State Agricultural Experiment Stations, IR-6 Office, Suite 101, Commonwealth Building, 1300 Wilson Boulevard, Rosslyn, VA 22209. (IR-6 Information Report 61). 2) *Inventory of Agricultural Research FY 1979, FY 1980*, USDA, Cooperative State Research Service, Oct. 1982.

[y]From Kunz and Purcell.

[x]The value added total includes tomatoes, lettuce, dry edible beans, onions, sweet corn, mushrooms, cucumbers, celery, cabbage, carrots, snap beans, sweet potatoes, broccoli, asparagus, green peppers, green peas, cauliflower, spinach, garlic, green lima beans, escarole/endive, mint, dry edible peas, eggplant, beets, and artichokes.

[w]The value added total includes apples, grapes, almonds, peaches, strawberries, cherries, pears, prunes and plums, muskmelons, walnuts, avocadoes, pecans, watermelon, cranberries, hops, blueberries, apricots, honeydew melons, nectarines, olives, red raspberries, figs, pistachios, filberts, dates, and blackberries.

[v]The value added total includes oranges, grapefruit, lemons, tangerines, temples, limes, and tangelos.

[u]Includes beets and cane.

[t]Includes grain sorghum.

[s]Includes sheep, lambs, and wool.

[r]Includes eggs, turkeys, and chickens.

[q]Corresponds to the "milk" category in Kunz and Purcell.

[p]Corresponds to the "cattle and calves" category of Kunz and Purcell.

The productivity of the U.S. agricultural research system since World War II has, in my judgment, induced a sense of complacency about the gains that might be realized by closer collaborations among the research systems of the developed countries. While the number of scientists in the U.S. system has remained static since the mid-1960s, the number of scientists in national agricultural research systems in Western Europe, Japan, and the U.S.S.R., have experienced substantial growth (8).

There is inadequate effort on the part of the U.S. agricultural research

Average USDA Research Expenditure
per $1,000 of Commodity Value Added.

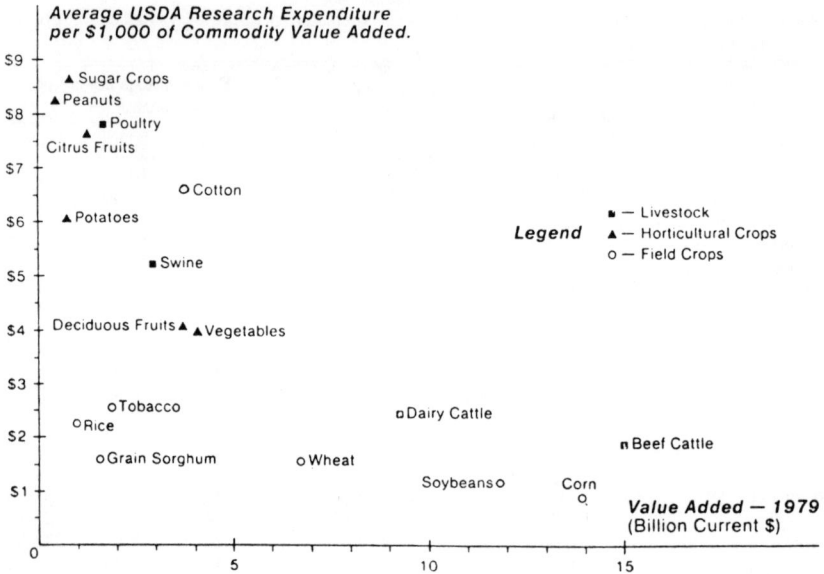

Fig. 5.   Average USDA research expenditures per $1000 of commodity value added.

system to a) monitor the progress of agricultural research, b) support participation in scientific meetings, or c) engage in systematic exchange of scientific staff with the agricultural research institutions in other developed countries. These efforts vary greatly among commodity areas. They are perhaps strongest in the area of wheat breeding. But in most commodity areas such exchanges appear to be much less well-organized.

I am concerned about our continuing inability to bring information and analytical capacity from the natural and social sciences to bear on research resource allocation decision processes.

The issue of research resource allocation and planning is one that often generates a strong emotional response on the part of both research scientists and managers. This response is frequently induced by concern about who will have the authority for research planning. In spite of these concerns, central management and planning staffs have been mandated by the legislative and budget agencies responsible for allocating resources to research. Central management and planning staffs have been strengthened in most national agricultural research systems.

The planning staffs and administrators responsible for research resource allocation have not found it easy to respond to the expectations that their efforts would contribute to greater efficiency in the use of research resources or to greater relevance in research resource allocation. They have been pressed to respond to a succession of styles in analysis and planning: project and priority weighting or scoring of research objectives in the mid-1960s, program planning and budgeting in the early 1970s, and the rhetoric of technology assessment in the mid-1970s. By the late 1970s, the program planning and budgeting methodology, which had temporarily fallen into disrepute as a result of the gap between promise and performance, had been resurrected under the rubric of zero-based budgeting.

As research-planning staffs have struggled with the demands placed on them, it has become increasingly obvious that effective research planning requires close collaboration among natural and social scientists. This is because *any research resource allocation system, regardless of how intuitive or how formal, cannot avoid making judgments about two major questions.*

The first question is: *what are the possibilities of advancing knowledge or technology if resources are allocated to research on a particular commodity, a particular resource problem, or a particular disciplinary or scientific field?* If, for example, resources are allocated to the transfer, development, or enhancement of nitrogen-fixing capacity to grasses, what is the probability of success? The answer to such questions can only be provided with any degree of authority by scientists who are on the leading edge of the research discipline or problem being considered. The intuitive judgments of research administrators, even those who were formerly scientists, or research planners and economists must be discounted severely in attempting to answer such questions.

The second question is: *what will be the value to society of the new knowledge or the new technology if the research effort is successful?* If efforts to develop nitrogen-fixing capacity in maize are successful, for example, will it

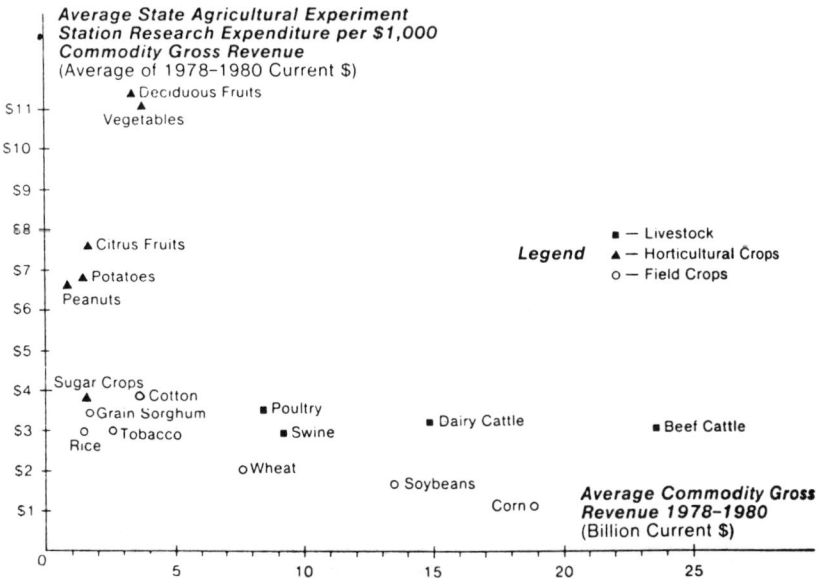

Fig. 6. Average state agricultural experiment station research expenditures per $1000 of commodity gross revenue.

become an efficient source of plant nutrition when evaluated in relation to the economic and environmental costs and returns to other forms of fertility enhancement? The answers to such questions require the use of formal economic and other social science analysis. The intuitive insights of research scientists and administrators are no more reliable in answering questions of value than the intuitive insights of economists and planners in evaluating scientific and technical potential.

Yet the planning of research resource allocation remains largely intuitive. Formal methods have been tested and largely rejected (21, p. 275-294). The new six-year research plan prepared by the USDA Agricultural Research Service drew on very little analytical capacity in making judgments about the value of alternative research priorities (1). The research resource allocation decisions at the state experiment stations are made primarily at the department—rather than the experiment station—level.

The research resource allocation model implicit in the questions that commonly are raised by both scientists and administrators has been called the parity or the congruence model. The question that is usually asked in the application of the parity or congruence model is how do research expenditures by commodity compare to the relative economic importance of a particular commodity. Does the expenditure of $13 per $1000 of sales in the case of potatoes and less than $3 per dollar of sales in the case of soybeans represent an efficient allocation of research resources? (Fig. 2-7).

One implicit assumption of the parity or congruence model of research

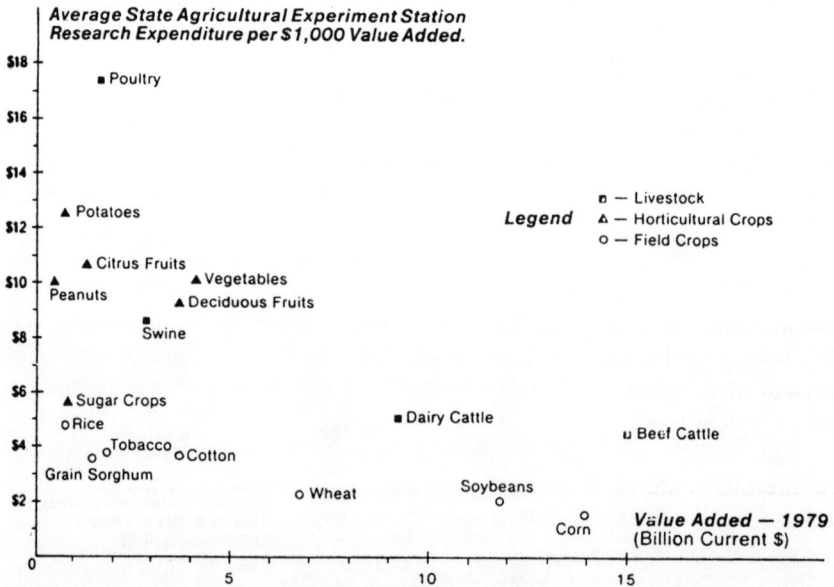

Fig. 7.   Average state agricultural experiment station research expenditures per $1000 of commodity value added.

resource allocation is that the benefits from research are proportional to the size of the research budget relative to the economic importance of the commodity sector, resource input, or field of science to which the research effort is directed. A second assumption is that the opportunities for productive scientific or technical effort are equivalent in each area of commodity, resource, or disciplinary research activity. Both assumptions are clearly naive. No one believes that either assumption is valid.

In the absence of specific knowledge of research opportunities and payoffs, application of the parity or congruence model may not be entirely inappropriate. But whether one accepts the model as a primary criterion for the allocation of research resources or as a point of departure for the fine-tuning of research budgets, a research manager can hardly begin to make useful allocation decisions in the absence of at least the following congruence calculations:

●A comparison of the ratio of research expenditure by commodity to the value added to national product by each commodity.

●A comparison of the ratio of research expenditure by factor (or resource input) to the cost or economic value of the factor in production.

●A comparison of the ratio of research expenditure to the value added at each stage in the food production chain from purchased inputs to the consumer.

The compilation of a set of research parity or congruence accounts does not imply that resources should be allocated by the parity or congruence model. It does suggest that an explicit rationale should be developed for any departures from the parity rule. When departures are observed, there should be a reason. There should be a reason why our public research system pursues research on peanuts more than four times as intensively and on wood more than fifteen times as intensively as on wheat. Is it because a dollar saved on wool import [missing copy]

But if the parity rule is inadequate, where can one look for more adequate criteria for research resource allocation? I have reviewed the several formal methodologies in considerable detail (21, p. 267-294). In my judgment, the formal analytical approaches represent useful methodologies for refining the judgments of research scientists and administrators. But they divert too many resources from the practice of science when implemented on a regular basis. And they have great difficulty in achieving compatibility between decision-making at the individual scientist or scientific team level and decision-making at the research system level.

Increasingly powerful methodologies are, however, becoming available to the directors of individual research programs, research institutes, and experiment stations for interpreting scientific, technical, and economic information in a manner that can increase the effectiveness of research efforts, whether evaluated in terms of advance in knowledge or technology. To have access to those methodologies, resources must be devoted to interdisciplinary experimental and systems modeling research in areas described by rubrics such as yield constraint and crop loss modeling, plant growth modeling, and selection indexes.

The major advantage of these methodologies is that they can be carried out as an integral component of ongoing research programs. Their results become directly available to individual scientists and research teams. The results can be fed back immediately into research planning and design. And the results can also be fed forward to the central research management and budgetary units. These methodologies add precision to decentralized research decision-making where the relationship between knowledge generation and decision-making is most fully informed. They

[missing copy].

NOTES

1. Agricultural Research Service. 1983. Agricultural Research Service program plan: 6-year implementation plan, 1984-1990. USDA Agricultural Research Service, Washington, D.C.

2. Anderson P. P. 1982. The role of agricultural research and technology in economic development. Longman, New York.

3. Becker, S.L. 1976. Donald Jones and hybrid corn. Conn. Agr. Expt. Sta. Bul. 763.

4. Busch, L. and W.B. Lacy. 1982. Science, agriculture and the politics of research. Westview Press, Boulder, Colo.

5. Bush, V. 1945. Science: the endless frontier; a report to the President in a program for post-war scientific research. National Science Foundation, Washington, D.C. (reprinted July 1960).

6. Council on Agricultural Science and Technology. 1980. Impact of government regulation on the development of chemical pesticides for agriculture and forestry. Ames, Iowa. (CAST Report 87).

7. Eddleman, B.R. 1982. Impacts of reduced federal expenditures for agricultural research and education. National Agricultural Research Planning Project, IR-6 Information Rpt. 60.

8. Evenson, R.E., P.E. Waggoner, and V.W. Ruttan. 1979. Economic benefits from research: an example from agriculture. Science 205:1101-1107.

9. Hadwiger, D.F. 1982. The politics of agricultural research. Univ. of Nebraska Press, Lincoln.

10. Huffman, W. 1981. Research training: PhD degrees awarded in fields associated with agriculture and home economics by land grant universities, 1920-1979. Dept. of Economics, Iowa State Univ., Ames. (mimeo.)

11. Judd, M.A., J.K. Boyce, and R.E. Evenson. 1983. Investing in agricultural supply. Yale Univ. Economic Growth Center, New Haven, Conn. (mimeo).

12. Kuhn, T.S. 1962. Scientific discovery and the role of invention, p. 450-457. In: R.R. Nelson (ed.). The rate and direction of incentive activity: economic and social factors. Princeton Univ. Press, Princeton, N.J.

13. Layton, E.T., Jr. 1979. Scientific technology: the hydraulic turbine and the origins of American industrial research. Technology & Culture 20:69-89.

14. Mansfield, E., J. Rappaport, A. Romeo, S. Wagner, and G. Beardsley. 1977. Social and private rates of return from industrial innovations. Quart. J. Econ. 91:221-404.

15. Nelson, R.R. 1959. The simple economics of basic scientific research. J. Political Economy 67:297-306.

16. Office of Technology Assessment. 1982. An assessment of the U.S. food and agricultural research system. National Technical Information Service, Springfield, Va.

17. Otto, D.M. and J. Havlicek, Jr. 1981. An economic assessment of research and extension investments in corn, wheat, soybeans and sorghum. Virginia Polytechnic Institute and State Univ., Department of Agricultural Economics Research Rpt. SP-818, Blacksburg, Va.

18. Perkins, J.H. 1982. Insects, experts and the insecticide crisis: the quest for new pest management strategies. Plenum Press, New York.

19. Press, F. 1982. Rethinking science policy. Science 218:28-30.

Financial Crisis in Agriculture: Discussion

Mark Drabenstott*

The United States has just endured the most severe, protracted period of farm financial stress in nearly half a century. This invited papers session serves the helpful purpose of sorting out the effects of the farm recession, distilling the policy issues that emerge from this period, and directing the profession to a number of important research questions.

Boehlje and Eidman advance a theoretical framework for examining farm firm survival. The model they present, containing some new approaches and directing emphasis to new decision variables, should be a worthy construct to address public policies and their impacts on farm firms. The authors make an excellent case for focusing more attention on the collateral and liquidity characteristics of assets. These attributes have been largely overlooked by economists and the Boehlje-Eidman theoretical structure provides appropriate variables and rules to incorporate them into prudent management decisions.

The Boehlje-Eidman paper follows a conceptual approach, not an empirical one. Nonetheless, greater discussion of the lessons farm producers learned from agriculture's financial crisis would have established more fully the real-world setting of their model. The extended farm recession has driven home a number of management principles, both new ones and revisited ones, and these warranted greater attention than the paper accorded them.

---

*Mark Drabenstott is a senior economist with the Economic Research Department of the Federal Reserve Bank of Kansas City.

The views and opinions expressed herein are solely those of the author and do not necessarily represent those of the Federal Reserve Bank of Kansas City or of the Federal Reserve System.

From *American Journal of Agricultural Economics*, December 1983, pp. 955-57. Reprinted with permission.

Two primary implications of the financial crisis for producers can be noted. First, growth strategies must account for changing economic ground rules. As real interest rates rise, firms must shift from debt to retained earnings to finance expansion, a lesson many aggressive producers have learned only belatedly. Second, farm producers must be total risk managers—making simultaneous decisions to manage production, marketing, and financial risks. The prospect of continued interest rate volatility as a result of deregulation and Federal Reserve operating procedures will continue to accentuate financial risk management, as have the past three years.

Boehlje and Eidman discuss bankruptcy as an alternative method of firm survival. Realistically, this option may exist for only a relatively small number of farmers since rising bankruptcy numbers would rather quickly lead to higher borrowing costs, thus negating some benefits. Moreover, bankruptcy does highlight a number of questions involving the equitable treatment of various creditors, as noted in a recent *Wall Street Journal* article.

The Boehlje-Eidman framework inspires a number of farm policy issues relating to financial stress and farm firm survival. Perhaps most fundamental among these is, what is the appropriate role for public policy in the cyclical adjustment process? Should the United States provide a safety net for all producers in farm sector downturns, or should some market adjustments be allowed to occur? Answers to these questions must recognize at least three factors: the role of past policies in influencing current conditions, the desired long-run equilibrium productive capacity of the sector, and the distributional impacts of policies designed to smooth the adjustment process.

The long-run structure of the farm sector is a related and substantial policy issue. The size of the sector obviously will depend on growth in domestic and foreign markets, as well as policies directed at these objectives. The types of firms that make up the sector will be determined by economic efficiency and farm policies. Should farm programs focus on more efficient farms, the largest firms that control the vast majority of farm sales? Or should program benefits be based more on equity, providing assistance to smaller farms that rely more heavily on off-farm income?

Barry and Lee identify the numerous types of risk that lenders currently face and examine the impact of the farm recession on all agricultural lenders during a period of significant change in the regulatory and financial market environment. They conclude that farm credit problems have been serious but manageable for lenders. Against a backdrop of prominent media attention to the farm crisis, this conclusion may deserve more emphasis. Forthcoming work by Hughes, including additional empirical results, further shows that the financial condition of farm lenders remains strong (Hughes).

Barry and Lee correctly identify the mix of risks that lenders now encounter in a fast-changing operating climate shaped by two dominant forces—farm recession and deregulation. In sorting out lenders' responses to change, however, one might delineate the effects according to their causes and their potential long-term significance more completely than did the authors. The most fundamental implication of the farm recession for lenders may be a shift from equity-based loans to cash flow-based loans. Deregulation, on the other hand, carries two primary implications. First, it highlights lenders' portfolio risk. Second, it underscores the competitive nature of today's financial services marketplace, in terms of both price and service offerings.

The authors accurately assert that increased farm loan delinquencies have kept farm loan rates higher, portfolio spreads wider, loan maturities shorter, and loan volume lower than otherwise would have occurred. As lenders adapt to deregulated financial markets, however, some of these cyclical responses to financial stress may be less pronounced in the future because increased competition will tend to diminish spreads and increase loan volume.

Banks have sought greater flexibility from examiners during the farm financial crisis, as noted by Barry and Lee. Indeed, the farm recession has highlighted the appropriate measures banks and regulators must consider in the face of mounting farm loan problems. It should be added, however, that with continued weakness in the farm economy, loan classifications at rural banks are still increasing, thus signalling some continued stress for these banks.

Barry and Lee refer to the potential removal of agency status as a significant regulatory risk for the farm credit system (FCS). The system does, however, face other substantial regulatory risks. For example, the removal of agency status may be linked to some offsetting benefits that might be negotiated as a *quid pro quo*, such as the right to accept deposits or to make loans to nonagricultural businesses. Should this occur, the FCS would become more like a national financial service institution and would encounter new risks as a consequence.

Barry and Lee acknowledge the large role of government credit programs in absorbing serious problem loans during the farm financial crisis. They conclude that efficient lender responses to financial stress of the types discussed lessen the need for additional public credit programs. Nonetheless, the future role of such programs remains a substantial and political issue. If future farm policy is more market oriented, with reduced public credit programs, private lenders likely will feel the effect of future farm recessions more acutely than the most recent one.

Both papers leave unaddressed two broader aspects of the farm financial crisis. First, U.S. agriculture has undergone significant secular as well as cyclical change. National economic policies oriented toward reducing inflation, changing export patterns and policies, financial markets that pass through higher and more volatile interest rates to the sector—these and other factors have reshaped U.S. agriculture and its future. Important questions arise concerning the substantial adjustments that the farm sector is undergoing. How much cyclical adjustment to the farm recession has been made? What more basic, long-term adjustments remain? For producers, secular change will redefine appropriate growth strategies and financial management. For lenders, managing portfolio risk and competing for deposits and loans likely will be a more enduring challenge than coping with farm recession.

Second, the implications of farm financial crisis extend well beyond just producers and lenders; agribusinesses also have been seriously affected. The weakened financial position of many suppliers, processors, and farm cooperatives likely will leave a legacy of businesses that are streamlined and fewer in number. This holds implications for producers that rely on this infrastructure as well as for lenders who provide credit to both producers and agribusinesses. The plight of agribusinesses also raises the issue of how farm program benefits should be distributed to improve the total farm economy.

U.S. agriculture is passing through a dynamic era. The policy challenges are and will continue to be many. Determining the proper role for emergency government lending, providing appropriate assistance to new entrants to agriculture, preventing programs that smooth cyclical adjustment from distorting long-term market price signals, examining the structural changes in lending institutions to agriculture—these are but a few of the issues that confront economists and policy makers.

REFERENCES

Hughes, Dean W. "The Financial Condition of Agricultural Lenders in a Period of Farm Sector Distress." *Econ. Rev.* Federal Reserve Bank of Kansas City, July/August 1983.

Wall Street Journal, "Farmer's Recovery Reflects the Strengths and Weaknesses of U.S. Subsidy Programs," 18 July 1983.

Financial Crisis in Agriculture: Discussion

John R. Blake*

These two papers present useful views of financial stress and implications. Missing, however, was a definition of financial stress. Financial stress results from a perceived inability to meet planned cash flow commitments. Such commitments stem from family living needs, cash farm expenses, debt service, etc.

Financial stress is a cash flow concept and does not directly coincide with net income or profitability, though obviously they are related. For example, an investment in durables or real property may be profitable based on rate of return. Yet the investment may still create cash flow problems and financial stress.

Inability to meet financial commitments reflects unfavorably on the business and the manger or operator. It indicates a need for decision on someone's part: the operator, to make adjustments and/or revisions in commitments so they can be met; or the lender, to salvage his investment before further losses occur. When a business cannot meet commitments or gets too far in arrears, the game is over and the business is terminated. Hence, the time frame for adjustment is typically short term once a business starts to experience financial stress.

With respect to the current financial stress in agriculture, certainly few operators, or lenders for that matter, would have made contractual commitments they did not expect to keep. Simply put, expectations were erroneous. Economic events did not occur as expected. Further, the economic downturn was severe enough to shake expectations of continued future capital gains. In 1982, twenty-seven years of uninterrupted land value appreciation were broken with a value decline.

Financial stress in 1981-83 began with lower farm incomes. However, it

---

*The author is the W. I. Myers Professor of Agricultural Finance at Cornell University.

From American *Journal of Agricultural Economics*, December 1983, pp. 953-954. Reprinted with permission.

differed from previous periods of stress with at least two new components. *(a)* The expected ability to borrow periodically on capital gains disappeared with the reality of asset value decreases. *(b)* Of much more importance, the cash flow required to service previous debt commitments became substantially larger with rapidly rising interest rates. Floating interest rates on a substantial amount of outstanding debt were passed through to the borrower in a magnitude well beyond previous experience. Given the important influence of debt service burden on financial stress, those hardest hit, in general, were operators who recently started farming or recently undertook a major debt-financed expansion. These events turned our focus to financial stress, cash flow problems, and means for adjustment.

Boehlje and Eidman consider implications for producers. The refer to debt/income ratio, higher interest rates and interest payments as evidences of financial stress. However, what is really needed is a measure of debt service burden of farmers. Data on gross cash flows of the agricultural sector including scheduled term debt repayment would permit a much improved analysis compared to the net flows and net changes in outstanding debt now being published.

Boehlje and Eidman state that farmers restructured their balance sheets during the 1970s, shifting current assets to long-term assets. It is true that sector balance sheets were less liquid by 1981 than in 1973. But, the question is, did farmers choose to restructure or did the market restructure their balance sheets? My perception is that the aggregate restructuring resulted less from farmers' actions and more from changes in market values. Boehlje and Eidman suggest the need for a higher proportion of current assets relative to long-term assets for liquidity purposes. If current assets/current liabilities is a measure of liquidity, then liquidity could also be improved by shifting current liabilities to long term.

The differentiation Boehlje and Eidman make between collateral value of an asset and liquidity (or liquidation) value leaves me a bit uneasy. Are these really measures of the same thing viewed from two different perspectives? The lender assigns collateral value supposedly based on what he could net in case of default. Liquidity (liquidation) value is also an estimate of net salvage value, but presumably from the asset owner's standpoint. Were Boehlje and Eidman trying to say that liquidity value in a period of financial distress may be well below expected liquidity or collateral value in more normal times? Or are they differentiating based on who receives the proceeds? At any rate, liquidity value is not a new concept. It is no more than the salvage value of an asset. When the return of a factor in the business becomes less than its value for salvage, the appropriate decision is to sell it. The changed emphasis from Boehlje and Eidman is that liquidation value and future returns may have to be evaluated in terms of contribution to survival of the firm rather than to profits. Future returns may have to be truncated since, without short-run survival, there are no future returns.

Boehlje and Eidman present a model for discussing financial stress. The model specifies fourteen factors that affect financial stress. All fourteen of these factors are described as stochastic. In emphasizing the many factors of importance, they did not elaborate on possible relationships. In periods of severe financial stress such as 1981-83, most, if not all, of these factors are highly correlated. Substantially lower earning rates on assets tend to be associated with decreased net cash flow, reduced or negative capital gains, reduced liquidity, and lower collateral values. While debt-servicing requirements need not be correlated with the others, from 1979-82, the debt-servicing burden also contributed to financial stress. What are the implications for producers when the factors affecting survival are not only stochastic in nature but are highly correlated as well?

Boehlje and Eidman discussed several useful strategies for dealing with financial stress. Their discussion of chapter 11 bankruptcy was particularly appropriate as a means of reorganization. Perhaps some producers might even consider using the threat of chapter 11 as a means to pressure informal acceptance of a plan for debt restructuring.

The Barry and Lee paper is an excellent summary of the current situation and adjustments being made by lenders. Let me reemphasize a few points. *(a)* Rural areas and farmers are no longer insulated from national money markets and interest rates. As future changes in financial markets occur, these changes will be quickly transmitted to rural areas. *(b)* With deregulation of financial markets and institutions, there are many more, and more complex, decisions for rural bank management to make. Bank management, as they said, must become more sophisticated to remain competitive.

One intriguing part of their paper concerns PCA losses in the Fourth Farm Credit District where 60% of total loan loss reserves were charged off. Why were losses so severe in that area? Was it an institutional phenomenon, a type of farming phenomenon, or neither? Were there no implications for lenders or lessons to be learned from that experience? The shift in non-real estate debt from PCA to government lenders in the fourth district suggests there are some implications to lenders from the severe financial stress in that district.

Barry and Lee mention the Economic Emergency and Emergency Annual Production loan programs of FmHA. Did some of the riskier debt get transferred from conventional lenders to FmHA in the late 1970s before the current period of stress? If so, how much more severe would the financial stress of 1981-85 have been if this shifting had not occurred? Perhaps risk of government policy changes should be included as a seventh risk in their list.

Does financial stress contribute to changes in market shares of agricultural lenders? Is there evidence that recent financial stress led to greater retrenchment by one lender group than another? Were there differences by region? These are questions which might have been addressed. My own reading of market-share changes is that these are affected more by alternative opportunities of various lender groups than by markedly different reactions to financial stress in the sector. But, I would like to hear what Barry and Lee have to say on this.

Comparative Advantage in an Interdependent World: The Need for a Realistic Agricultural Policy for the U.S.

Orville L. Freeman*

Let me tender my apologies for this ambitious title. When Dean Rusk invited me to address this important export conference he, reasonably, asked me to address myself to "some aspect of agricultural exporting." But the more I thought about it, the more it became clear to me that there is no aspect of agricultural exporting that can be usefully addressed in isolation. Indeed, U.S. agriculture—both its fabulous and problem-fraught productive capacity and its vital function in the U.S. trade balance and in the role the U.S. plays in the current world economy— cannot be assessed, or even described, without analyzing the connections and complexities that constitute reality today.

So I decided to go for broke and share with you my thoughts on what is needed to hammer out a comprehensive agricultural policy for the U.S. that will be responsive both to domestic concerns and international requirements.

I would like to emphasize my profound conviction that the active participation of every one of you here is essential in defining and structuring such a policy and in assisting the process of implementation.

This is, I believe, a vital task. If the United States of America is going to continue its world leadership as well as improve the well-being of her own people, it is critical that we have a policy with clear-cut goals and objectives. I am certain that if there is public understanding, support and participation, an agricul-

---

*Chairman, Business International Corporation; Export Conference Dean Rusk Center School of Law March 30, 1984.

"Comparative Advantage in an Interdependent World: The Need for a Realistic Agricultural Policy for the U.S.," in *Perspectives on the Future of American Agriculture,* hearing before the Joint Economic Committee, September 27, 1984, pp. 7-19.

tural policy will evolve that is responsive to reality, and that the President of the U.S. will be able to provide the leadership to put such a policy in place and carry it forward to execution.

FACTS AND FIGURES

Before addressing directly what I think an agricultural policy for this nation should encompass, permit me to identify the facts and forces that must be factored into a realistic policy. First and foremost is the critical importance of American agriculture to the well-being of our people and to our constructive role as leader of the free world. It is not an overstatement, I believe, to describe the accomplishments of American agriculture as the number-one production miracle in the history of mankind. Today only 2% of the population of the U.S. is on the farm. On the average, each of the farmers feeds 76 Americans at prices that are lower as a percentage of personal income than they are anywhere else in the world. In addition, agriculture, directly and indirectly, is responsible for approximately 25% of U.S. employment.

Between 1965 and 1980, while farm population decreased by one half, annual output in constant dollars tripled, increasing by over $100 billion. Between 1970 and 1982, grain production in the U.S. climbed from 170 million metric tons to 330 million metric tons. And while U.S. exports climbed from 38 million MT to 150 million MT, Soviet imports climbed from 8 million MT to 43 million MT. American family farm agriculture accomplished this with 350 million acres of land under plow, in contrast to the 500 million acres cultivated in the Soviet Union. The $44 billion worth of American agricultural exports in 1981 were an essential offset to our otherwise rapidly deteriorating balance of trade and current account.

AT THE CROSSROAD

Despite this unexcelled record, American agriculture today stands at a troubled and uncertain crossroad. All is *not* well on the farm. Aggregate income is the lowest it has been in 50 years. Farmer return on equity in 1981 and 1982 was a negative 9.2% and 6.5 %, respectively, and will probably be negative again in 1984. Land values declined for the first time in 27 years. Exports have slipped in the last two years, suffering a 20% shrinkage. The debt/equity ratio is way up as farm debt climbed 300% between 1971 and 1983. Bankruptcies and foreclosures are sharply on the rise. The cost of price-support production control programs has zoomed, reaching a record $18.9 billion in fiscal 1983. If one includes the cost of the PIK program, price support costs were actually $28.3 billion, 10 times the average annual cost in the 20-year period from 1961 to 1981, and five times higher than the largest expenditures in those two previous decades.

WHAT WENT WRONG?

It is my contention that these adverse developments call for a careful, thoughtful reexamination of where we have been, where we are, and where we want to go. Only if there is recognition and understanding of the massive change that has taken place in American agriculture can we develop a viable and workable policy that will make it possible for this nation to regain lost ground and to take appropriate advantage of the magnificent productive plant that we have built over the past generation.

How, then, did we lose ground? How did we get ourselves into the mess we're in? The answer to that question is, of course, complex. But the key point is that agricultural policy, as implemented over the last two decades, has not reflected the fact that American agriculture is no longer national in scope. It is international. We are no longer relatively isolated from the rest of the world in any way.

To illustrate: In the 1950s, agricultural exports were less than 10% of cash farm receipts. Today, exports represent 30% of total cash receipts and 54% of crop receipts; production of four acres out of every 10 is destined for foreign markets. Typically, we export a fourth of the U.S. corn crop, half of the soybean crop, 60-65% of the wheat crop, and over 40% of cotton and rice crops.

THE GLOBAL CONNECTION

What these figures demonstrate, dramatically and incontrovertibly, is that for the U.S. agricultural plant to be continuously operated at an acceptable capacity level, foreign market share must be maintained and expanded. Farmers and agribusiness alike now have a vital stake in international conditions, economic and political, a stake that did not exist before the last decade.

THE NEW UNCERTAINTIES

Agriculture, as all of you are aware, has always been subject to great uncertainties. Historically, these uncertainties were predominantly on the supply side. No one can control the weather. Disease and pests, equally unpredictable, also seriously affect supply. Adjusting production to signals in the marketplace is much more difficult, and the lead time required much longer than that for industry. These uncertainties continue. But uncertainties in demand have now become as great, or even greater, in the internationalized marketplace. Let me sketch for you two scenarios that will manifest these new uncertainties.

A GROWTH SCENARIO

The first scenario can be properly labeled a growth scenario. It starts with the fact that the middle-income developing countries increased their imports of grain from 12.7 million MT in the years 1960-63 to 44.7 million MT in 1977-79. With their own annual economic growth in a 5-7% range, these countries became an explosive market for agricultural products, particularly grain, resulting in firm and growing prices. Had the world not slipped into a major recession in 1980 and, with it, the threatening debt overhang we face today, U.S. agricultural exports would not have slumped. As a matter of fact, had economic growth continued in those countries and around the world, the 38 low-income developing countries, whose increase in agricultural imports had climbed only to 8.7 million MT a year, would have accelerated their purchases as well.

It follows from this that, if the world returns to a reasonable level of growth and prosperity, with favorable growth rates in the developing world, the demand for food, and particularly for protein, would again explore. That is where future markets will be found. In fact, a number of studies projecting such growth conclude that there is actually a serious threat of major shortfalls. Some studies estimate a shortfall of as much as 70 million MT of grain by the turn of the century. Obviously, if this should happen, U.S. agriculture would respond, assuming we still have the productive capacity. Prices would move up solidly and American agriculture would prosper. That is one scenario.

A COMPETITIVE SCENARIO

A more realistic scenario, given the current world economy still largely bogged down in recession, with the heavy debt overhang inhibiting growth and expansion of developing world markets, is that for at least the next four or five years, there will be strong competition for commercial world markets. During the late 1970s, the U.S. became, in many respects, a residual supplier. This occurred in part because of a very strong dollar, and also because of price-support levels that were higher in some instances than the prices our competitors in world markets were able to offer. This we can no longer afford.

U.S. policy, resting solidly on our comparative advantages as an agricultural producer, must be to move more aggressively into world markets and be prepared to meet competition everywhere. I emphasize *meet competition*. We would make it crystal clear that the U.S. will not *initiate* export subsidies.

However, we should also send a strong signal that if our competitors in the world market engage in export subsidies we will match them.

THEREFORE . . .

This nation, built on private enterprise in a competitive market place, should firmly set the course for an open, competitive world, with agriculture in the lead. In the process we can point the way for the industrial side of our economy to reverse its current tilt toward protectionism.

THE SKEWED STATE OF AFFAIRS

Currently, world agricultural markets are in an abnormal state. On a global basis, production has been expanded significantly as our competitors have been favored by excellent yields in the last few years.

At the same time, global demand has fallen sharply because of the world recession. The result is a glut of grain. The total carryover of grain stocks, plus the equivalent of idle acres in the U.S., had climbed to an all-time high of 283 MT or, in terms of world consumption days, to 68 days. For perspective, this carryover compares to 104 days in 1961 when I became Secretary of Agriculture. The problem we face in these terms is thus not a new one.

The immediate result is weak market prices and an acute recession in the agricultural sector of the U.S. economy. Given these circumstances—and they are likely to recur in unpredictable but inevitable cycles—the U.S. must have in place a domestic farm program to support and assist the American farmer. To make the program work, experienced and competent management must be in place.

POLICY PREMISES

The policy premise for this program is twofold:

First, the production capacity of the U.S. agricultural sector must not be seriously eroded. History has shown that we, at home, and the world internationally, will need American production capacity when global economic cycles emerge from their trough.

Second, and equally important as a policy imperative, both fairness and equity demand support by the government of this nation to the farmers who have contributed so much to our economic well-being, and who are uniquely subject to uncontrollable external causes, and to cyclical movements and global interactions.

Nevertheless, a policy and program to accomplish what, for want of a better word, I will call this defensive purpose, must be sensitive to global realities and designed in a fashion that does not result in the U.S. pricing itself out of world markets.

A FEASIBLE PROGRAM

Let me offer some ideas on how I think this can be done and on what it will take to design an agricultural policy for the US that will effectively integrate both domestic and international realities.

It must be recognized that this offensive will be a different kind of game than we have known in the past, requiring a wider range of skills, resources and initiatives. An exporting strategy based on the notion that it can expand sales simply by writing orders will fail. We will have to do our homework. Americans will have to research potential customer countries in terms of their total requirements. We will have to look at consumer needs and wants, purchasing power, political pressures, the needs for infrastructure such as port facilities and transportation, and customer countries' needs for new production, storage, and processing technology, as well as farm products. In short, we will have to size up these opportunities in terms of packages that meet the customer's needs.

Happily, the U.S. is solidly positioned to put such packages together and to tie them to a sensible domestic farm program.

Since 1954, and the passage of PL 480, this country has, on a concessional basis, moved over $100 billion of food and fiber to meet human needs, contribute to economic development, and build commercial export markets in developing countries all over the world.

Shipments since 1954 have ranged from 15.3 million MT of grain in 1967 to an estimated 4 million MT in 1983. In the process we have learned how food abundance can be effectively utilized. We have also learned how, if carelessly managed, it can be counterproductive.

AN INTERNATIONAL INITIATIVE

It is my conviction that the time has come to combine that knowledge and our farm abundance into a solid, efficient, international agricultural initiative.

Such an initiative should have four components.

Humanitarian

We should reach out all over the world to help feed truly needy people. A major effort with a significant U.S. contribution is now under way in drought-stricken Africa. That effort must be strengthened and expanded. In addition to relief, food aid should be tied into self-help projects focused on improving production potential, aimed especially at small producers.

Developmental

The U.S. should expand its economic development assistance program to many more developing countries. Food aid can be used to stimulate agricultural development in developing countries. Food-for-work programs, building needed infrastructure, can be highly successful if well managed.

Title 3 of PL 480 provides for the U.S. to grant money it receives for agricultural commodities back to the country to finance agricultural development projects, with forgiveness of funds if the project is successful. The authority of Title 3 could be expanded to help finance investment by American agribusiness companies in developing countries. The present initiative of the Bureau for Private Enterprise in the AID Agency can make good use of Title 3. It should be given more support and resources.

THE INDUSTRIAL POLICY CONTEXT

Our nation is engaged today in a great debate on industrial policy. We are trying to identify what should be the relationship between the government and the private sector as American industry faces new technology, new challenges, and new competition around the world. One can hardly pick up a newspaper or tune in a television station without exposure to the question of how to relate government and the private sector as we go forward to meet competition in world markets and successfully accommodate basic structural change.

There is no doubt in my mind that the private sector moves technology to use more efficiently than does the government, and that this is true in developing countries as much as in industrialized ones. Obviously, profit and risk criteria must be met if private agribusiness companies are to invest in the developing world and move modern technology in production and marketing to small farmers in developing countries. My point here is that identifying these win-win opportunities for private sector activity in the developing world, and encouraging U.S. companies to respond, could and should be an important ingredient of our national agricultural policy. Designed in close cooperation between government and business at the highest level, this kind of global enterprise would have a triple dimension for the U.S.: It would yield profits; it would build export markets; and it would make friends in the political arena.

A GRAIN "SDR"

Another innovative way of putting American food abundance to constructive use in solving pressing global problems would be for the U.S. government to make available to the International Monetary Fund a substantial volume of wheat, in addition to the credit already recommended by the President. The IMF could use this wheat to alleviate the debt loads that now plague many of the developing countries. The wheat could be supplied by the IMF to grain-importing LDCs, with payment negotiated over a period of time at appropriate levels of interest. Such a move would make it possible for hard-pressed LDCs to use foreign exchange they would otherwise spend on grain imports to meet their international obligations, or to invest in internal growth and development.

Marketing-Minded

We must expand our market development activities, coordinating them closely with our economic development initiatives. Since the mid-1950s, the U.S. has run a remarkably successful foreign market development program for agricultural products. It is a cooperative program between the Foreign Agricultural Services of the U.S. Department of Agriculture and some 60 private commodity organizations, ranging from wheat and flour to raisins. The costs of these programs are shared by government and the commodity groups. These market development efforts need to be expanded. They should command top priority and adequate resources.

Competition-Oriented

The U.S. must fight unfair trade competition wherever it occurs, particularly in nations that use export subsidies, or have erected import barriers for agricultural products. This means developing a long-term strategy to prevent some countries from putting up new protective barriers and getting other nations to reduce unfair levels of protection, such as Japan still has for beef and citrus. Measures to fight protection and subsidies must be specifically targeted. The U.S. must convince other nations that we are serious about unfair practices and that we will take steps to make these practices so costly that others will be discouraged from using them. Measures the U.S. can use range from instituting countervailing subsidies to limiting access to the U.S. market if we don't have fair access to other markets.

A PROFILE OF U.S. AGRICULTURE TODAY

Before I proceed further with my policy recommendations on the domestic side, let me sketch for you a concise profile of what American agriculture looks like today. You may find the portrait surprising.

At present, approximately 112,000 farms—5% of the total number of farms—produce just under 50% of the entire output of food and fiber originating in the continental U.S. These are operations that had annual sales of $200,000 or more in 1981. It is important to remember that these major producers are mostly family farms, not what we think of as corporate farms. The great bulk, somewhere around 95%, are individually owned and operated family farm businesses.

At the other end of the scale are the large majority of farms, 1.7 million of them, comprising 71% of all economic units classified as farms by the USDA. These are generally small farms, frequently worked part time, with off-farm income covering a major portion of the family living expenses. These 1.7 million farm units, with annual farm sales of less than $40,000, produce only 12.5% of total U.S. output.

The final feature of the profile consists of the medium-sized traditional family farms. These make up a little less than our fourth of all farms, some 580,000. They are predominantly family-owned and -operated, with the owner-operator engaged full-time in farming pursuits. Sales run between $40,000 and $200,000 annually. In the aggregate, these medium-sized farms produce 38.5% of the output of U.S. agriculture.

So we have three general classes of farming enterprise that are different in size, productivity and income requirements. How then should a comprehensive, national farm program relate to each of these three groups?

A THREE-PRONGED APPROACH

Let us consider first the largest farms—the 5% who produce approximately 50% of the total output. According to a number of studies, these farms have cost structures that allow them to be profitable. They have, in recent years, benefited greatly from government programs, but there is considerable question as to how important those programs really are to the continued economic vitality of these larger farms; they could probably make it on their now.

The small farmers, too, are economically strong, albeit in a different way. Because their off-farm earnings are sufficient to fully offset the small losses of income from farming, these small farmers are relatively well off in economic terms, and apparently satisfied with their ability to live in rural areas and pursue farming as a secondary, part-time, or in some cases "hobby" operation.

The middle group, however, is in a different situation. Recent research by Texas A&M University covering cotton farms in Texas' southern high plains clearly suggests that government farm programs have been of major benefit to these medium-sized farm operators. The Texas study found that, without a program along the lines of the farm program of 1981, only 42% of the medium-sized traditional family farms would survive over the next decade. In contrast, the Texas A&M Study found that 98% of the smallest farms would be able to survive for 10 years without any program. And the largest farms—those over 4,400 acres—would survive without any government programs. I think we can conclude that it is the middle category of farms where a long-range farm program is needed for economic survival.

NO CHANGE

Let me stress in this context that I foresee no drastic alterations in this profile. All the evidence from agricultural scholars concurs that, for the foreseeable future, the composition of the U.S. agricultural sector will remain much as it is now.

The real question, therefore, is how can a program or programs be developed to meet the economic, social and cultural conditions of these diverse groups?

I have already cited evidence that the small producers would survive without any programs. National agricultural policy can do little to help or hurt this group of farms. However, state programs in the areas of education, health, medical service, roads, schools, etc. *are* important to the economic and social well-being of this group of nearly two million American families.

The group of large farmers would also do well without federal farm programs. These are educated, innovative producers, well financed, efficient, highly mechanized. They can compete effectively in both domestic and world markets. They are fully poised to take advantage of the food requirements of the world for the remaining years of this century.

The needs of this group will be best served by constructive trade and macroeconomic policies. These producers will benefit from government development efforts to stimulate the national economies of the world so that there is capability to purchase the needed food commodities, including those produced in the U.S. Export credit assistance efforts; export market development assistance; sensible, consistent international trade policy; stable and reasonably valued currency; good infrastructure in the way of transportation and port facilities—these are the policies that will benefit this group of highly efficient farm businessmen. Domestically, they need some assistance from public institutions in research, and a stable, economic climate of growth.

There is, however, one additional policy element to be considered for these large farm producers: However well trained, educated, financed, mechanized and efficient, they are still subject to the vagaries of nature. And because their market is international, they are also subject to global uncertainties and shifts in the economic and political climate. These factors, coupled with the large capitalization and credit requirements of farms with sales of $200,000 or more, subject these larger farmers to a much higher level of risk than many other businesses. Long-term policy should therefore provide a way to cushion the risk faced by this very important part of our productive economy.

At a minimum, a long-range farm program should provide a world market cleaning non-recourse loan program for the large producers. This loan program would enable them, in periods of extreme adverse conditions, to assure orderly marketing and some degree of risk-sharing with the public. Such price support loans could be based on a three-year or five-year moving average of the world market prices or some significant percentage of that level.

An additional idea, which deserves further study and consideration, is the possibility of providing a mechanism whereby these large producers would have both the legal and economic ability to limit their production in periods when favorable weather conditions and unfavorable market conditions have combined to produce excess supplies. I have in mind a system in which, under a government-refereed and -sanctioned referendum, large producers of the major commodities could vote to decide if they wanted to have mandatory acreage and production adjustments so as to maintain a reasonable supply-demand balance. There would be little or no expenditures of public funds to carry out such a program. It would provide the economic and legal mechanisms to avoid wasteful and economically disruptive short-term surplus buildups.

Finally, and undoubtedly the most difficult challenge, is the effort to devise a sensible program to deal with the medium-sized family farmers. I believe we need to offer these farmers some system of income transfer protection, perhaps similar to the existing target-price concept. A scheme could be developed that would assure these farms a return from the marketplace, and from the farm program, that would enable the most efficient of them—and this would be a majority—to continue to be viable contributors to our society. Not incidentally, such a program might well include a requirement that the farmer follow sound soil-conserving practices.

Dealing fairly with these farmers is important to the national weal, not only because they produce nearly 40% of our total food and fiber output, but also because they are a vital part of the social and cultural fabric of rural American and, indeed, the nation. A modest expenditure of well under 1% of the national budget could, in my judgment, be justified to protect and preserve this important part of our society.

THE NEED FOR COORDINATION

A meaningful agricultural policy, responsive to international and domestic realities, requires effective coordination of private and public programs and initiatives. As matters now stand, a wide range of activities need to be tied into logical and sensible packages. Currently, no person or group is performing this function. Recently, at the initiative of the Ohio Farm Bureau, a number of agricultural leaders got together in Chicago to discuss the need for a new leadership position to represent the private sector in export development for agriculture. I find much merit in their recommendations. But I believe we need more than a new leader in the private sector. We need a leader/spokesman to articulate and coordinate a new agricultural policy for this nation, indeed for the world. I suggest he, or she, be a presidential appointee with Cabinet rank. This Cabinet member should not have direct line responsibility, but should have the complete confidence of, and direct access to, the President. This would make it possible for him, or her, to coordinate across the entire U.S. government and the private sector, speaking with one voice for, and on behalf of, the President on all issues and topics involving U.S. agricultural policy. This person would also maintain direct contact with foreign governments, at the highest level, to measure, in concert with the resident U.S. Ambassador, the Secretary of State, the Administrator of AID, and the U.S. Secretary of Agriculture, how U.S. agricultural policy is being carried out.

LOOKING BACK—AND FORWARD

Twenty-three years ago, John F. Kennedy named me U.S. Secretary of Agriculture. I was privileged to serve in that capacity for eight years. Then, the importance of agriculture to the well-being of the people of the U.S., and of the world, did not receive priority attention. Today, as we approach the mid-point of the decade of the '80s, the critical importance of agriculture, if mankind is to advance toward its goal of human betterment, is universally recognized. The time has come for this country, as the leader of the free world, to put in place a sound agricultural policy, and to give the highest priority to carrying it out—at home and around the globe.

IV
Selected Bibliography

SELECTED
BIBLIOGRAPHY

BOOKS

Abee, Cleveland. *A First Report on the Relation Between Climates Crops*. U.S. Department of Agriculture. 1978, Ayer Co.

Ananyeva, G.E. *An Outline Theory of Population*. 1980, Imported Publications.

Bach, Wilfrid. *Our Threatened Climate*. 1982, Kluwer Academic.

Bach, W. *Edminteractions of Food and Climate*. 1982, Reidel.

Barrons, Keith, C. *Are Pesticides Really Necessary?* 1981, Regnery-Gateway.

Bandyop, Adh Yaya. *Climate World Order*. 1983, Humanities.

Baum, Kenneth H., and Schertz, Lyle P. *Model for Farm Decisions for Policy Analysis*. 1983, Westview.

Bayles, Michael D. *Morality, Population Property*. 1980 ALA Press.

Bates, Robert H. *Markets and States in Tropical Africa: The Political Basis of Agriculture*. 1984, University of California Press.

Batie, Sandra, and Healy, Robert G. *The Future of American Agriculture*. 1980, Conservation Foundation.

Barnett, Larry D. *Population Company Constitution (Studies in Human Issues)*. 1982, Kluwer.

Bayliss, Smith. *Understanding Green Revolutions: Agrarian Change and Development Planning in South Asia*. 1984, Cambridge University Press.

Boserup, Ester. *Conditions of Agricultural Growth: The Economics of Agrarian Change under Population Pressure*. 1965, Aldine Pub.

Brown, Lester R. *U.S. Soviet Agriculture: The Shifting Balance of Power*. 1982, World Watch Institute.

———. *State of the World*. A World Watch Institute on Progress Toward a Sustainable Society. 1984, Norton.

Brown, Peter G., and Shue, Henry, eds. *Food Policy: The Responsibility of the U.S. in the Life and Death Choices*. 1977, Free Press.

Calder, Nigel. *The Weather Machine*. 1977, Penguin.

Campbell, Keith O. *Food for the Future: How Agriculture Can Meet the Challenge*. 1979, University of Nebraska.

Chambers, Janice E., and Yarbrough, James D., eds. *Effects of Chronic Exposures to Pesticides on Animal Systems*. 1982, Raven.

Choucri, Nazli, ed. *Multidisciplinary Perspectives on Population and Conflict*. 1984, Papt, Text. ed.

Clark, Colin. *The Myth of Over Population*. 1975, Lumen Christi *Crop Production Levels and Fertilizer Use with Bulletins*. 1981, Unipub.

225

Crossmon, Pierre R., and Stout, Anthony T. *Productivity Effects of Cropland Erosion in the United States.* 1984, Papt. Text ed. 64.

Delong, Peter, ed. *Pest Management in Transitions.* 1979, Westview.

Dickson, H. *Climate and Weather.* 1976, Gordon Press.

Dumont, Rene, and Cohen, Nicholas. *The Growth of Hunger: Concerning a New Politics of Agriculture.* 1980, M. Boyars.

Ecobichon, D.J., and Joy, R.M., eds. *Pesticides and Neurological Diseases.* 1982, CRC Press.

Embar, Chellam. *People, People Everywhere.* 1983, Concepts Unlimited.

Environmental Studies Board, National Research Council. *Pest Control: An Assessment of Present and Alternative Technologies.* 1976, National Academy Press.

Fite, Gilbert C. *American Farmers: The New Minority.* 1979, Indiana University Press.

Flint, Mary L., and Kobbe, Brunhild. *Integrated Pest Management for Citrus.* 1983, Ag. National. Res.

Flint, Mary L. and Van Den Bosch, Robert. *Introduction to Integrated Pest Management.* 1981, Plenum Pub.

Food and Agriculture Organization. *Drought in Thesahel: International Relief Operations.* 1973-1975, Unipub.

Forry, Samuel. *The Climate of the U.S. and its Endemic Influences.* 1980, Elsevier.

Fowden, L. and Grahm, Bryce, eds. *Crop Protection Chemicals: Directions of Future Development.* 1981, Scholium International.

Friedrich, Robert A. *Energy Conservation for American Agriculture.* 1979, Ballinger Pub.

Gardner, Bruce L. *The Governing of Agriculture Studies in Government and Public Policy.* 1981, U. of Press.

Gaskell, T.F., and Morris, Martin. *World Climate. The Weather, The Environment and the Man.* 1980, Thames Hudson.

Georghiuou, G.P., and Saito, Tetsuo, eds. *Pest Resistance to Pesticides.* 1983, Plenum Pub.

Gilmore, Richard. *A Poor Harvest: The Clash of Policies and Interests in the Grain Trade.* 1982, Longman.

Green, M.B. *Pesticides: Boom or a Bane.* 1976, Westview.

Gregor, Howard F. *Industrialization of U.S. Agriculture: An Interpretive Atlas.* 1982, Westview.

Grigg, David. *The Dynamics of Agriculture Change: The Historical Change.* 1984, St. Martin: 8.

Hartley, G.S. *Physical Principles of Pesticide Behavior: The Dynamics of Applied Pesticide in the Local Environment in Relation to Biological Responses.* 1980, Academy press.

Hassal, Kenneth A. *The Chemistry of Pesticides: Their Metabolism, Mode of Action and Action Uses in Crop Protection.* 1982, Verlag Chemie.

Hauser, Phillip M., et al. *Population and the Urban Future.* 1982, State University of New York Press.

Hayes, Wayland. *Pesticides Studies in Man.* 1982, Williams and Wilkins.

Hopkins, Raymond F., and Puchala, Donald J. *Global Food Interdependence: Challenge to American Foreign Policy.* 1980, Columbia University Press.

Huffaker, C.F., and Messenger, P.S., eds. *Theory and Practice of Biological Control.* 1977, Academic Press.

Johnson, D. Gale, and Schuh, George E. *The Role of Markets in the World Food Economy.* 1983, Westview.

Keyfitz, Nathan. *Population Change.* 1984, Text Ed.

Knutson, Ronald, and Penn, J.B. *Agricultural and Food Policy.* 1983, ISBN.

Land Planning Committee, U.S. National Resources Board. *Report of the Land Planning Committee*. 1976, Ayer Comp.

Levy, Maurice and Robinson, John L., eds. *Energy and Agriculture: The Interacting Futures Policy and Implications and Global Models*. 1983, Harwood Academic, Vol. 42.

Marshall, Catherine. *A Man Called Peter*. 1980, Chosen Books, Pub. 42.

Martin, Hubert. *The Scientific Principles of Crop Protection*. 1973, Crane-Russak Co.

Mercier, M., ed. *Criteria (Dose Effect Relationships): For Organichlorine Pesticides: Report of a Working Group of Experts Prepared for the Commission of the European Communities*. Pap Text Ed.

Nair, Kusman. *Transforming Traditionally: Land in Labor Use in Agriculture in Asia and Africa*. 1983, Riverdale Comp.

Nutty, Keslie. *The Green Revolution in West Pakistan: Implications of Technological Change (Special Studies in International Economics and Development)*. 1972, irvington.

Osborn, Fairfield, ed. *Our Crowded Planet: Essays on the Pressures of Population*. 1983, Greenwood.

Overbeek, Johannes, ed. *The Evolution of Population Theory: A Documentary Sourcebook*. 1977, Greenwood.

Paarlbert, Don. *Food and Agriculture Policy*. 1978, An Enterprise.

Perring, F.H. and Mellanby, K. *Ecological Effects of Pesticide (A Linnean Society Symposium)*. 1977, Academic Press.

Pirone, Pascal P. *Diseases and Pests of Ornamental Plants*. 1978, Wiley.

Pittock, A.T., et al., eds. *Climate Change and Variability*. 1978, Cambridge.

Population Policies for an Economic Era. 1983, Unipub.

Porter, Phillip W. *Food and Development in the Semi Arid Zone of East Africa*. 1979, Syracuse University Foreign Comp.

Post, John D. *The Last Great Subsistence Crises in the Western World*. 1977, Johns Hopkins.

Renich, F. *When the Chisel Hits the Rock*. 1980, Victor Books.

Resource Trends and Population Policy: Time for Reassessment (World Watch Paper No. 29). 1979, Unipub.

Resource Trends and Population Policy: A Time for Reassessment. 1979, World Watch Institute.

Ridker, Ronald G. *Population and Development: The Search for Selective Interventions*. 1977, Johns Hopkins.

Rose, Claud. *Forecast of Disaster: Our Changing Weather*. 1981, Zebra.

Schwerdtferberger, W. *Weather and Climate of the Antarctic (Development in the Atmospheric Science)*. 1984, Elsvier.

Sheets, T.J., and Pimental, David, eds. *Pesticides: Contemporary Roles in Agriculture*. 1979, Humana.

Simon, Julian L. *The Economics of Population Growth*. 1977, Princeton University Press.

Smic, James A., ed. *Climates of the States, 2 Volumes*. 1971, MIT Press.

Smith, R.W., and Gittins, A.R., eds. *Pest Management for the Twenty-first Century*. 1973, University Press of Idaho.

Spengler, Joseph J., ed. *Zero Population Growth: Implications*. 1975. Carolina Population Center.

Steinmann, G., ed. *Economic Consequences of Population Change in Industrialized Countries: Proceedings of the Conference on Population Economics Held at the University of Palderborn West Germany*. 1983, Springer-Valeg.

Tickell, Crispin. *Climatic Change and World Affairs*. Harvard Studies in International Affairs. 1977, Harvard University International Affairs.,

Trewartha, Glenn. *The Earth's Problem Climates.* 1981, University of Wisconsin Press.
Van Heemstra-Lequir, A.H., and Trodoir. *Education and Safe Handling in Pesticide Application.* 1982, Elsevier.
Veatch, Robert M., ed. *Population Policy and Ethics: The American Experience.* 1977, Irvington.
Wallace, Robert. *Dissertation on the Numbers of Mankind in Ancient Modern Times.* 1976, Clark University Press.
Warwick, Donald P. *Bitter Pills: Population Policies on Their Implementation in Eight Developing Countries.* 1982, Cambridge University Press.
Wogaman, Phillip J., ed. *Population Crises and Moral Responsibility.* 1973, Public Affairs Press.
Woods, Richard G., ed. *Future Dimensions of World Food and Populations.* 1981, Westview.

PERIODICALS

"Agriculture and the Environment: An Examination of Critical Issues for Food Policies." *Agriculture,* January 1984.
"Agriculture Land Preservation by Local Government." *West Virginia Review,* 1982.
"Agriculture Nonpoint Pollution Control: A Time for Sticks." *Journal of Soil and Water Conservation,* 1985.
"Agriculture Nonpoint Pollution Control: An Assessment." J.B. Braden and D.L. Uchtmann. *Journal of Soil and Water Conservation,* 1985.
"Agroecosystem Diversity and Pest Control: Data, Tentative Conclusions, and New Research Directions." *Environmental Entomology,* 1983.
"Agricultural Land: Will There be Enough?" *Environment,* 1984.
"American Horticulture Exports: How They Stack Up." *Foreign Agriculture,* 1983.
"Biotechnology of Plant Foods." *Food Technology,* October 1985, pp. 12-42.
"Charting the Path of U.S. Exports." *Foreign Agriculture,* January 1985, pp. 12-17.
"Collective Bargaining for Farm Workers—Should There be Federal Legislation." H.M. Levy. *Santa Clara,* Spring 1981, pp. 333-55.
"Conservation Programs Amidst Faltering Governmental Commitments." *Environmental Affairs Law Record,* 1982-83, p. 96.
"Cost-Effective Targeting of Agricultural Nonpoint-Source Pollution Controls." R.J. Johnson. *Journal of Water and Soil Conservation,* January 1985, pp. 108-11.
"Cost Sharing to Promote Use of Conservation Tillage." *Journal of Soil and Water Conservation,* November/December 1984, pp. 395-7.
"Cross-Compliance for Erosion Control: Anticipating Efficiency and Distributive Impacts." *American Journal of Agricultural Economics,* August 1984, pp. 637-38.
"Detoxifying EPA." R. Sandler. *Environment,* 1983.
"Early Warning Sought for Deserification." *Conservation News,* October 1984, pp. 10-11.
"Ecological Aspects of Agricultural Policy." S. Pimental. *Natural Resources,* July 1980, pp. 555-85.
"Economic Instability in Agriculture: The Contributions of Prices, Government Programs and Exports." *American Journal of Agriculture,* December 1983, pp. 922-31.
"Economic Environment and Agricultural Development: The Importance of Macroeconomic Policy." *Food Policy,* February 1985, pp. 29-40.
"Evaluating the Economic Benefits of Pesticide Usage." R.F. Settle. *Agricultural Ecosystem and the Environment,* March 1983, pp. 173-85.
"Exposing Pesticides to the Clear Light Reason." L. Mott. *Garden,* January 1983, pp. 2-5.

"Factory Farming: An Imminent Clash Between Animal Rights, Activities, and Agribusiness." *Environmental Affairs Law Review,* 1980, pp. 423-61.

"Farmland Preservation: A Vital Agricultural Law Issue for the 1980's." J.C. Juergensmeyer. *Washburn,* Spring 1982, pp. 443-77.

"Financial Stress in Agriculture: Implications for Agricultural Lenders." *American Journal of Agriculture,* December 1983, pp. 945-52.

"Food Crises Detection: Going Beyond the Balance Sheet." *Food Policy,* August 1984, pp. 189-92.

"Future Directions for Agricultural Policy." *American Journal of Agriculture,* May 1984, pp. 234-39.

"Future Direction for Food and Agricultural Trade Policy." *American Agriculture,* May 1984, pp. 240-1.

"General Agreement on Tariffs and Trade: What it Means to U.S. Agriculture." *Foreign Agriculture,* June 1984, pp. 16-17.

"Global Crop Sales: Assessing the U.S. Competitive Challenge." *Agricultural Engineering,* 1985, pp. 17-20.

"Helping Farmers and Saving Farmland." G. Torres. *Oklahoma Law Review,* Spring 1984, pp. 31-65.

"Hunger Relief: A Bigger Bowl of Numbers?" *Food Policy,* August 1985, pp. 10-188.

"Insecticide Use and Crop Rotation Under Risk: Rootworm Control in Corn." W.F. Lazarus and E.R. Swanson. *American Journal of Agricultural Economics,* November 1983, pp. 738-47.

"International Impact of U.S. Domestic Farm Policy." D.G. Amstutz. *American Journal of Agricultural Economics,* 1984.

"International Trade Environment for Food and Agriculture in the Late 1980's." J.S. Hillman. *American Journal of Agriculture,* December 1984, pp. 567-71.

"Introduction: Weather Modification Symposium." *Agricultural Water Usage,* Spring 1983, pp. 152.

"Legal Aspects of the U.S.S.R. Grain Embargo." *Denver Journal of International Law,* Winter 1981, pp. 95-97.

"More Land Protection From Soil Erosion." *Soil and Water Conservation News,* June 1984, pp. 5-13.

"New Approaches to Commodity Programs and Conservation Goals." M.E. Mekelburg. *Journal of Soil and Water Conservation,* August 1983, pp. 324-5.

"New Directions in the U.S. Food Aid: Human Rights and Economic Development." J.R. Walczak, *Denver Journal of International Policy,* Spring 1979, pp. 543-71.

"New Perspectives on Soil Conservation Policy: Conservationists Must Begin to Address Some Tough, New Policy Questions." P. Crosson. *Journal of Soil and Water Conservation,* August 1984, pp. 222-5.

"Paying the Nonpoint Pollution Control Bill." L.W. Libby. *Journal of Soil and Water Conservation,* January/February 1985, pp. 3-36.

"Pesticide Demand and Integrated Pest Management: A Limited Dependent Variable Analysis." T.M. Burrows. *American Agricultural Economics,* 1983, pp. 807-10.

"Productivity of Soils: Assessing Long Change Due to Erosion." *Journal of Soil and Water Conservation,* January 1983, pp. 39-44.

"Section 301: Access to Foreign Markets From an Agricultural Perspective." M.A. Echols. *International Trade,* Fall/Winter, 1980-81, pp. 4-23.

"Small Farms: The USDA, Rural Communities and Urban Pressures." J.B. Wadley. *Washburn Law Journal,* Spring 1982, pp. 478-514.

"Soil Erosion Reduces Yields." M.S. Gillespie. *Soil and Water Conservation News,* January 1984, pp. 4-14.

"Soil, Water, and Conservation Quality Improvement." *Journal of Soil and Water Conservation,* January/February 1983, pp. 15-20.

"Soil Conservation: 'The Search for Solutions.'" N.A. Berg and R.J. Gray. *Journal of Soil and Water Conservation*, January/February 1984, pp. 18-22.

"Soil Conservation Institutions of the Future." *Journal of Soil and Water Conservation*, March/April 1985, p. 182.

"Soils and Society, and Sustainability." W.K. Reilly. *Journal of Soil and Water Conservation*, September/October 1984, p. 286.

"Technological Change, Government Policies, and Exhaustible Resources in Agriculture." D. Ziberman. *American Journal of Agricultural Economics*, December 1984, pp. 634-40.

"The Effects of Cashing Out Food Stamps on Food." D. Hollenbeck. *Agricultural Econ.*, August 1985, pp. 609-13.

"The Future of Food and Agricultural Policy." C.W. MacMillan. *Food Drug Cosm.*, January 1985, p. 84.

"The Macro Implications of Complete Transformation of U.S. Agricultural Production to Organic Farming Practices." *Agricultural Environment*, December 1983, pp. 323-33.

"The Migrant and Seasonal Agricultural Worker Protection Act." *Arkansas Law Review*, 1984, pp. 253-92.

"The Potential of Ecosystem Management for Pest Control." *Agricultural Ecosystem Environment*, September 1983, pp. 183-199.

"The Question of Small Development: Who Teaches Whom?" *Agricultural Ecosystem Environment*, July 1983, pp. 401-5.

"The Soviet-American Grain Agreement and the National Interest." *American Agricultural Economics*, 1985, pp. 651-6.

"The Wild Rice Mystique: Resource Management and American Indians Rights as a Problem of Law." *William Mitchell Law Review*, 1984, pp. 804-11.

"U.S. Public Policies and Institution in an Unstable Future." *American Agricultural Economics*, December 1984, pp. 592-6.

"U.S.-Soviet Agricultural Trade: Post Embargo Update." *Foreign Agriculture*, July 1983, pp. 14-16.

"U.S. Surplus Worldwide Undernourishment." *Agricultural Engineering*, July 1984.

"Weather Climate and the Land." *Journal of Soil and Water Conservation*, November/December 1984, pp. 350-3.

"When are Export Subsidies Rational." *Agricultural Econ. Res.*, Winter 1985, pp. 1-7.

"Will Plant Genetics Really Save the World From Starvation." *World Crops*, September/October 1984, p. 154.

GOVERNMENT DOCUMENTS

"Administration's Budget Proposals for The Food and Nutrition Service Programs," Hearings before the Senate Committee on Agriculture, Nutrition, and Forestry, 98-1, April 11, 1983.

"Agriculture Act of 1982", Hearing before the Senate Committee on Agriculture, Nutrition, and Forestry, 97-2, December 9, 1982.

"Agricultural Act of 1983", Hearings before the Senate Committee on Agriculture, Nutrition, and Forestry, 98-1, February 3, 1983.

"Agricultural Development in the Carribbean and Central America", Hearings before the Senate Committee on Agriculture, Nutrition and Forestry, 97-2, July 20, 1983.

"Agricultural Export Trade," Hearings before the Senate Committee on Agriculture, Nutrition, and Forestry, 98-1, February 17, 1983.

"Agricultural Productivity Act of 1983," Hearings before the Senate Committee on Agriculture, Nutrition, and Forestry, 98-1, August 3, 1983.

"Agricultural Research," Hearings before the Senate Committee on Agriculture, Nutrition, and Forestry, 98-1, June 22, 23, 28, 29, 1983.

"Agricultural Trade Legislation", Hearings before the Senate Committee on Agriculture, Nutrition, and Forestry, 98-2, February 23, 1984.

"Agricultural Trade and Export Commission Act," Hearings before the House Committee on Agriculture, 98-2, July 26, 1984.

"Alternatives to Ethylene Dibromide (EDB)," Hearings before the House Committee on Agriculture, 98-2, May 9, 1984.

"Announcement of Acreage Limitation and Set-Aside Programs," Hearings before the House Committee on Agriculture, 98-1, July 21, 1983.

"Amendments to the Perishable Agricultural Commodities Act," Hearings before the House Committee on Agriculture, 98-1, November 8, 1983.

"Benefits of Processed and Value-Added Products in Agricultural Exports," Hearings before the Senate Committee on Agriculture, Nutrition, and Forestry, 97-2, September 21, 1982.

"Cultivation of Marihuana in National Forests," Hearings before the House Committee on Agriculture, 97-2, September 30, 1982.

"Economic Conditions in Agriculture and FY84 Department of Agriculture Budget Proposals," Hearings before the House Committee on Agriculture, 98-1, February 9, 1983.

"Effects of Interbasin Water Transfers on Agriculture," Hearings before the House Committee on Agriculture, 98-1, June 15, 1983.

"Emergency Agriculture Credit Act of 1983," Hearings before the House Committee on Agriculture, 98-1, February 14, 1983.

"EPA Pesticide Regulatory Program Study," Hearings before the House Committee on Agriculture, 97-2, December 17, 1984.

"Farm Products Buyers' Protection Act of 1983," Hearings before the House Committee on Agriculture, 98-2, July 25, 1984.

"Federal Insecticide Fungicide and Rodenticide Act Extension," Hearings before the Senate Committee on Agriculture, 98-1, May 11, 1983.

"Highly Erodible Land Conservation Act of 1983," Hearings before the Senate Committee on Agriculture, Nutrition, and Forestry, 98-1, November 2, 1983.

"Hunger in the U.S. and Related Issues," Hearings before the Senate Committee on Agriculture, 98-2, March 2, 1982.

"Improved Standards for Laboratory Animals Act; and Enforcement of the Animal Welfare Act by the Animal and Plant Health Inspection Service," Hearings before the Senate Committee on Agriculture, 98 2, September 19, 1984.

"Information Technology for Agricultural America," Hearings before the Senate Committee on Agriculture, 97-2, December, 1982.

"Lending Policies and Administration of the Economic Emergency and Disaster Emergency Loan Programs (Farmers Home Administration)," Hearings before the Senate Committee on Agriculture, 98-2, February 2, 1984.

"Long-Term Farm Policy to Succeed the Agriculture and Food Act of 1981, Part 1," Hearings before the Senate Committee on Agriculture, 98-2, February 28, 29, 1984.

"Long-Term Farm Policy to Succeed the Agriculture and Food Act of 1981, Part 2," Hearings before the Senate Committee on Agriculture, 98-2, May 2, 1982.

"Maintaining Current Efforts in Federal Nutrition Programs to Prevent Increases in Domestic Hunger," Hearings before the Senate Committee on Agriculture, 98-1, July 29, 1983.

"Meat, Poultry and Egg Products Inspection Act of 1982," Hearings before the Senate Committee on Agriculture, 97-2, August 17, 1982.

"Miscellaneous Conservation," Hearings before the Senate Committee on Agriculture, 98-1, May 4; September 20, 1983.

"National Aquaculture Act Authorization, FY84," Hearings before the Senate Committee on Agriculture, 98-1, June 1, 1983.

"National Aquaculture Authorization Act of 1983," Hearings before the Senate Committee on Agriculture, Nutrition, and Forestry, 98-1, July 20, 1983.

"Nutrition Education and Training of Health Professionals," Hearings before the Senate Committee on Agriculture, 98-1, November 10, 1983.

"Operations of the Agriculture Stabilization and Conservation Committee System," Hearings before the Senate Committee on Agriculture, 98-2, September 11, 1984.

"Oversight on General Farm and Food Programs," Hearings before the Senate Committee on Agriculture, Nutrition, and Forestry, 98-2, August 21, 1984.

"Oversight on Matters Relating to the Commodity Futures Trading Commission," Hearings before the Senate Committee on Agriculture, Nutrition, and Forestry, 98-2, March 15, 1984.

"Perishable Agriculture Commodities Trust Protection Plan," Hearings before the Senate Committee on Agriculture, Nutrition, and Forestry, 98-1, November 7, 1983.

"Problems of Hunger and Malnutrition," Hearings before the Senate Committee on Agriculture, Nutrition, and Forestry, 98-1, February 28, 1983.

"Protection For Purchasers of Farm Products," Hearings before the Senate Committee on Agriculture, Nutrition, and Forestry, 98-2, September 26, 1984.

"Proposed Changes in the Federal Tobacco Program," Hearings before the Senate Committee on Agriculture, Nutrition and Forestry, 98-1, June 14, 1983.

"Payment in Kind Program," Hearings before the House Committee on Agriculture, 97-2, December 16, 1982.

"Regulation of Pesticides," Hearings before the House Committee on Agriculture, 98-1, February 22, 1983.

"Regulation of Pesticides," Hearings before the House Committee on Agriculture, 98-1, June 9, 1983.

"Regulation of Pesticides Vol. 3," Hearings before the House Committee on Agriculture, 98-1, 1983.

"Regulation of Pesticides Vol. 4," Hearings before the House Committee on Agriculture, 98-1, 1983.

"Review Alternatives to Administration Proposals Relating to Agriculture." Hearings before the House Committee on Agriculture, 98-1, October 19, 1983.

"Review of Agricultural Exports and Trade (Secretary John R. Block)," Hearings before the House Committee on Agriculture, 98-1, October 18, 1983.

"Review of Agricultural Trade Issues," Hearings before the House Committee on Agriculture, 97-2, August 11, 1982.

"Review of Agricultural Trade Issues," Hearings before the House Committee on Agriculture, 98-1, April 7, 1983.

"Review of Dairy Price Support Program," Hearings before the House Committee on Agriculture, 98-1, March 23, 1983.

"Review of Export Promotion Credit Programs," Hearings before the House Committee on Agriculture, 98-2, March 7, 1984.

"Review of Federal Crop Insurance Program," Hearings before the House Committee on Agriculture, 98-1 April 20, 1983.

"Review of FY84 Budget for the Food and Nutrition Service, U.S. Department of Agriculture," Hearings before the House Committee on Agriculture, 98-1, April 20, 1983.

"Review of FY85 Budget for the Food and Nutrition Service, U.S. Department of Agriculture; The Hunger Relief Act of 1984; and Related Matters," Hearings before the House Committee on Agriculture, 98-1, 1983.

"Review of Problems Related to Purchase of Mortgaged Agricultural Commodities," Hearings before the House Committee on Agriculture, 98-1, November 16, 1983.

"Review of Studies of the Domestic Hunger Problem and Proposed Solutions," Hearings before the House Committee on Agriculture, 98-1, October 20, 1983.

"Review of the Commodity Futures Trading Commission," Hearings before the House Committee on Agriculture, 98-2, February 8, 1984.

"Review of the General Agricultural Situation in Hawaii," Hearings before the House Committee on Agriculture, 98-1, August 20, 1983.

"Review of the Surplus Commodity Distribution Program," Hearings before the House Committee on Agriculture, 98-1, August 3, 1983.

"Review of Tobacco Price Support Program," Hearings before the House Committee on Agriculture, 98-1, February 25; March 18, 1983.

"Review of Tobacco Price Support Program Costs," Hearings before the House Committee on Agriculture, 97-1, October 7, 1982.

"Review the Payment in Kind Program," Hearings before the House Committee on Agriculture, 98-1, May 24, 1983.

"Review of the World Hunger Problem," Hearings before the House Committee on Agriculture, 98-1, October 25, 1983.

"Soil Conservation Service Fiscal 1985 Budget Proposals," Hearings before the House Committee on Agriculture, 98-2, March 16, 1984.

"Stabilization Programs Announced for the 1984 Crops of Wheat and Feed Grains," Hearings before the House Committee on Agriculture, 98-1, October 20, 1983.

"To Extend the Effective Date of Amendments to the U.S. Grain Standards Act," Hearings before the House Committee on Agriculture, 98-2, April 12, 1984.

"To Provide Disaster Assistance to Agricultural Producers and Ranchers," Hearings before the House Committee on Agriculture, 98-1, October 6, 1983.

NTC Debate Books

1986/87 Topic
A Comprehensive Agricultural Policy for the United States,
  Goodnight, Harris, Dauber
The Agriculture Crisis, *Hynes, Campbell*
The Future of American Agriculture, *Flaningam*

Debate Theory and Practice
Advanced Debate, Third Edition, *Thomas, Hart*
Basic Debate, Second Edition, *Fryar, Thomas, Goodnight*
Cross-Examination in Debate, *Copeland*
Forensic Tournaments: Planning and
  Administration, *Goodnight, Zarefsky*
Judging Academic Debate, *Ulrich*
Modern Debate Case Techniques, *Terry et al.*
Strategic Debate, *Wood, Goodnight*
Student Congress & Lincoln-Douglas Debate,
  Fryar, Thomas

Debate Aids
Debate Award Certificates
Debate Lectern
Debate Pins
Debate Timer
Case Arguments Flow Charts
Plan Arguments Flow Charts
Lincoln-Douglas Debate Casette Tape

For further information or a current catalog, write:
National Textbook Company
4255 West Touhy Avenue
NTC Lincolnwood, Illinois 60646-1975 U.S.A.